The Essence of Marketing

The Essence of Management Series

Published titles

The Essence of Total Quality Management
The Essence of Strategic Management
The Essence of International Money
The Essence of Management Accounting
The Essence of Financial Accounting
The Essence of Marketing Research
The Essence of Information Systems
The Essence of Personal Microcomputing
The Essence of Successful Staff Selection
The Essence of Effective Communication
The Essence of Statistics for Business
The Essence of Business Taxation
The Essence of the Economy
The Essence of Mathematics for Business
The Essence of Organizational Behaviour
The Essence of Small Business
The Essence of Business Economics
The Essence of Operations Management
The Essence of Services Marketing
The Essence of International Business

Forthcoming titles

The Essence of Public Relations
The Essence of Managing People
The Essence of Financial Management
The Essence of Change
The Essence of Marketing
The Essence of Business Law
The Essence of International Marketing
The Essence of Women in Management
The Essence of Mergers and Acquisitions
The Essence of Industrial Relations and Personnel Management
The Essence of Influencing Skills
The Essence of Services Management
The Essence of Industrial Marketing
The Essence of Venture Capital and New Ventures

The Essence of Marketing

Simon Majaro

Prentice Hall
New York   London   Toronto   Sydney   Tokyo   Singapore

First published 1993 by
Prentice Hall International (UK) Limited
Campus 400, Maylands Avenue
Hemel Hempstead
Hertfordshire, HP2 7EZ
A division of
Simon & Schuster International Group

Typeset in 10/12pt Palatino
by Goodfellow & Egan Phototypesetting Ltd,
Cambridge

Printed and bound in Great Britain by
Redwood Books, Trowbridge, Wiltshire

Library of Congress Cataloging-in-Publication Data

Majaro, Simon.
    The essence of marketing / Simon Majaro.
        p.   cm.
    Includes bibliographical references and index.
    ISBN 0-13-285354-X
    1. Marketing.   I. Title.
    HF5415.M2692   1993
    658.8—dc20
                                                    93-22068
                                                    CIP

British Library Cataloguing in Publication Data

A catalogue record for this book is available from
the British Library

ISBN 0-13-285354-X (pbk)

3 4 5   97 96

*This book is dedicated to my grandson Jonathan —
the consumer of the future*

Contents

Preface   xi

1 An introductory note   1
The role of marketing in a modern firm: a holistic approach   3

2 The marketing concept revisited   10
Marketing as a corporate attitude   11
Marketing as a function   16

3 The marketing mix   25
Marketing mix analysis   30

4 The input for effective marketing   40
How much knowledge?   41
Marketing profile analysis   46
The value of intelligence   48
The market and marketing research process   52
Methods of forecasting demand   54

5 Product policy and planning   64
The product life-cycle reviewed   68
Product portfolio management   79
Branding   87

6 Price and pricing policy   93
Supply and demand   94
Pricing in a monopoly   97

Pricing in an oligopoly 99
Different ways of looking at price 99
Pricing and costs 100
Price and the product life-cycle 103
The product portfolio 105
Price and the customer perspective 107
Pricing and image 111
The use of discounts 112
Summary 113

7 **The promotional mix** 118
Promotional channels 120
Promotion objectives 121
Advertising 124
Promotions 131
Direct marketing 133
Preparing the communication plan 135

8 **Distribution and logistics** 140
Marketing channels 141
The choice of intermediaries 143
Power in the distribution channel 144
Channel motivation 146
The logistics of distribution 147
Customer service 150
Developments in distribution 154

9 **Selling** 158
The sales force: its role and objectives 158
Improving the productivity of the sales force 165
Sales force size 171
The salesperson's 'profit and loss account' 172

10 **Marketing planning** 178
Benefits of marketing planning 179
Understanding the process 180
Aids to marketing planning 188
Formulating marketing strategies 201

11 **Marketing control** 208
Different types of control 208
Strategic control 210
Managerial effectiveness and efficiency control 212

Operational controls 216

12 Organizing for marketing 224
The development of organizations 224
The subactivities of an effective marketing organization 228
Types of marketing organization 231
Centralization versus decentralization 236
Marketing organizations at the integrated phase of
development 237
Main considerations 239

13 Marketing integration 244
The meaning and scope of integration 246

References and further reading 256
Index 258

Preface

During a recent seminar which I conducted for a group of engineers and scientists working for a large company that considers itself as highly marketing orientated, I was very disappointed to discover how little they all knew about the subject. Moreover, the overall reaction of the group was that the technical people are the 'added value' generators whereas their marketing counterparts are the ones who squander the company's resources for little real return. I had to cope with cynicism and a fair amount of hostility towards 'marketing'.

It became clear to me that the company in question masquerades as a marketing-orientated organization. In reality, no firm should consider itself as market led or customer orientated until all the functions of the firm accept the validity of such a concept. Every person in the organization, irrespective of his or her functional affiliation, must believe in the marketing creed and its value for success. As long as only marketing personnel believe in such a philosophy, the firm as a whole is unlikely to benefit from it.

As a consultant and academic who has spent a good portion of my life propagating the marketing gospel among thousands of managers, I felt frustrated and defeated. I came to realize that the marketing profession has failed to 'market' marketing among non-marketing personnel. Undoubtedly considerable progress has been achieved in improving the marketing skills of people in that function during the last decade. Yet the true challenge is to turn every manager, regardless of his or her role in the firm, into a potential marketer. Engineers, accountants, R & D personnel and computer people must all learn to understand and love the marketing concept.

xi

Otherwise the benefits of the marketing creed for corporate excellence are of dubious value.

When the editor of the Essence of Management Series invited me to write a book on the essence of marketing I was delighted. It gave me an opportunity to review the whole subject of marketing and to reduce it to simple and concise concepts and tools. My main aim was to bring all this material to a much wider audience than just marketing people. I have tried to approach it in a 'user-friendly' way and, in particular, to help non-marketing managers develop warmth and empathy towards this vital and exciting topic. I shall gauge the success of the book by the number of non-marketing people who will have read it! At the same time I hope that it will provide marketing specialists with a fresh perspective on the main principles of the subject.

Most chapters are accompanied by 'audit questionnaires', designed to help readers see how their own firms measure up to a checklist of effectiveness in each area of the process. These audit questionnaires are meant to alert readers to areas in which their organizations can improve, not to provide definitive proof of either excellence or poor quality. They are purely a basis for reflection and development work.

I should like to place on record my thanks to John Leppard. He was most helpful in guiding me towards simplicity and concision whenever I was leaning towards the more complex and less readable. I appreciate his steadfast help.

Simon Majaro

1

An introductory note

Many books, articles and papers have been written about marketing. The literature on the subject is vast and one is almost embarrassed by the choice available. Yet when students ask me for a book which could give them a simple and succinct overview of the main principles underlying marketing, I have some difficulty in pointing them in the right direction. Most authors have favourite topics which they succeed in bringing into prominence while shunting others into the sidelines. The result is that the reader tends to gain an unbalanced view of the relative significance of the various subjects covered. If an author decides that planning is the main component of effective marketing, the inevitable result is that the book acquires a bias towards that activity. If the author happens to have gained most of his experience in market research, the book tends to be skewed in that direction. The overemphasis on research procedures and methodologies can easily diminish the book's holistic value to the reader.

This is precisely what this book is endeavouring to avoid. As *The Essence of Marketing* implies, I am not seeking to break new ground in the field of marketing and/or marketing management. I am trying to provide a simple, verbiage-free and, above all, holistic compendium of principles and concepts pertaining to what is one of the most important areas of modern management.

Marketing can be looked at from a variety of positions. If one accepts the organizational model (Figure 1.1) that divides a firm into three distinct, albeit interrelated, levels – strategic, management and operational – one faces the problem of deciding on the vantage point from which the main principles and concepts should be examined. Marketing at the strategic level places an emphasis upon directional

1

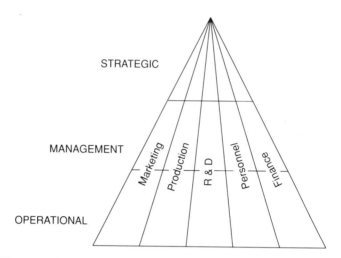

Figure 1.1 The three levels of the organization: a conceptual model

issues such as corporate mission development, the choice of strategies, the development of a corporate image to match the firm's aims
and objectives, the decision to apply undifferentiated or niche
marketing, product innovation and so on. At the other extreme,
operational marketing deals with the minutiae of marketing, such as
researching markets, selling and advertising. The former deals with
macro issues; the latter deals with the 'nitty gritty' activities of the
marketing process. A choice has to be made as to whether one
explores marketing principles from the top or delves into the detailed
methodologies practised at the sharp end of the function.

The aim of this book is to paint the subject with a broad brush and
not to delve too deeply into the operational details of each sub-
activity of marketing management. My main objective is to provide a
framework for reflection and analysis at the risk of appearing thin on
operational methods and procedures. These are amply covered by a
plethora of excellent books. More emphasis is placed on the need for
integration between marketing and the rest of the organization than
on skills development. Similarly, the importance of marketing as a
corporate attitude and part of the firm's shared values system is
highlighted, somewhat at the expense of an assemblage of 'how to do
it' techniques. The book should be regarded as an overview of what
marketing encompasses and not as a detailed account of how best
practice can be developed.

Many of the chapters are accompanied by simple auditing questionnaires inviting readers to test their company's performance in

the various areas under discussion. The questionnaires are designed as food for thought and not as a definitive test of prowess. However, any reader who discovers that his or her score is particularly low in a specific area should seriously consider taking steps to amend the firm's approach to that sector of its activities.

The role of marketing in a modern firm: a holistic approach

Many thinking firms agonize, from time to time, about what marketing actually means to them. Firms have been known to be very successful without having a complex marketing organization. On the other hand, some companies have been known to possess a comprehensive marketing department, supported by a myriad of subactivities belonging to the marketing function, and yet fail to achieve excellence.

The reason is simple: marketing is not simply a structural matter. Above all, it must be an integral part of the firm's culture and its shared values system. A marketing infrastructure that operates in a corporate culture that sees the customer as king will attain far greater heights than a complex marketing organization that functions in a climate that resents its customers, or regards them, at best, as a necessary evil. A senior manager in a well-known airline who had been heard to say: 'Life could be great if we did not have f... passengers!' nullified at a stroke all the good work that marketing personnel were attempting to achieve.

We shall examine the attitudinal aspect of marketing in the next few chapters. In this introductory note I want to explore briefly the role of marketing within a holistic model of the firm and as seen from the top of the pyramid. Looking at the firm as a total edifice is always a valuable basis upon which to build one's approach to organizational development and task allocation.

Business gurus have attempted over the years to identify the key elements which make companies excellent. Many valuable and interesting books have been written with a view to telling us about the panaceas for corporate success. In the highly fashionable field of quality, people like Demming, Crosby *et al.* tell us about the importance of getting the quality right, almost to the exclusion of everything else. Michael Porter has taught us about the enormous value of competitive advantage (Porter, 1985). Gifford Pinchot in *Intrapreneuring* has tried to explain why big business, despite spending most of the world's R & D money, has such a disproportionately low share of major innovations.

Few of the literature gurus appear to view businesses as a total system. They concentrate their attention upon specific areas of the corporate ecology, while the reader runs the risk of not being able to see the wood for the trees. The one guru who always seems to view businesses in a holistic way is Peter Drucker. This is perhaps the main reason for his books having passed the test of time.

Peters and Waterman's book *In Search of Excellence* (1982) views enterprises from a holistic vantage point and has created a stir by forcing many managers and corporate strategists to gaze at their corporate navels and ask themselves many searching questions about the main elements of corporate excellence. Whether the book really provides the answer is a secondary matter. The fact that managers reflect upon such an important subject is in itself an achievement.

The Peters and Waterman model has undergone a number of modifications and is referred to in many publications. I have used it myself quite often in my work and writings. For the sake of those who are not familiar with the model, it is reproduced as Figure 1.2.

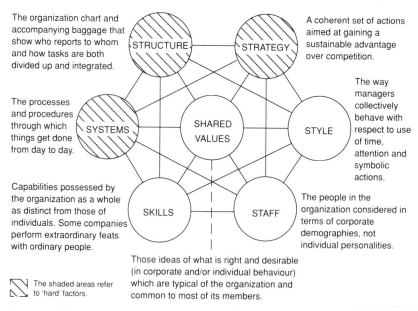

The organization chart and accompanying baggage that show who reports to whom and how tasks are both divided up and integrated.

A coherent set of actions aimed at gaining a sustainable advantage over competition.

The processes and procedures through which things get done from day to day.

The way managers collectively behave with respect to use of time, attention and symbolic actions.

Capabilities possessed by the organization as a whole as distinct from those of individuals. Some companies perform extraordinary feats with ordinary people.

The people in the organization considered in terms of corporate demographies, not individual personalities.

STRUCTURE · STRATEGY · SYSTEMS · SHARED VALUES · STYLE · SKILLS · STAFF

The shaded areas refer to 'hard' factors.

Those ideas of what is right and desirable (in corporate and/or individual behaviour) which are typical of the organization and common to most of its members.

Figure 1.2 The seven Ss framework for effective organizations (Source: Peters and Waterman (1982))

The model, which is referred to as the seven Ss framework for effective organizations, is based on the thesis that organizational effectiveness stems from the interaction of seven factors: structure, systems, style, staff, skills, strategy and shared values. The last one is sometimes referred to as 'superordinate goals'. Figure 1.2 shows the seven Ss and highlights their interconnectedness. The shape of the diagram and the position of the Ss *inter se* is non-hierarchical, and each one of the seven Ss can be the driving force of change at a given point in time. The important message is that 'shared values' is the centrepiece of the paradigm. The meaning and role of each of the other Ss are probably self-explanatory and the interconnectedness is fairly obvious.

The seventh and central S – shared values – calls for some exploration in the context of this book. By 'shared values' Peters and Waterman mean guiding concepts – a set of values and aspirations, often unwritten, that go beyond the conventional formal statement of corporate objectives. They are the postulates upon which the firm's climate, corporate philosophy and attitudes are based. The drive for their accomplishment pulls an organization together; it provides the engine that pulls the firm in a desired direction.

During my own consultancy work I collected a number of examples of corporate statements describing such guiding concepts and shared values (see Figure 1.3). Some are customer orientated, others high-

---

- Closeness to the customers
- Marketing orientation
- What is good for the customer is good for our business
- Commitment to quality
- Ideas are 'gold dust'
- Let us learn from our lead user
- We need your creativity
- Watch the 'bottom line'
- A bias for action
- A learning culture
- A culture of pride, climate of success
- Nothing is sacred
- 'Stick to your knitting'
- Let us add value through systems development
- A climate of entrepreneurship

Figure 1.3 Examples of shared values

light the importance of creativity and ideas, while yet others underline results, profits and 'the bottom line'. My own observation of 'excellent' companies, coupled with a period of research and reflection upon the fundamentals of managerial effectiveness, taught me an important lesson: companies that have recognized the importance of 'satisfying the customer at all times' as a corporate ethos have fared better than those who have shunned such a philosophy. Moreover, some companies declare their belief in such an orientation but act in the opposite direction. The essence of the process of satisfying the customer is *thinking, dreaming, planning* and *acting* in a customer-friendly and market-orientated way. 'Come close to the customer' is one of the prescriptions of Peters and Waterman's book. It summarizes the whole concept most succinctly.

My own starting point is based on the premise that every enterprise (and that includes institutional bodies and nonprofit organizations) exists to satisfy the needs of its customers. A firm that fails to attain such a simple and fundamental objective is unlikely to become excellent. Some readers may not agree with the premise stated. I invite them to reflect long and hard about the underlying philosophy of their own business. After all, developing a corporate creed and shared values is probably one of the main tasks of top management. I am convinced that even those who would wish to argue with my statement will sooner or later come to the conclusion that my suggested premise is a valid one.

For the purpose of this book, then, the success of any business depends on its ability to satisfy the customer. This statement implies that the whole panoply of the marketing function as well as other functions of the organization must be harnessed to assist in fulfilling the basic task of satisfying customers and their expectations. The enterprise stands to win or lose by its ability to attain such a goal.

So far so good, but the whole concept begs many questions.

(1) Who is our customer and what exactly are his or her needs? Any company that cannot answer this question with precision is unlikely to provide the level of satisfaction implied by the premise stated earlier. In this connection it is important to remember that the word 'customer' often conceals the fact that a complex assemblage of individuals may be involved in the buying process. This is particularly true in the marketing of industrial goods and services. The expression 'decision-making unit' refers to the list of players who help or impede a buying decision. Thus when a firm buys a computer many individuals may be involved in the decision as to which computer should be purchased. One normally talks about *deciders, buyers, influencers, users* and *gatekeepers.* Each has opinions and an impact on the final decision. They all have needs and expectations and these must be satisfied. Possession of detailed knowledge about their relative importance can provide a powerful input to effective marketing.

(2) Who is responsible for satisfying the customer? Is this purely the job of marketing personnel, or should it be a company-wide process? The obvious answer is that it must be part of the whole firm's ethos and shared values. Other departments like R & D, manufacturing and finance must be involved. Everybody in the firm from top to bottom and from left to right has a role to play in attaining maximum customer satisfaction. Obviously top management must be the prime mover in masterminding the development and implementation of such a creed.

(3) What do we need to 'know' before we can commence the task of planning the process of satisfying our customers, now and in the future? Knowledge is the essence of effective management. The more we know, the safer we are in taking correct decisions. In fact knowledge is one of the prime assets of excellent organizations and a most valuable competitive advantage. Customers prefer to deal with companies that know more about their own business and environment than they know themselves. The whole world of information technology is at management's disposal, and companies that do not exploit this powerful tool in coalescing, diagnosing and analyzing knowledge pertaining to the marketplace and customers are unlikely to become winning players in their sector. In this connection one must remember that the essence of information is 'knowing what one needs to know'. Information *per se* is normally of limited value.

(4) To what extent do our customers expect us to be creative and innovative in whatever we do? We hear a lot about the need for creativity, which in turn leads the firm towards innovation. This can affect every aspect of a firm's existence. In the marketing area it can have a significant influence upon the company's product development, promotion, after-sales service and so on. Do the customers want us to be innovative? To the extent that creativity and innovation help the marketing firm to be dynamic and responsive to a changing world, the answer must be a loud 'yes'. Research has shown that many consumers are starting to rebel against the frequency with which electronic appliances are being changed and deliberately made obsolescent. Being able to identify such a change in consumer mood and reaction to it also needs creative thinking. The mistake that people often make is to assume that innovation necessarily means the introduction of new products. Improving an existing product or finding ways of making it more cheaply also calls for creativity and innovation.

Figure 1.4 describes a model reflecting a holistic approach to building an effective and creative organization. The model offers a blueprint of the main components that top management must orchestrate if the firm is to achieve its ultimate purpose of satisfying its customers in an effective and creative manner. Like the seven Ss model described by Peters and Waterman, the important feature here is the interconnectedness of the four 'satellites' shown. They must all work in total harmony within the company's environment, present and future, with a view to developing the appropriate 'satisfiers' in order to keep the customers happy. In turn, such happiness is guaranteed to promulgate and maintain the firm's overall success. The four satellites are like a juggler's plates which rotate in unison but each of which periodically needs a further twist in order to ensure its continuous rotation. Moreover, each in turn can act as the major driving force that propels the enterprise towards the fulfilment of its aims.

The main purpose of Figure 1.4 is to provide the reader with a framework for reflection and analysis relating to his or her business environment. It also seeks to raise the level of this reflection to the strategic decision-makers. If the people at the top think clearly about their role, the likelihood is that the rest of the firm will think and act in a more cohesive manner. It must be recalled that my main aim is to highlight the corporate context within which marketing can operate. It is probably unnecessary to emphasize that companies in which marketing operates in an intellectual and philosophical vacuum are less likely to excel.

In subsequent chapters we shall have an opportunity to explore a few of the 'satellites' in greater detail. However, it is important to stress a couple of important points:

- The model described in Figure 1.4 is only relevant in the context of firms that have undertaken to pursue a customer-orientated route. Those who resist the discipline envisaged by the 'marketing concept' are not really concerned about the need to satisfy their customers. In fact, if they do satisfy customers it is more by luck than by judgment. They achieve it in spite of themselves.

- The four satellites must be viewed as an integrated assemblage.

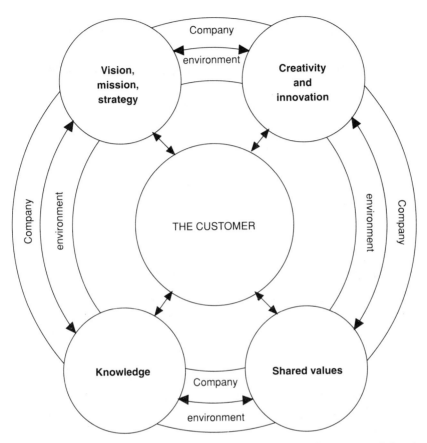

Figure 1.4 Satisfying the customer: a holistic approach to the company's input

They interact and fructify each other. Knowledge enriches vision and vision stimulates the development of shared values. The right shared values help the firm to harness creative ideas and these may lead to innovation. All of them together help to maintain a special relationship with the customer.

Viewed in the terms described in this brief introduction, the firm represents an exciting anatomy. Within this anatomy marketing is the vital organ which provides the firm with its true *raison d'être*. It creates and maintains customers, and provides the firm's stakeholders with a payoff for the time, money and effort invested in the whole business cycle. It is within this context that we shall review the essential elements of marketing.

2

The marketing concept revisited

Marketing is one of the concepts in management studies that one often finds it difficult to define. If one scans the literature, one is surprised by the plethora of definitions that one encounters. Why is it so difficult to find a single and all-embracing definition which applies to every company and to every situation? The definition used by the Chartered Institute of Marketing is as follows: 'Marketing is the management process responsible for identifying, anticipating and satisfying customer requirements profitably'.

Broadly speaking, this is an elegant description of what marketing means. Of the many definitions in the literature, it is one of the most succinct. Yet it belies the full meaning of the word and the extent to which marketing can and should pervade the whole organization if it is to extract full value for the enterprise. It describes the process, but it fails to highlight the full significance of the 'marketing creed'. It implies that 'marketing' is a discrete process which operates in isolation from the rest of the organization. A full understanding of the essence of marketing demands that this perception is broadened beyond its functional limitations.

In this book, 'marketing' involves two distinct, albeit highly interrelated, notions:

- Marketing as a corporate attitude, philosophy and ethos – part of the firm's shared values.
- Marketing as a function – a set of activities.

On the face of it, these two statements are difficult to reconcile. A few words about each will place them in their proper perspective.

Marketing as a corporate attitude

'Marketing orientation', 'market orientation', 'customer orientation' and 'market-led companies' are phrases that one often encounters when the subject of marketing is being taught or discussed. Received knowledge suggests that companies that have adopted these desirable philosophies are more likely to attain success than those that have adhered to other attitudinal patterns of behaviour, such as 'production orientation' or 'profit orientation'.

The evidence in support of such a belief is indeed powerful. The annals of modern marketing history demonstrate that in a competitive environment companies that have pursued a market-led approach to running the business have fared better than those that have not. It is difficult to find examples where this axiom does not apply. Nevertheless it is not always easy to identify which company is truly marketing orientated and which is not. The accolade is frequently given to those who have managed to project a suitable image in this regard: to those who keep shouting about their desire to look after the consumer. In practice it is not unusual to discover that the truly customer-orientated firm often achieves such a standing without excessive protestations of its 'love for the consumer'. Genuine and steadfast behaviour is often more important than costly and insincere manifestations of corporate ethos.

The important point to remember is that being a marketing-orientated firm does not simply involve a pious statement being issued from above on a solitary occasion. It requires a well-developed and deeply rooted corporate philosophy that guides every part of the organization in all its activities and operations. This attitude and mode of behaviour should apply to all departments and not only to the marketing people, and should apply with equal rigour to all members of the firm regardless of their functional affiliations. Thus production personnel, accountants and human resource people should all come close to the customer and behave in a 'marketing-orientated' manner. The company's ethos should be detected not only in public statements and published material but also in the way people on the switchboard respond to telephone calls.

When talking about their products or services, marketing-orientated firms think in terms of what the customers buy rather than what the company manufactures. When customers buy light bulbs they buy 'lighting' and not incandescent lamps. When car manufacturers buy ball bearings they buy them because they have a friction problem to overcome and not because they love the shape of spherical objects. Companies that adhere to the 'marketing concept' attempt to identify and solve customers' problems rather than to supply discrete products. This means that they are always ahead of the game. They anticipate events and needs, and seek to provide solutions.

If all this sounds somewhat theoretical, let us bring the whole subject back down to earth. In order to highlight the practical significance of this aspect of marketing, a simple questionnaire is provided to help the reader to determine whether he or she works for a truly 'marketing-orientated' company.

The main aim of the questionnaire is to make the reader reflect upon a number of important issues with which marketing-orientated companies grapple. The reader is invited to append the answer which seems the most appropriate in the circumstances of his or her organization. A recommended scoring system is shown at the end of the audit. However, it is important that the reader does not emerge at the end of the exercise rather frustrated about his or her firm's performance. The audit is a learning exercise and seeks to provide food for thought rather than to check the virtuosity of specific companies in respect of their corporate culture.

MARKETING-ORIENTATED AUDIT

Score
0 1 2

1. **Does top management recognize the importance of focusing the firm's strategies and operations on meeting the needs of chosen markets?**

    Possible responses and recommended scores:
    (a) The firm develops products without reference to the marketplace and then simply seeks to sell them to whoever wants to buy them.   (*Score 0*)
    (b) The marketing effort is focusing on identified needs, but the firm is not paying much attention to the dynamism of the market.   (*Score 1*)
    (c) The firm recognizes the need to solve customers' problems and meet their needs in a dynamic way. It is fully aware of market needs and anticipates them in advance for a longer-term perspective. (*Score 2*)

▶

2. **Does the firm's mission/purpose describe the nature of the business in a marketing- or customer-orientated way?**

    (a) The business described by top management is centred around products and/or technology.   (*Score 0*)
    (b) The business is centred around markets but these are fairly vague.   (*Score 1*)
    (c) The business is centred around well-defined markets and a well-defined cluster of needs.   (*Score 2*)

3. **Is marketing represented at board level, or is its functional role centred around lower levels of management only?**

    (a) Marketing is understood to mean selling and its operations are at middle and operational levels only.   (*Score 0*)
    (b) The marketing function encompasses a wide array of activities but is not represented at the top.   (*Score 1*)
    (c) Marketing is considered as a vital function for success and is strongly embedded at the top.   (*Score 2*)

4. **Does the planning of marketing play an important role in the firm's business planning cycle?**

    (a) The company does not prepare marketing plans. The only plans are business ones and these are based mainly on financial extrapolations.   (*Score 0*)
    (b) The business plans incorporate some marketing input.   (*Score 1*)
    (c) Marketing plans are the basis upon which the firm develops its overall planning cycle.   (*Score 2*)

5. **Does the firm's management understand in detail the competitive forces that may affect marketing performance?**

    (a) The company is only aware of the existence of 'brand' competitors which offer similar products under different names.   (*Score 0*)
    (b) The company possess full details of both 'brand'

▶

competitors and those which offer 'substitutes'
('functional' competitors).   (*Score 1*)
(c) The firm's marketing personnel understand the
competitive scene fully, including strengths and
weaknesses of all types of competitors and potential
new entrants. It has its finger on the competitive
pulse.   (*Score 2*)

6. **Does the company offer products or does it seek to
    solve clients' problems?**

    (a) The company always thinks in terms of the
    product it manufactures or the service it renders
    regardless of who buys it and why.   (*Score 0*)
    (b) Company personnel seek to respond to market
    needs and provide products and/or services which
    meet such needs.   (*Score 1*)
    (c) The whole philosophy of the company is to
    understand customers and their problems and
    provide solutions thereto. In fact the marketing
    personnel know more about their customers'
    problems than the latter know
    themselves.   (*Score 2*)

7. **Does management undertake marketing and market
    studies?**

    (a) The firm never undertakes such
    studies.   (*Score 0*)
    (b) Markets are investigated from time to time but
    without a clear set of objectives.   (*Score 1*)
    (c) The firm seeks to understand the markets in a
    dynamic fashion, and information is gathered
    regularly and consistently.   (*Score 2*)

8. **Does marketing management attempt to integrate its
    activities with other functional areas such as R & D,
    production, finance, etc.?**

    (a) Seldom or never.   (*Score 0*)
    (b) Sometimes. Occasional meetings are being
    arranged to highlight disagreements and/or potential
    conflicts.   (*Score 1*)
    (c) The importance of integration is fully recognized
    and acted upon at all times. It is part of the firm's
    'shared values' system.   (*Score 2*)

▶

Score
0 1 2

9. **Does marketing management seek to measure the cost-effectiveness of the various items of expenditure on marketing activities?**

    (a) Seldom or not at all.   *(Score 0)*
    (b) Spasmodically.   *(Score 1)*
    (c) Regularly.   *(Score 2)*

10. **How effectively does management anticipate and/or respond to changes in the market?**

    (a) Management seldom anticipates events and has to deal with crises which have not been anticipated.   *(Score 0)*
    (b) Management does try to anticipate events but often gets it wrong.   *(Score 1)*
    (c) Management spends time in developing a vision of the future and seeks to validate its future assessment of events through many discussions with experts in the field.   *(Score 2)*

The questions listed in the audit are fairly straightforward. However, scoring calls for an honest appraisal of one's perception of managerial and organizational realities. The total score may indicate where the firm stands in the process of becoming a marketing-orientated company:

15–20   **Excellent.** Companies that achieve such a score are likely to be successful and to remain so.

10–14   **Good to very good.** A good start has been achieved. More effort is needed to improve further and to attain excellence.

5–9   **Fair.** Considerable works needs to be undertaken in developing the marketing concept throughout the organization. The firm may be quite vulnerable to competitive action.

0–4   **Poor.** The extent of the problem should be quite obvious. Any reader who is in the position of doing something about it should undertake an immediate programme of work designed to change the firm's culture and orientation with a view to its 'coming close to its customers'. Otherwise the firm runs a grave risk of not surviving.

Marketing as a function

The main thrust of this book is centred around the marketing function as practised by marketing-orientated companies. We now assume that the company has understood the importance of the marketing concept and has taken the appropriate steps to improve the firm's orientation towards customers, markets and consumers.

It is important to understand that a firm can be market orientated and yet have a very small marketing department or none at all. The reverse is also true: a firm can have a whole panoply of marketing activities and fail in its aim to come close to its customers. In my opinion it is better to fall into the former category than the latter. A truly market/marketing-orientated firm can be very successful without having a plethora of individuals or departments bearing titles associated with marketing tasks and subtasks.

Marks and Spencer is universally recognized as a well-managed firm manifesting an excellent bias towards satisfying the needs of its customers. At the same time it does not have a vast marketing function. It is a firm which believes that everybody who works for the company has a marketing role to play regardless of his or her level of management and key tasks. Marketing at Marks and Spencer is a way of life which pervades the whole firm, and is not left to an army of marketing personnel who perform the discrete activities that one normally associates with the function.

At this point it is useful to provide a framework for reflection and analysis based on the Chartered Institute of Marketing's definition provided earlier. It will be remembered that the definition contains the following elements:

1. A management process
2. Responsible for:
   (a) identifying
   (b) anticipating
   (c) satisfying customer requirements
3. Profitability.

Each of these elements deserves a brief exploration.

A management process

The main significance of this phrase is the notion that marketing is a continuous process. Some companies fall into the trap of pursuing marketing activities on a spasmodic basis, undertaking activities such as *ad hoc* market studies, periodical promotional campaigns and sudden motivational research projects. All these projects suffer from a lack of integration and consistency. In other words, marketing does not function in such circumstances as a process; it is simply a hotch-potch of disjointed activities.

This may sound a simple and obvious proposition. However, it is quite remarkable how many companies believe that they operate an effective marketing function while in practice it is no more than a series of badly planned and poorly integrated acts.

Identifying, anticipating and satisfying customers' requirements

Identifying requirements

The identification of customers' requirements is a major task for a marketing function. All the input-gathering activities of marketing are designed to find out what customers' needs and wants are. Marketing aims to satisfy such requirements (the combination of needs and wants) and this means that a dynamic process for their assessment and measurement has to be put in place. Two questions must be addressed.

(1) Whose requirements are we interested in identifying? The obvious answer is the customer's. However, the word 'customer' can be very misleading. The customer may be a single individual, but in most instances the customer is represented by a myriad of 'players'. When a housewife buys a deodorant stick for her husband, is she the customer or is he? Yet each of them needs to be satisfied with the offering.

One normally talks about the need to satisfy the requirements of all the members of a 'decision-making unit'. The decision-making unit encompasses all the people who are involved, directly or indirectly, in the purchasing and consuming process. Thus the housewife in question may well be the 'buyer', but in this case her husband is the 'user'. She may have selected a specific product in response to a suggestion by one of her close friends, who has therefore acted as an 'influencer'. Yet the actual 'decision' to buy a specific product or brand may have been taken by the husband himself.

In other words, the customer is a conglomerate of the following:

- Buyer(s).

- Decider(s).
- User(s).
- Influencer(s).

The aim of effective marketing is to understand their requirements, to identify the relative importance of each of them, and to plan for the full satisfaction of them all.

The same concept applies to industrial goods. When one seeks to sell an industrial product, one must remember that the 'customer' can be a complex group of stakeholders. When one sells a computer to an industrial user, it is useful to bear in mind that the buying process entails a diverse and complex group of interested parties, and each member of that group may have a different range of expectations and requirements. Sometimes these expectations can be in a state of conflict. The purchasing officer, who acts as the 'buyer', is looking for the lowest price; the EDP manager, the 'user', is looking for a user-friendly product; the finance director, who may be the ultimate 'decider', is looking for cost–benefit and tax advantages; the chief executive as an important 'influencer', may consider whether the purchase of the computer in question will enhance the firm's image. Finally, the chief executive's personal assistant may act as a significant 'gatekeeper'. This term relates to an individual who, through personal likes or dislikes, can facilitate or impede the whole transaction.

In analyzing the 'decision-making units' involved, a subtle difference exists between consumer goods and industrial goods. In the former one seeks to collect information which enables the marketer to *generalize* his or her approach. One endeavours to understand how the majority of the people in the target audience behave and then to prepare a generalized approach to provide 'the greatest happiness of the greatest number'.

On the other hand, in the case of industrial goods one must be *specific*. One accepts the notion that every customer is unique and that this is manifested in the interplay among the members of the decision-making unit. This means that an in-depth understanding of every customer and its decision-making process must be assembled and the requirements of individuals therein must be clearly tabulated and acted upon. One can seldom extrapolate from the knowledge gained from one customer to others. The marketing approach must literally be 'customized'.

The point about the different approaches to consumer goods and industrial goods marketing is summarized in Figure 2.1.

DECISION-MAKING UNITS		
	CONSUMER GOODS	INDUSTRIAL GOODS
	Buyers Deciders Influencers Users	Buyers Deciders Influencers 'Gatekeepers' Users Others
MAIN MARKETING TASKS	1. To analyze the behavioural patterns that exist in the marketplace. 2. To develop a *generalized* approach capable of providing maximum satisfaction to the largest number of consumers.	1. To analyze the behavioural pattern of each customer. 2. To identify the main 'players' in each company and list their specific expectations. 3. To maintain an up-to-date dossier about each significant customer and/or potential customer. 4. To develop a 'customized' approach to each company incorporating the *specific* needs of each member of the decision-making unit.

Figure 2.1 The decision-making units and their implications in consumer and industrial goods markets

(2) What kind of requirements do we need to identify? When customers purchase a product they seek to satisfy a range of requirements, some tangible and some intangible. The tangible ones are easy to articulate and measure. The intangible ones are often elusive and difficult to identify. Nonetheless creative marketers always attempt to gauge the latter with the same vigour as they seek to determine the former. Moreover, as we shall see in Chapter 5, the intangibles often represent a fraction of the total cost but can create a very significant level of satisfaction.

Intangible requirements include psychological and emotional needs. For instance, when a person buys a product as a status symbol it is not always easy to extract such a motive during a simple interview. Customers are either unaware of their true motivation or not prepared to expose their inner feelings. Yet it is important to verify the existence of such an intangible dimension and to add it to the cluster of requirements that one must attempt to satisfy.

Examples of tangible and intangible requirements are listed in Table 2.1 (below).

Anticipating requirements

Many marketers often overlook the fact that part of their job is to anticipate future requirements.

It is important to stress at the outset that the essence of effective marketing entails a full acceptance of the dynamism of the process. The marketplace is fast moving, and successful marketing means that the team must be prepared to respond immediately to changes that are likely to take place. This in turn involves the marketer in the task of developing and forecasting a vision of things to come.

Being 'proactive' is one of the hackneyed expressions of modern jargon. Yet it does portray the importance of anticipating the future with creativity and imagination, coupled with a thorough understanding of trends in human behaviour and attitudes. It is not an easy task and one cannot always be sure of being right in one's prediction of future events and environments. At the same time there is little doubt that the marketer who is able to coalesce a realistic vision of customers' future requirements is more likely to succeed in the competitive area. There is considerable talk about the need to develop a competitive advantage as the main ingredient of corporate success. Anticipating the future is probably one of the most important sources of competitive advantage.

A number of useful techniques are available to assist the marketer in the task of anticipating the future environment for the business. We shall look at a few of them later. Some of these techniques, such

Table 2.1 Tangible and intangible requirements

Tangibles	Intangibles
• Physical comfort	• Social acceptability
• Reliability	• Minimum after-purchase doubt (cognitive
• Convenience	dissonance)
• Ease in use	• Matching peer-group expectations
• Labour saving	• Patriotic sentiments
• Security	• Location of purchase point (e.g. Harrods-type
• Physical features and benefits	stores)
• Investment value	• Product's name or badge (e.g. Lacoste)
	• Product novelty

as time-series, regression and correlation analysis, are quantitative in nature; others, such as scenario writing and scenario day dreaming, are qualitative.

Satisfying customer requirements

The main task of marketing is to satisfy customer requirements (tangible and intangible). However, on many occasions customers are simply *unaware* of the fact that they have such requirements. These have to be awakened before the customer realizes that he or she 'needs' and 'wants' such an offering. This is particularly true if the marketing company is ahead of its customers in assessing their future requirements. Therefore part of the marketing task is, through a communication programme, to convert needs and wants into requirements waiting to be satisfied.

Thus, if a car manufacturer anticipates that the consumer of the future (say, in four to five years' time) may derive satisfaction from a small, non-polluting, electric vehicle, it will need to undertake a thorough process of pre-launch communication as part of the marketing task. The needs may be there but they are latent, and marketing communication must awaken them and translate them into wants. Only then will the customer be ready to consider a purchase and expect satisfaction. In other words, the communication process itself has an important role to play in moving customers, in a proactive fashion, towards their ultimate satisfaction.

Satisfaction of customers' requirements is a major ingredient in the marketing task. It is achieved through the development of an effective *marketing mix*. The marketing mix is the essence of the modern marketing concept. It is a simple concept and any marketer worth his or her salt should understand it fully. Unfortunately, owing to its simplicity it is often relegated to the status of a semi-academic notion that should be understood but not used. As we shall see later, the marketing mix is a means by which multi-faceted customer requirements can be satisfied to the fullest economic extent. It represents an amalgam of all the elements which must be put in place if the customer is to have all his or her expectations and requirements fulfilled. In basic terms, the marketing mix is an attempt to respond to the fundamental question: 'As a marketing-orientated company, what do we need to offer the customers in order to satisfy their requirements fully?' This is a straightforward question, but the answer is not always easy to formulate without thorough research into customers' needs and expectations.

The answer lies in a full understanding of the marketing mix concept and an appreciation of the interplay among its various components. The marketing mix encompasses in one assemblage all those elements that help to satisfy the customer and his or her needs. The subject will be treated fully in Chapter 3. At this stage we need consider only the framework of the concept.

Satisfying customers entails dealing with a number of fundamental and interrelated components:

- The product.
- The price.
- The place – the location where the product can be purchased.
- The promotion – the communication system that creates awareness of the product, its features and benefits, and its location of purchase, and also reassures the customer after the purchase has taken place.

This assemblage of 'satisfiers' is known among marketers as 'the four Ps model'. The model is further complicated in so far as each of the four Ps is normally broken down into subcomponents and varies from industry to industry and in relation to different marketing strategies. At this stage it suffices to emphasize that the ability to 'mix the optimum mix' is an essential part of effective marketing.

Profitability

'Profitability' is the last word in the definition at the beginning of this chapter and rounds off the whole proposition. Marketing seeks to satisfy customers' requirements, but at the same time it must make profits for the company. Satisfying customers while losing money is clearly not very smart marketing.

The definition would have been more complete if instead of specifying profits it had said that the company needs to satisfy customers 'while meeting its objectives'. Profitability is not always an organization's objective. Nonprofit organizations, such as charities, also have a marketing task to perform. The Family Planning Association pursues a vigorous marketing programme, yet one cannot measure its effectiveness in profit terms.

Figure 2.2 provides a framework for the marketing function. It is based on the definition explored and the various activities that are encapsulated in the process described.

In summary, it is worth highlighting again the notion that marketing effectiveness involves the company in a dual initiative: (a) a

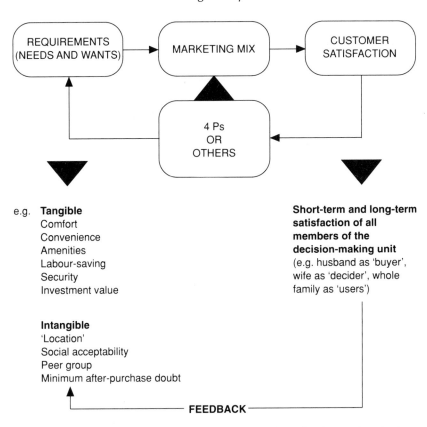

Figure 2.2 The marketing function: a framework for reflection and analysis

total commitment to an honest and wholehearted championship of the 'customer cause'; and (b) the development of a cluster of activities designed to bring about a multifaceted and profitable customer satisfaction at all times. The former runs as a theme throughout this book. The latter forms a basis upon which the main subfunctions of marketing will be explored in greater depth.

3

The marketing mix

The marketing mix is one of the most fundamental concepts associated with the marketing process. It is well understood by most
modern marketers and is systematically applied in many industries,
especially those that deal with physical products. Yet it is easy to
assume that, because most managers have heard about it and/or use
it, there is no need to mention it again in a book on marketing.

The sad truth is that quite often the precise role and scope of the
concept and its underlying principles are not fully appreciated by
those who talk about it or use it. It is regarded by many managers as
no more than a theoretical model that helps in understanding the
breadth of activities encompassed by the marketing task. In many
situations it is considered as no more than an aid to highlighting the
fact that 'marketing' is a much broader concept that just 'selling' or
'promoting'.

A brief review of the main principles surrounding the marketing
mix can help to clarify its true role in the development and execution
of an effective marketing effort.

As stated earlier, the marketing mix represents an assemblage of
tasks and subtasks which ultimately will help to satisfy the customer's requirements in such a way as to enable the firm to attain its
objectives in an optimum fashion. The subtle part of the concept is
that different companies in the same business may opt to develop
different 'mixes'. In fact it is this difference that may provide one
company with a competitive advantage over its competitors.

Let us consider a simple analogy. A pastry cook is invited to
prepare a cake for a given clientele, based on a number of ingredients
which are placed in front of him. At the same time he is told that

most of his customers are on a diet. Obviously he would use the available ingredients in such a way as to meet the dietary requirements of his customers. He would probably use less sugar but increase the use of less fattening components. If the 'mix' were right, he would satisfy the requirements of his clients and would gradually develop customer loyalty to his offering.

The same applies to the marketing mix. The marketer has at his or her disposal a number of components. The ability to mix them in response to an identified set of requirements, coupled with a number of other objectives, is one of the major requirements of effective marketing.

The 'four Ps model' of the marketing mix (see Chapter 2) has probably gained acceptance because of its elegance rather than its validity in all situations. Regrettably, what has been gained in simplicity has been sacrificed in universal appropriateness. It is easy to find examples of marketing programmes which do not fit into the four Ps model. It is therefore important to emphasize at the outset that this model is not of universal validity.

The theory underlying the Four Ps concept is that, if one manages to achieve the right *product* at the right *price* with the appropriate *promotion* and in the right *place*, the marketing programme will be effective and successful. However, one must bear in mind that each of the four Ps can be broken down into a number of subcomponents. Table 3.1 lists some of these.

In other words, it is not sufficient to think in terms of the four Ps. One needs to identify the significant subcomponents which underlie the firm's marketing strategy. A few simple examples of the marketing mixes of various companies will help to illustrate the point.

Table 3.1 The subcomponents of the four Ps

Product	Price	Place	Promotion
Brand	Credit terms	Channels	Advertising
Packaging	Payment period	Locations	Sales promotion
Warranties	Discounts	Transport	Publicity
Service	Instalments	Delivery	Selling
Features	Commissions	Stocks	
Guarantees	General cost/ benefit in use	Customs clearance	

Cosmetics: A major cosmetics company has declared that its marketing mix consists of the following components (referred to as 'the seven Ps and one A'):

- Product.
- Packaging.
- Price.
- Promotion.
- Personal selling.
- Publicity.
- Physical distribution.
- Advertising.

Domestic appliances: An international manufacturer of domestic appliances places its emphasis upon the following components:

- Product.
- Price.
- Promotion.
- Place.
- Service.

Automotive components:

- Product.
- Quality.
- Price.
- Place ('just-in-time').
- Selling.

No mention is made of promotion and/or advertising.

These are three very simple but disparate illustrations. The message is clear: what is right for a cosmetics company is not appropriate for a company manufacturing and selling automotive components to car manufacturers. The situation is probably even more complicated inasmuch as the components company may have different mixes, depending on whether it sells its products to original equipment manufacturers (OEM) companies or for the replacement market. In the former case there is little point in spending resources on promotion and/or advertising, whereas in the latter case advertising may be quite relevant because one is seeking to reach a market with a large number of consumers in it.

Every situation calls for a careful analysis of the key points where marketing resources must be allocated. The marketing mix represents those key points. More specifically, the main reasons for such an analysis are as follows.

(1) The marketing mix concept provides a valuable framework for allocating financial and human resources. Every company has to allocate a certain amount of resources towards its marketing effort. These resources are precious and must be used in the most effective way. Different businesses will need to allocate different amounts and personnel to each component of the mix. Before starting to allocate such resources one must determine with some precision which of the various ingredients available is likely to provide maximum customer satisfaction on the one hand, and optimum response from the marketplace on the other. This duality of roles must pervade the whole concept at all times.

(2) It can help to allocate responsibilities. Part of the marketing process entails the allocation of responsibilities to members of the marketing team. Some members of the team are responsible for product management, others for selling and yet others for physical distribution. The task of allocating such responsibilities is greatly facilitated if a logical and thoroughly researched framework for the 'perfect' mix is at hand. It is much easier to allocate responsibilities when one understands fully the nature and scope of the main activities that need to be undertaken.

Thus in the case of the domestic appliances company above, the 'service' component has been identified as a major element in the mix. Moreover, the company has recognized that the service department can be organized as a separate profit centre. It can function as a separate unit responsible for guaranteeing the product for the warranty period and thereafter can provide expeditious and efficient maintenance and repair at a fee. During the warranty period it derives its income from the manufacturing sister unit. In this particular company, everybody understands that the quality of the service rendered by the service unit can determine the difference between having happy and unhappy customers. Clearly this justifies the notion that 'service' deserves a separate existence in the mix. If anything goes wrong with the service element, there is no difficulty in apportioning blame.

(3) It provides an opportunity to analyze elasticities. Resources allocated to marketing mix ingredients are designed to yield results. For example, the number of sales personnel can be increased in order to increase sales. Similarly, by increasing the advertising budget one is seeking to increase the level of awareness of a product and/or the level of interest among potential customers. The most complicated task that every marketer has to grapple with is the decision as to which of the various ingredients at his or her disposal is likely to yield the best returns. Is it better to increase the sales force or to increase the promotional budget? Alternatively, is a faster and more efficient distribution system likely to yield better results?

The situation becomes more complex because the response to many of these expenditure areas is not linear. Life would be truly wonderful if by doubling the sales force one could double one's sales. In reality, there comes a point at which an increase in the number of sales personnel only generates a marginal increase in sales volume. The 'law of diminishing returns' sets in sooner or later, with the result that an increase in expenditure is not always followed by a commensurate increase in results.

Figure 3.1 illustrates a hypothetical relationship between expenditure and possible response rates in terms of sales revenue of three

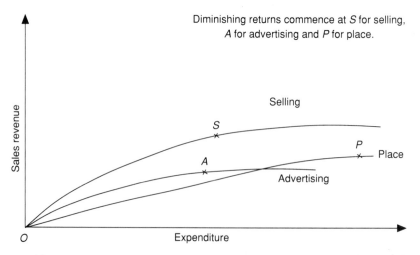

Figure 3.1 Elasticities of expenditure versus sales revenue of selling, advertising and place for a hypothetical product

components of the mix (selling, advertising and place). For the purpose of this illustration, the interaction among the three components is ignored. The diagram seeks to highlight how the three curves vary in respect of their elasticities and also in relation to the point at which the diminishing returns set in. With this kind of knowledge at hand it is much easier to develop a meaningful approach to allocating resources to the various ingredients of the mix.

To the extent that the chart describes a realistic state of affairs it is evident that the selling ingredient is the most productive, although at the point marked S the law of diminishing returns is setting in. At this point it ceases to be useful to increase costs inasmuch as the extra costs do not generate adequate sales. The advertising curve crosses the distribution curve, which means that a better (and more costly) distribution system continues to yield results after the point at which advertising has ceased to be productive.

In real life one has to consider the cumulative effect of these multiple tools upon each other. Nevertheless it is clear that different tools carry different elasticities and that the marketing mix concept helps to analyze such a proposition.

The perfect mix is based on full recognition of the relationship between cost and response, and identification of the point at which it does not pay to increase expenditure because the extra net revenue does not cover the extra cost. In other words, this kind of analysis can be undertaken only in the context of a marketing programme that has identified clearly the components that are effective in stimulating market response.

(4) It can facilitate communication. A cursory analysis of the organization charts of a number of companies would soon highlight the confusion that often prevails in the use of terms associated with the marketing function. Different organizations ascribe different meanings to subactivities of the marketing function.

A recent random comparison conducted by myself of a number of organization charts indicated a plethora of confusing and conflicting titles, such as 'marketing and promotion manager' side by side with 'brand managers', and 'promotions and publicity manager' side by side with 'sales and contracts manager'. Another company talks about a 'market research and promotion manager'. One sometimes encounters a position described with a perfectly neutral title such as 'commercial manager' when in fact the job entails substantial parts of the marketing task.

Titles *per se* can be fairly meaningless. It is the description ascribed to each job which matters. As long as members of the organization understand what the job entails, the title is quite irrelevant. On the other hand, it is quite helpful if people in other departments and/or even in the marketplace can relate to a person's responsibilities through a title which means what it says.

A full understanding of the main ingredients of the marketing mix can certainly provide a framework around which jobs can be allocated and their respective tasks communicated to the world at large. Thus, if one talks about a 'promotion manager', it should be fairly clear to everybody inside or outside the firm what the subactivities of such a job are. In other words, a well-defined and well-understood marketing mix analysis has a role to play both in the firm's organization development and in the communication system of the firm.

Marketing mix analysis

Identifying the major components of an effective marketing mix is an essential task for every marketer. This should be pursued at regular intervals:

- Whenever a new marketing programme is being developed.
- During the annual planning and review process for marketing.

When a new product is being launched, the most effective marketing mix must be determined. Similarly, when the company wishes to enter new markets or market segments with an existing product, it ought to consider what kind of mix is likely to yield the best results. With existing products the mix is already in place and the planning task in such situations is to review whether it is still appropriate and cost-effective.

It is important to remember that one of the main characteristics of the marketing process is its dynamic nature. Planning is designed to respond to the dynamism of the marketplace, and that includes the need to analyze and review the relevance of the mix which was selected when the product was first launched. Many companies fail for no other reason than not having identified the need to change the mix in response to changing market conditions.

Let us explore the two situations in greater depth.

The marketing mix for new marketing programmes

As we saw earlier, the simplest mix structure consists of the so-called four Ps. It was emphasized that these four headings belie the existence of a myriad of subcomponents of each of the four ingredients. The four Ps simply provide a simple and elegant structure for analysis and reflection. When one is planning to launch a totally new marketing programme, one must attempt to identify with clarity which of the subcomponents is likely to provide the company with the maximum cutting edge.

Let us draw an analogy with the way military campaigns are planned and conducted. If analysis shows that use of the air force will give faster and better results than use of tanks and infantry, obviously one chooses the former approach. The fact that the infantry could attain the same objectives but at a greater cost and on a longer time-scale needs to be recognized and brought into consideration during the planning of the campaign.

Moreover, if one has intelligence about the enemy's approach, strategy and tactics, one can deploy resources in the best way to surprise and defeat them. The important thing is to be fully aware of the relative effectiveness of the tools available. With this analogy in mind one should attempt to analyze as accurately as possible the relative value of each of the subcomponents of the marketing mix.

Figure 3.2 provides a simple checklist of the marketing mix and its main subcomponents. On the right-hand side of the checklist a score card is provided ranging from 0 for totally irrelevant to 4 for very important.

The main aim of this checklist is to provide the marketer with an opportunity to reflect upon the relative importance and relevance of the various tools which could be developed to facilitate a successful marketing effort. Many of the elements could be considered on the basis of the information available; others may need some additional research and/or advice; yet others may be based on previous experience and even entrepreneurial flair. However, it is important to emphasize that the checklist is an aid to the thinking process, not a substitute for reflection and analysis.

At the end of the marketing mix analysis, a useful insight should be gained into the relative value of the various components and subcomponents of the mix. The conclusions reached during such an analysis must be kept constantly under review and cannot be taken as constant in the long term. For instance, price may be judged as fairly unimportant at the beginning, but as the product life-cycle

	Relevance				
	0	**1**	**2**	**3**	**4**
Scoring: 4 = essential; 3 = important; 2 = worth considering; 1 = unimportant; 0 = irrelevant					
PRODUCT					
Brand name					
Packaging					
Warranties					
Service					
Features					
Guarantees					
Quality					
PRICE					
Credit terms					
Payment period					
Discounts					
Instalments					
Commissions					
Cost/benefit in use					
PROMOTION					
Advertising					
Sales promotion					
PR and publicity					
Selling					
Direct marketing					
PLACE					
Channels					
Locations					
Transport					
Delivery					
Stocks					
Speed of order					
Customs clearance					

Figure 3.2 Marketing mix analysis

progresses it may prove to be a crucial element in the game. Similarly, advertising may be vital during the launch period, but once a high level of awareness is reached its value may diminish. Marketing mix analysis should be treated as a continuous and dynamic process and not as a one-off exercise. On such a basis it can prove a most powerful tool in the armoury of marketing personnel.

In Figure 3.3 an attempt has been made to illustrate typical marketing mix patterns by industry types. The chart should not be read as a definitive recommendation of the emphasis that marketers in such sectors should place on the various ingredients of the mix listed. It is purely a judgmental perception of the relative importance of these ingredients *inter se*.

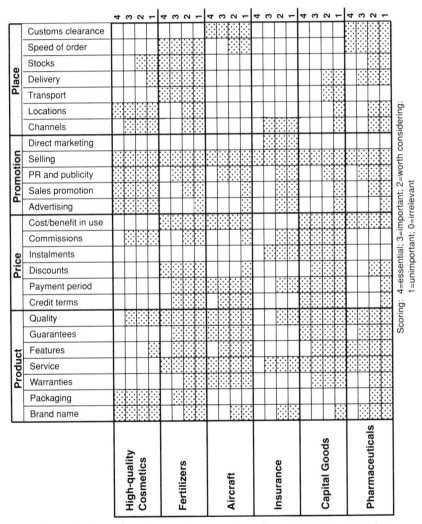

Figure 3.3 The marketing mix in a number of industries (for illustration purposes only)

Clearly the pattern will vary in accordance with the firm's marketing objectives and strategy. It will also vary in the way different segments could be approached. Nonetheless the chart demonstrates how the emphasis upon subcomponents can vary from industry to industry. It is up to each marketer to carry out his or her own analysis in relation to a particular marketing programme.

The marketing mix for existing marketing programmes

As we have seen, the marketing mix is not a constant edifice. The real challenge that marketers have to face is the delicate process of fine-tuning and honing the mix over time. Truly experienced and creative marketers can do this as a second nature. Like competent sailors they adjust their sails in response to changing conditions. They even attempt to anticipate changes and plan accordingly. The ability to do this is the acid test of excellence in the marketing function.

The marketing planning cycle provides the forum for reviewing the marketing mix assemblage and attempting to translate it into quantitative costs and revenues. Normally people who are continuously immersed in the marketing programme of a specific product or range of products, and over a fairly long period, are more sensitive to the need to amend the mix than those who arrive fresh to a well-established marketing activity. The reason is simple: old hands at marketing specific products have up-to-date knowledge of the product's history as well as full empathy towards its customers. Newcomers have to rely on quantitative information which does not provide the same feel for the realities of the situation.

If one traced the mix history of successful products and placed it on a comparative bar chart, it would be apparent that significant changes had taken place over the life of the product. Of course, this is natural and one would expect to see such changes in emphasis. Nevertheless very few marketers bother to record the relationships that have taken place among mix ingredients over a number of periods. Carrying out such an exercise can be most valuable for two reasons:

- It can help to identify trends in expenditure and the allocation of resources. This in turn can be of particular value during the monitoring and measurement process.
- It can provide a useful case study for analysis and future planning, especially where a programme for a similar product is under consideration. While a product history is not always a

perfect model for future launches, lessons learnt from a previous marketing effort do provide valuable insights for future projects. It is strongly recommended that a fairly detailed log-book is always kept by product or brand managers, in which the various steps relating to mix adjustments and the resultant outputs are recorded. Without such a record any change of personnel may mean that the true lessons learnt disappear from the firm's corporate memory.

The marketing mix of a high-quality cosmetics company was mentioned earlier. It was stated that the marketing personnel in that company talk about a mix consisting of 'seven Ps and one A': product, packaging, price, promotion, personal selling, publicity, physical distribution and advertising. This mix concept has been published in a small booklet with a wide distribution. Its main aim was to ensure that a homogeneity of approach and nomenclature existed throughout the firm. The booklet highlighted the fact that each of the eight ingredients has a number of further sub-ingredients, and their scope and role were explained in clear terms. The marketing director introduced a system whereby every brand manager was instructed to monitor the pattern that the mix took over time.

Figure 3.4 illustrates the kind of information that the company expects to be included in the marketing planning dossier. It relates to an exquisitely packaged deodorant. The bar charts illustrated in the diagram cover four periods: at launch and on the three subsequent anniversaries. The bars were calculated by amalgamating quantitative data (costs) and qualitative input (time spent and level of emphasis). Each chart was supported by a full explanatory narrative and figures. Although the differences are fairly subtle, a number of significant points can be highlighted:

- The expenditure on the product in the form of brand management was constant. The marketing personnel recognized that success demands a continuous and steadfast attention to detail throughout the product's life.
- Resources allocated to packaging were very high at the beginning and during the launch period. They dropped substantially during the next two years because little had to be done during that period. On the other hand, additional expenditure was spent during the fourth year to reposition the product and enhance its packaging once again.
- Price was not considered a sensitive element in the mix until the

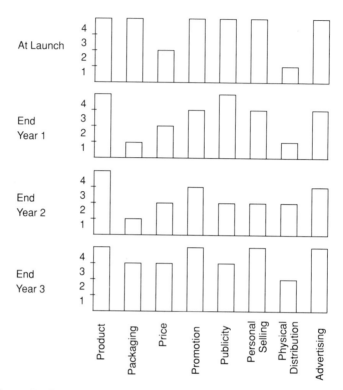

Figure 3.4 The marketing mix at launch and in three subsequent years (illustration only)

fourth year. At that point it was necessary to cope with competitive pressures and to allocate some resources to special discounts for bulk buying and special premiums.

- Some fine-tuning can be observed in the resources allocated to promotion, publicity and advertising. Once again the cumulative expenditure was higher at launch and in the fourth year. Some relaxation took place in between. In the second and third years the product was enjoying the fruits of the enormous effort that went into the launch of the product. In the fourth year fresh energy was needed to cope with competitive pressures and to communicate the refurbished image.

MARKETING MIX AUDIT

Score
0 1 2

1. **Is the marketing mix concept understood and used by the marketing personnel?**

    (a) No.   (*Score 0*)
    (b) It is understood but never found of practical
    use.   (*Score 1*)
    (c) Yes. It is understood and used. Detailed marketing
    plans are based on it.   (*Score 2*)

2. **Does the marketing department attempt to quantify the levels of expenditure that should be allocated to each of the mix ingredients?**

    (a) No.   (*Score 0*)
    (b) Yes, but in a fairly vague way.   (*Score 1*)
    (c) Detailed expenditure is allocated to each element
    of the mix and its relative effectiveness
    measured.   (*Score 2*)

3. **Are the elasticities of the various mix ingredients understood by the marketing department?**

    (a) No.   (*Score 0*)
    (b) An attempt is made to identify elasticities after the
    money has been spent.   (*Score 1*)
    (c) Part of the research budget is allocated to
    determining elasticities of mix ingredients in advance
    of expenditure.   (*Score 2*)

4. **When does the marketing department review its marketing mix?**

    (a) Never.   (*Score 0*)
    (b) When major marketing problems
    arise.   (*Score 1*)
    (c) Continuously and in particular during the
    marketing planning cycle.   (*Score 2*)

5. **Does the firm take steps to develop an optimum mix when planning new product launches?**

    (a) No.   (*Score 0*)

▶

(b) A number of mixes are
considered.   (*Score 1*)
(c) Careful analysis is carried out in order to identify
the most effective and the most economical
mix.   (*Score 2*)

6. **Does the firm attempt to analyze its competitors'
    marketing mix?**

(a) Seldom.   (*Score 0*)
(b) Yes, but only when we can get hold of the
appropriate input.   (*Score 1*)
(c) Yes. We consider the understanding of
competitors' mixes a most valuable piece of
knowledge. We allocate resources to this kind of
study.   (*Score 2*)

7. **Does the company adjust its marketing mix in
    relation to specific segments?**

(a) No. Everybody gets the same
treatment.   (*Score 0*)
(b) Yes. We adjust one component of the mix at a
time, e.g. different prices for different
segments.   (*Score 1*)
(c) The whole mix is reviewed in detail, and each
segment gets its own assemblage of mix
components.   (*Score 2*)

8. **Is a 'log-book' of changes in the mix over the product
    life being kept?**

(a) No.   (*Score 0*)
(b) We do not keep a log-book, but we try to
remember how the mix has changed.   (*Score 1*)
(c) Yes. Every product and brand manager is
instructed to monitor the mix development in a
systematic way.   (*Score 2*)

9. **Do other departments understand the marketing mix
    concept, and are they invited to take part in its
    development?**

(a) No.   (*Score 0*)

▶

Score
0 1 2

(b) Yes. We advise them of our decisions in this
regard. *(Score 1)*
(c) We recognize that marketing strategies must be
integrated with other functions. We therefore try to
have as wide a dialogue as possible with other
departments. *(Score 2)*

10. **When briefing outside contractors (such as research
and/or advertising agencies) does the company
provide them with details of the marketing mix plan?**

(a) No. *(Score 0)*
(b) We give them some idea of our mix but expect
them to tell us what the right mix should
be. *(Score 1)*
(c) We provide them with full details of our thinking
on the subject, supported by a marketing mix plan for
the period(s) during which we invite them to help
us. *(Score 2)*

The maximum score possible is 20. Very few companies could achieve
such a score. Lower scores can be interpreted as follows:

15–20 **Excellent**
10–14 **Good to very good.**
5–9 **Fair**
0–4 **Poor**

4

The input for effective marketing

The phrases 'market research', 'marketing research', 'intelligence gathering', 'information gathering' and 'motivation research' are all popular terms in the marketing field. They have been deliberately omitted from the title of this chapter because they represent only a fraction of the 'knowledge' requirements underlying effective marketing decisions. The word 'input' is synonymous here with 'knowledge'.

Knowledge is an essential aid to marketing. The more one knows about markets and customers, the easier it is to coalesce an assemblage of 'satisfiers' to address to the target audience. Marketers with inadequate knowledge operate like archers who aim at a target in darkness. Conversely, the well-informed archer knows how external conditions like temperature and breeze can affect the trajectory of the arrow.

Ideally one should detach oneself periodically from day-to-day marketing operations and pose the question: 'What do we need to know in order to improve our marketing effort?' This question forms an integral part of the planning process. Nonetheless the 'input' needed for planning and the 'input' required for effective marketing operations are somewhat different. The former relates to 'macro' strategic thinking, whereas the latter is highly operational and can provide some immediacy to one's response to a changing market environment. For example, the fact that customers are unhappy with the literature that accompanies the product can be acted upon quickly, but it has little influence on the firm's planning cycle unless its rectification offers the firm a significant competitive advantage. Moreover, the firm can respond to such a complaint only if it knows all about it. Unfortunately, many marketers are often completely ignorant about 'micro' issues that irritate the customers.

In response to the question, 'What do we need to know in order to improve our marketing effort?' it is important to remember to be selective in the amount of knowledge one collects. It may be true that a 'little knowledge is a dangerous thing', but one must also remember that too much knowledge can overwhelm its recipient. In a dynamic environment the knowledge acquired must be capable of assisting in dynamic and cost-effective decisions. It is important to distinguish between truly valuable facts and those which are simply 'nice to know' but of limited practical value. One of the dangers, often encountered in organizations that have a so-called market research department, is that the researchers undertake many interesting projects which are not of practical value to those who take decisions in an operational context. As we shall see in Chapter 13 this is a common problem with organizations which fail to integrate the various subactivities of the marketing function. 'Input gathering' is an aid to marketing and not an end in itself.

How much knowledge?

Many companies operate with very little knowledge. At the other extreme, some companies are submerged in so much knowledge that they simply do not have time to operate. A happy medium has to be struck between these two extremes. With very little effort one can list areas of knowledge which might be useful in improving one's relationship with existing and potential customers. Here are a few such areas:

- Demographics.
- Socioeconomic factors.
- Ethnic/religious data.
- Geographic/regional data.
- Attitudes of customers and users.
- Motivational factors.
- Life-styles.
- Consumption habits.
- Shopping habits.
- 'Shopping baskets' related to socioeconomic segments.

- Legal and quasi-legal factors.
- Competitive practices.
- Peer-group influences.
- Attitudes to channels and store patronage.
- Understanding price elasticity.
- Levels of awareness of products or brands.
- Segmentation possibilities in a given market.

These are just a few of many possible areas, and each one of these could be broken down into a myriad of potential input-gathering exercises. Where does it all end?

In industrial marketing there are many examples of the danger of over-proliferating the range of potential projects for in-depth studies. Figure 4.1 describes in a diagrammatic form the number of 'cells' that one can assemble if a steel manufacturer with a range of six products and eight major applications wants to study the market in detail in six countries or continents. Altogether one can list $6 \times 8 \times 6 = 288$ potential areas for survey projects. If an additional dimension becomes relevant, thousands of potential research projects are possible.

It is evident that some method for prioritizing the value of

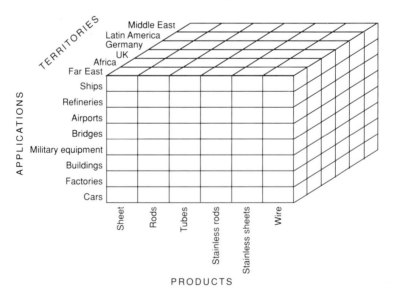

Figure 4.1 Potential areas for market survey projects of a steel manufacturer

input-gathering activities is an essential part of the whole process. While it is good to know everything, one must be content with acquiring knowledge which can satisfy two interrelated requirements:

- It is capable of having a significant impact upon marketing decisions.
- It can be obtained at a reasonable or acceptable cost.

Competent researchers can normally provide valuable information from the answers to survey questions. There are very few areas of marketing investigation which cannot yield the desired input. On the other hand, there are many areas in which the relationship between costs and anticipated benefits simply do not warrant the proposed expenditure.

For example, a firm of opticians with 100 outlets wants to know how many of their customers have blue eyes. Gaining such information is not technically difficult. Every optician in every outlet may simply be asked to add 'colour of eyes' details to the normal form and in due course the figures collated over a statistically valid period can be grossed up. Now the legitimate question arises as to what one can do with this input. In fact one should not waste time and resources on such an investigation unless one can simulate a 'payoff' statement to justify the proposed study. The opticians in the various outlets could probably use the same time either to carry out useful work or to ask other and more relevant questions, which in turn may provide valuable knowledge for immediate application.

Two practical steps can be taken to alleviate the danger described.

An impact/cost matrix

Figure 4.2 describes a simple matrix which can help to screen multiple research projects that may emerge during the 'What do we need to know?' exercise. It is not a foolproof system, but at least it forces the marketer to reflect upon the relationship between the value of the project and its likely cost. The project with the highest potential impact and the minimum cost is much more desirable than the one with little impact and high cost!

Cost–benefit analysis of research projects

In a multiproduct and multimarket organization there is a strong case for introducing a research authorization procedure. In most com-

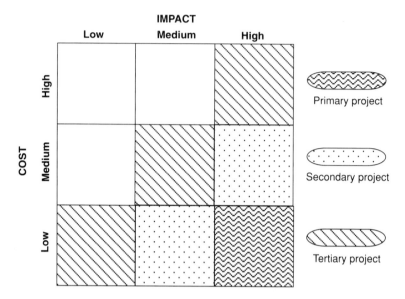

Figure 4.2 Impact/cost matrix

panies very little capital expenditure is allowed without a prior authorization procedure being complied with. Such a procedure asks for information about the reason for the expenditure, investment recovery prospects and so on. In many firms, however, market surveys are undertaken without the slightest justification procedure being pursued. When one remembers that such projects often cost much more than the purchase of pieces of equipment which, in normal circumstances, need to go through rigorous authorization procedures, it seems a strange omission!

A system for evaluating and authorizing market research activities is proposed in Figure 4.3. The system may appear like an additional piece of bureaucracy. It is not meant as such. The sheer process of responding to the various questions incorporated in the questionnaire is of great value. It should force the submitters of the proposed programme of work to consider all the implications and the potential 'payoffs' that the research project under discussion may yield.

The procedure itself is not easy to complete and support with quantitative accuracy, but the qualitative thinking underlying the whole task is most salutary. The aim is to discourage managers from undertaking research projects which are stimulating and 'nice to know', but which at the same time are unlikely to provide a sufficient payoff for the effort involved.

Procedures for evaluating marketing research projects

Research project title -

Purpose -

- -

- -

Likely methods to be used -

- -

- -

Specific activities / tasks to be undertaken -

- -

- -

- -

Resources needed and costs

INTERNAL		EXTERNAL		TOTAL COSTS
Days	Cost	Days	Cost	

Simulated Payoff

(Applicants must endeavour to quantify benefits that may accrue from the successful completion of the project. A simulated cost–benefit analysis must be appended to this form)

Supportive material to be included -

- -

Estimated payoff in money terms £ -

- -

Submitted by - - - - - - - - - - - - - - - - - - - Approved by -

Figure 4.3 Procedure for evaluating the cost/benefit of research projects

Marketing profile analysis

It is worth remembering that the planning of a successful marketing programme always takes place in an environment which is outside the marketer's control. The marketer must know as much as possible about such an environment, but in normal circumstances he or she can do little to change it. Although one can think of specific circumstances where marketers have managed to stimulate changes in the external environment, these on the whole are rare. The main role of marketing is to understand the environment and to develop a programme which responds to the realities that the marketplace offers.

The word 'environment' in this context encompasses a myriad of factors. In broad terms one can break it down into four major components:

- **The customer's environment:** This covers all the elements that relate to customers, their typologies, behaviour, present and future demand patterns, personal disposable incomes, tastes, attitudes, etc.

- **Competitive practices:** Here one is concerned with knowledge about competitors, their practices, behaviour, plans, etc. This includes both 'brand' competitors and 'functional' competitors. The former offer a similar product but under a different name. The latter offer substitutes that act as competition.

- **Institutions:** This includes bodies that can facilitate and/or impede the marketing process. Channels of distribution, media availability, organizations that compare qualities and bodies that lay down codes of practice can all be regarded as institutions. It is difficult to change them or avoid them, so why not join them? In order to do so, one must, of course, understand how they function.

- **Legal system:** Marketing decisions are surrounded by legal and semi-legal instruments which must be adhered to. Understanding their scope and limitations is essential for an effective marketing effort.

On reflection the reader will soon realize that most external factors that impact upon marketing decisions fall comfortably under these headings. In other words, the marketing mix must be developed within a cluster of environmental factors, each of which may have an impact upon each of the components of the mix. Thus, if we place the various elements of the mix on one side and the external factors that form a marketplace opposite, we get a picture like the one shown in Figure 4.4.

Alternatively, we can now place the 'internal' and 'external' elements in a matrix which looks like the one described in Figure 4.5. Essentially this is a spreadsheet-type diagram which consists of 16 rubrics. Each rubric represents the interface between one external and one internal element of knowledge required. The rubric does not provide information, but it helps to list the areas in which information may be required. It is an aid to reflection and analysis. Thus the rubric 'promotion/institutions' provides an opportunity to list such questions as:

'Availability of suitable media for promoting our new product?'

'Any institutions that prescribe an advertising code of practice in relation to this product offering?'

'Relative cost per spot, and is there a more economical way of buying space?'

The marketing profile analysis diagram is an aid to clear thinking, not a substitute for thinking. It is enormously helpful in analyzing

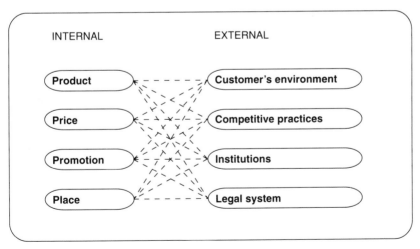

Figure 4.4 The interface between the internal ingredients of the mix and the external elements of the environment

CONTROLLABLE INGREDIENTS OF THE MARKETING MIX (4 Ps MODEL)			
Product	Price	Place	Promotion

		Product	Price	Place	Promotion
EXTERNAL / UNCONTROLLABLE ELEMENTS	Customer's environment				
	Competition				
	Institutions				
	Legal systems				

Figure 4.5 Marketing profile analysis: aid to listing 'knowledge' requirements

marketing environments when facing a market for the first time, such as in international situations.

The value of intelligence

Very few organizations understand the value of intelligence better than a nation's armed forces. If one studies the history of great military campaigns, one soon discovers that the quality of the intelligence available to the military machines was, in many instances, the determinant factor in their victories. It must be argued that armies attach this level of importance to intelligence because they know that defeat may mean ignominy or death. Marketing people are not exposed to such a cruel destiny and therefore often satisfy themselves with second-rate input.

At the outset it is useful to clarify a number of terms. Those involved in research activities use such terms as *data, information* and *intelligence* almost interchangeably. All three elements are part of the input-gathering process, but it is strongly suggested here that in the final analysis the only one that really matters in taking more effective marketing decisions is intelligence.

Data

Data means raw information generated in large quantities and often organized in a pattern which suits the convenience of the collector rather than of the user.

Imagine a telephone directory which lists all the telephone numbers in numerical sequence. It is very easy to produce but of limited value to anybody who wants to identify a named person. To find the telephone number of Ron Pinchingbottom, one needs to cast one's eye down the pages until that name is found. There is no need to emphasize what a gargantuan task that may be!

Data are available in great abundance either from external sources or from inside the company. Many companies do not realize what a wealth of data they have in their files or records. Unfortunately, a large quantity of data often negates its value in the eyes of its owners either through the discomfort of having to sift through it or through the owners' inability to distil it into a more manageable format.

Information

Information normally represents data which has been distilled and collated into a more user-friendly format. The needs of the user are borne in mind when information is presented. Returning to the telephone directory, the way that the names are arranged alphabetically can be of great help in searching for a subscriber's number. A telephone directory provides information of general value to those needing to find the numbers of given subscribers.

However, even the alphabetical format has its limitations. It seldom tells the user what the occupation of the subscriber is. It does not say whether the subscriber is young or old, rich or poor. It does not disclose what languages the names listed speak, nor does it tell us about any special interests they may have. If we were interested in identifying a list of left-handed golfers, the telephone directory would be pretty useless. What we need now is high-quality intelligence.

Intelligence

The truly valuable input for marketing decisions consists of intelligence. A telephone directory from which one can extract special input of particular interest to its owner could be a source of intelligence. To some extent classified directories seek to provide such a facility. Nevertheless the details given are provided for an undifferentiated global group of readers and therefore have little facility for translation into detailed intelligence. It is easy to find a list of dentists and their telephone numbers, but it is impossible to glean from the directory who among them likes Chinese food.

Intelligence must be accurate, detailed and focused upon specific objectives and tasks. It is therefore not surprising that some companies talk not about a market research department but about a marketing intelligence department. Companies that use the latter term purely as a cosmetic enhancement of research activities miss the point. Marketing intelligence, as against *ad hoc* research projects, must have the following qualities:

- It must be *relevant* within the firm's marketing aims and operations.

- It must be *accurate* in the sense that it consists of as many facts as possible rather than just opinions.

- It must be *dynamic* through the process of updating its accuracy when changes take place in the market environment.

In practice, data provide the raw material for information. Skilfully analyzed, distilled and interpreted information leads to the assembly of intelligence. Up-to-date and accurate intelligence is one of the most powerful areas in which a company can develop a competitive advantage *vis-à-vis* its competitors. As we saw earlier, those who possess the right 'knowledge' have a powerful competitive edge at their disposal.

Marketing intelligence can be acquired in three ways:

(1) *Ad hoc* **research projects:** We shall explore briefly the way such projects should be planned and managed.

(2) Continuous data collection and interpretation: This relates in particular to specific items of interest to marketing personnel in attempting to adjust objectives and control performance.

Thus, for instance, a pharmaceutical company may monitor on a continuous basis the number of prescriptions that are being issued by general practitioners for each of its products. IMS is an organization that assembles such information and provides a wealth of marketing intelligence derived from the data it collects.

In this connection we have already considered the use of marketing profile analysis (see Figure 4.5) as an aid to reflecting upon and identifying the various elements of knowledge which are significant for marketing planning and decision making.

(3) Marketing information system: This implies that the firm in general, and the marketing organization in particular, has developed a continuous and dynamic data, information and intelligence flow. Such a system is designed to encompass all the critical elements of a responsive organization which truly seeks to meet the challenges of a changing environment.

The challenge here is twofold:

- It calls for a high level of skill on the part of the system designer.
- It also requires a high level of conceptual awareness on the part of those managers who ought to derive benefit from the system.

A simple example will illustrate the value of such a system. A Japanese car manufacturer has established a worldwide system whereby any complaint, however small, made to one of its dealers must be immediately transmitted by the international electronic mail network to the company's headquarters. The system is geared to fan out details of such complaints to all the appropriate stakeholders with the aim of ensuring that, once identified, similar problems will never reoccur. The process is continuous, dynamic and certainly customer orientated.

In an ideal world every company should devote the time and resources to plan an all-embracing marketing information system which encompasses the critical intelligence needs. Such a system can derive its information from both external and internal sources. It is often forgotten that a wealth of information is available inside the company or can be easily collated from company personnel. One should never overlook the fact that the company's sales force represents a most fertile resource for information-gathering activities. Sales personnel come in direct contact with customers and have an opportunity to observe competitors. Moreover, they are often eager to communicate snippets of intelligence which they have gleaned during their travels. Alas, much too often nobody in the centre wants to listen to what they have to say.

The unequivocal message is that a company's marketing effort can be enriched through the introduction of a system that ensures that all company personnel are motivated and stimulated to communicate their impressions, opinions and factual observations in a structured manner. The system must be so organized that such input can be screened, collated and distilled into bits of intelligence.

The market and marketing research process

Considerable confusion exists in relation to the two terms 'market research' and 'marketing research'. They are often used inter-changeably.

Market research relates to data gathering about the market itself. Marketing research relates to the gathering, recording and analyzing of data about matters relating to the *marketing* of goods and services. In other words, the former seeks to research markets, their structure and the people in them. The latter attempts to study the most effective way of reaching such markets and to provide them with maximum satisfaction.

Within the context of a book dealing with the essential elements of marketing management it would be inappropriate to delve into the intricacies of research methodologies. Nonetheless it is important to describe the process and the logical steps that have to be pursued from the moment a decision has been made to undertake either a market research or a marketing research project.

The process is described in Figure 4.6. It consists of five main phases:

(1) Project definition: The purpose of the project must be defined (and redefined) with a view to establishing the underlying thinking and the relevance to the marketing task. At this stage it is useful to explore the following:

- Whether published material exists which may nullify the need to undertake such a project.
- The cost–benefit justification for the expense which may be incurred.

A number of pitfalls should be avoided:

- Using vague terms of reference.
- Stating the wrong problem.
- Undertaking projects with a covert or undisclosed purpose.

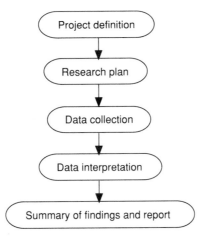

Figure 4.6 The marketing research process

(2) Research plan: The plan must list the following:

- Its objectives.
- Tasks involved (to include those that can be undertaken with internal resources as well as those that call for outside help).
- The most appropriate methodology to be used.
- Detailed plan and review procedures.

(3) Data collection: This is an important stage in the implementation programme of work. Sources of information must be identified and, if found to be useful, acquired. Internal sources should also be located and collated. More specifically, the following steps need to be pursued in a systematic way:

- The identification of sources of information – both external and internal. This step calls for a thorough analysis of published material, of which enormous quantities exist in libraries and other reference establishments.
- If the research involves interviewing of individuals, a sample interview/questionnaire-filling exercise needs to be carried out.
- Responses to be analyzed and errors, ambiguities or inconsistencies identified and corrected.
- Data collected and collated.

(4) Data interpretation: Now the time has come to analyze the data collected, distil its essentials, tabulate, classify and cross-classify.

Relevant data are to be integrated and organized into manageable format. Significant relationships are to be highlighted. Essentially, the data is gradually being turned into information and ultimately valuable intelligence.

(5) Summary of findings and report: This is the point at which effective communication is put to the test. The final report should be in a format which can be easily decoded by its 'audience', and if necessary acted upon. Quite often excellent research projects fail in their aims for the very simple reason that they are presented in a manner or style which the most significant recipients cannot relate to. Obviously, if they cannot relate to the report, they will not be able to act upon it either.

Methods of forecasting demand

One of the most important input-gathering tasks in marketing is attempting to forecast demand. Forecasting takes place during the planning cycle and is the basis upon which marketing objectives are determined. There are many different ways to undertake such an exercise. They vary from the very naive to the extremely sophisticated. It is important to remember that a forecast by its very nature is probabilistic and therefore should never be regarded as an immovable statement of events to come. All a forecast attempts to do is to quantify, to the best of one's ability and with the highest level of probability, what is likely to happen at a future date.

Clearly, when one seeks to forecast demand or sales, the higher the level of corroboration that one can obtain the better. Such corroboration may come from the extrapolation of the past into the future or from more analytical predictive models. Intuition can also play a role in the forecasting task. However, intuition which is supported by an array of more objective inputs is safer than intuition on its own.

Figure 4.7 illustrates the various methods which are open to marketing personnel during the forecasting process. The horizontal axis moves from a purely subjective mode on the left towards greater objectivity on the right. The vertical axis represents levels of analysis: low at the bottom, starting with naive methods, and culminating in a high level of analysis at the top, referred to as analytical methods.

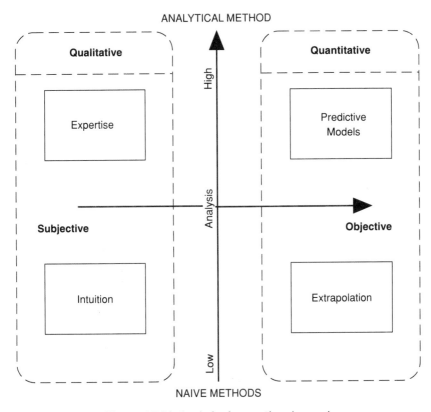

Figure 4.7 Methods for forecasting demand

The methods on the left are qualitative in nature. The methods on the right are quantitative.

Intuition

Some marketers, especially those with an entrepreneurial flair, have the gift of forecasting future demand and/or sales with amazing accuracy. Such people are very lucky. If one recalls the maxim that 'luck is the residue of good planning', one ought to come to the inevitable conclusion that plans based purely on intuition can be risky. However, if all the figures and all the analysis point in a certain direction, intuition has a valuable role to play.

Decision theory suggests that the intuition of many people is better than that of one person. This is the basis of such methods as the so-called *jury of executive opinion* and the *Delphi method*.

Jury of executive opinion

As its name implies, this method seeks to collate and average the opinions and intuitions of a large number of the firm's managers. Thus, if one invites the company's salespeople to express their opinions on the following year's sales, these opinions are likely to vary considerably. The optimists will provide higher forecasts than the pessimists. Yet the average among all these opinions may prove to be remarkably accurate. At least this is what the theory suggests.

Delphi method

This technique was originally developed in the USA by the RAND Corporation. The name is derived from the oracle of Delphi, who in ancient Athens used to offer predictions of events to come. National leaders used to solicit her opinions about the future and base their political and military strategies on an interpretation of what her rather equivocal messages communicated.

The technique, in effect, is a logical extension of the jury of executive opinion. The difference is that here one is seeking to integrate the opinions of many individuals who are not necessarily associated with the company. The aim is to attempt to average their opinions without sacrificing or compromising individuals' suggestions and ideas.

A panel of 'wise people' is asked to comment on a list of issues which may help to coalesce a vision of the future. The following couple of questions and the format represent the kind of items that the questionnaire might contain:

(1) *In the long term, the economic growth of the European Community will slow down to a maximum growth of 2%.*

I agree strongly | 1 | 2 | 3 | 4 | 5 | I disagree strongly

(2) *There will be only one currency in Europe by the year 2000.*

I agree strongly | 1 | 2 | 3 | 4 | 5 | I disagree strongly

Many other questions pertaining to some future date should be included in the questionnaire. Among these questions are those of particular relevance to the project. As one might expect, the answers are likely to produce a distribution curve, with the majority falling within the 2 to 4 zone and the minority at the extremities. An iterative questioning follows. The members of the panel are invited to reconsider and possibly revise their original opinions. Moreover, those insisting on remaining at the two extremes may have a valuable input relating to future scenarios. In other words, the whole process attempts to collate the collective intuition and opinions of a carefully selected panel.

Expertise

The higher the degree of expertise upon which opinions are based, the higher the quality of the forecast. To that extent it is important to identify the various scenarios published in the literature and to attempt to evaluate the level of expertise and knowledge that their authors possess.

The *jury of informed or expert opinion* is a subtle variation of the method described earlier. The one significant difference is that here one seeks to assemble the opinions of experts or of people who are known to be well informed in the area under study. A forecast relating to the price of cereal is more likely to be reliable if it is based on the collective opinions of cereal brokers. Similarly, a forecast as to exchange rates based on the opinions of money dealers or bankers would enjoy a higher probability of accuracy than one produced by ordinary managers.

Expert opinion can be gathered in a number of ways.

Group discussion
Experts are invited to discuss the situation and to reach some concurrence about a group estimate. The idea underlying this method is that the experts will ventilate openly their respective opinions and, once they have reached an agreement, will produce a joint forecast.

Pooled individual estimates method
Experts supply their estimators to a project leader, who in turn merges them into a single forecast. By monitoring the accuracy of individual estimates, the leader can ascribe an accuracy weight factor to each estimate for future exercises.

Delphi method
This method was discussed earlier under the heading of intuition. When the panel are selected for their *expertise*, the quality of the forecast carries a lot more weight than when they are simply a group of 'wise people'.

Extrapolation

Moving to the more quantitative side of the process, one can prepare forecasts on the basis of statistical–mathematical analysis of past data. The underlying logic is that the past data represent an enduring causal relationship. In the absence of evidence to the contrary, it is assumed that such a relationship will persist. Clearly, this is not always true and great caution must be exercised in relying upon such forecasts.

Prominent among the various techniques that can help to extrapolate past data into future trends are the following:

- Time series.
- Least squares method.
- Exponential smoothing.
- Regression and correlation.

It is outside the scope of this book to describe these methods in detail. The important point to remember is that every competent statistican will know how to extrapolate past data into a forecast. Moreover, with the increasing availability of computers on managers' desks, it is becoming very easy to produce demand analysis on the basis of the various extrapolation methods listed. However, the user must be aware of a number of pitfalls:

- The availability of too small a number of observations. This lowers the quality of a forecast based on such data.
- The emergence of new factors which have not been accounted for in the past.
- Where too much correlation exists among independent variables.
- Where a two-way cause and effect is in existence. Thus, the amount of paper sold by a photocopying machine manufacturer is affected by the number of machines sold. It would be wrong to take the sale of paper as the basis for extrapolative forecasting of the number of machines to be sold in the future.

Predictive models

This area represents the highest level of analytical quality and the maximum objectivity. A model has been defined by Philip Kotler as 'the specification of a set of variables and their interrelationships designed to represent some real system or process, in whole or in part'.

There are many different types of model which can be of value for marketing decisions. A diagram that represents the flow of goods from source to customer is a graphical model of a logical flow process. The network analysis technique which is normally reduced to a flow diagram is another model. It shows the interrelationship between activities and events with the critical path updated in a dynamic fashion.

Management science has taught us that in certain circumstances mathematical models can be powerful aids to planning and forecasting. For instance, a well-structured model can help the marketer to predict the relationship between such variables as advertising and sales. Where a few variables are in existence, one can resort to the multiple regression model, which can simulate the interplay among a number of such factors as advertising, selling, distribution points and their joint impact on sales. Models come in a number of forms.

Linear and nonlinear models

As its name implies, a linear model exists when the variables interact as a straight line. Assuming that every one degree increase in the temperature increases the sale of ice-cream by a constant amount, the relationship is linear. However, it is important to remember that a relationship may be linear initially, but ceases to be so after a while. If a company has a very small number of sales personnel, it is quite possible that in the beginning every additional sales person will increase sales by a constant amount. At this early stage the relationship is linear, but after a certain point it becomes nonlinear. The law of diminishing returns sets in, the increases diminish and the line becomes a curve. Linearity is generally only a first approximation for mathematical convenience.

Static and dynamic models

A static model occurs when cause-and-effect relationships take place regardless of time and environmental changes. Elementary supply and demand models described in books on economics tend to be static. They overlook the dynamism of the marketplace and possible real-life reactions. On the other hand, econometric models used by governments or fiscal institutes are dynamic. They seek to incorporate as many dynamic variables into the equation as possible. 'What if?' business models are normally dynamic ones.

Brand-switching models that seek to predict the interplay among brands in response to promotional expenditure and other factors are prime examples of dynamic models.

Deterministic and stochastic models

Deterministic models are those that allow little scope for chance. If 'A' happens, 'B' is sure to follow. Linear programming is deterministic insofar as, given a set of circumstances, it prescribes the optimum solution in terms of minimum costs or maximum returns or shortest route, etc. Stochastic models are those which allow for random variables or chance events. In fact, such elements are deliberately introduced into the relationship. Thus a brand-switching model is stochastic to the extent that brand choices are controlled by probabilities and one can never be sure how consumers are likely to respond.

The effective marketer must understand the role of models in the input-gathering game. The ultimate design and development of such models is a highly specialized task and belongs to the marketing management scientists, who know how to apply mathematics to the explanation, prediction and improvement of marketing processes.

INPUT-GATHERING AUDIT

Score
0 1 2

1. **Does the marketing organization undertake input-gathering activities on a regular basis?**

    (a) We carry out market research studies only before launching new products and only if we can afford them.   *(Score 0)*
    (b) We research markets from time to time in order to find out if we are on course.   *(Score 1)*
    (c) We research markets before, during and after launch, and attempt at all times to detect changes in the market environment.   *(Score 2)*

2. **What topics form the basis of the firm's research activities?**

    (a) Whether customers are happy with our product, and if not, why not.   *(Score 0)*
    (b) Altogether we seek to understand better our relationship with customers.   *(Score 1)*
    (c) We constantly define our 'knowledge'

▶

requirements and attempt to identify the most
important ones. These topics form the basis of our
input-gathering activities.   *(Score 2)*

3. **How much money is allocated for marketing research
    activities?**

    (a) As little as possible. We consider the whole subject
    as a luxury. Prior to launching a new product we
    allocate a percentage of our estimated sales
    target.   *(Score 0)*
    (b) We allocate every year a percentage of our annual
    sales targets.   *(Score 1)*
    (c) As much as is necessary to provide us with the
    appropriate insights into market realities. However,
    we always try to measure possible cost/benefit.
                                     (Score 2)

4. **Who is responsible for directing input-gathering
    policy?**

    (a) The sales manager or the market research
    department itself.   *(Score 0)*
    (b) Product or brand management. *(Score 1)*
    (c) 'Intelligence' is considered as an essential resource
    for success. Hence top marketing management feels
    responsible for laying down policy regarding 'input'
    required and frequency.   *(Score 2)*

5. **Does the company monitor the benefit derived from
    its input-gathering activities?**

    (a) As we spend so little, we do not consider it
    necessary to control results.   *(Score 0)*
    (b) Only if the project involves us in significant
    expenditure.   *(Score 1)*
    (c) We have a standing rule that a notional payoff
    analysis has to be undertaken in relation to each
    market/marketing research activity.   *(Score 2)*

6. **Who undertakes input-gathering activities in the
    firm?**

    (a) All research is undertaken by outside consultants,
    when we can afford them.   *(Score 0)*
    (b) Most of the work is carried out by a central

▶

marketing department at head office. They advise us
what should be researched and when. *(Score 1)*
(c) Everybody in our marketing organization,
including the sales force, are encouraged to collect
market intelligence at all times. We conduct training
programmes on this specific issue.   *(Score 2)*

7. **Are company personnel motivated in any way to
assemble and communicate bits of intelligence?**

(a) No. We do not feel that it is their
job.   *(Score 0)*
(b) Yes. We normally express our thanks to those who
communicate useful information.   *(Score 1)*
(c) One of the items we quiz people about during
appraisal sessions is the amount and frequency of
information they have assembled and submitted. It
can reflect upon their merit rating.   *(Score 2)*

8. **Does the marketing department have a system for
scanning the media for information about the market,
customers and competitors?**

(a) No. We have done it once and it does not seem to
pay.   *(Score 0)*
(b) We pay for such a 'news items' service. We receive
a lot of cuttings about our industry. However, nobody
seems to pursue them systematically.   *(Score 1)*
(c) We have trained our personnel to keep their ears
and eyes open for useful bits of information at all
times. We also have a system for collating and
analysing such an input.   *(Score 2)*

9. **Does the company maintain a databank about its
competitors as part of its input-gathering activities?**

(a) No. We know all we need to know about our
competitors   *(Score 0)*
(b) We maintain a dossier about each one of our
competitors. The dossiers include annual reports and
copies of their literature.   *(Score 1)*
(c) We maintain a detailed dossier about each
competitor. Our aim is to know as much about them
and their methods as they know themselves. We have
a small department responsible for such a task. We

►

Score
0 1 2

debrief every manager who joins us from a
competitor, within limits of propriety. (*Score 2*)

10. **How well are the input-gathering activities integrated
with other parts of the marketing organization?**

(a) Our marketing research people decide what
should be researched and when.   (*Score 0*)
(b) Marketing research personnel receive their
instructions from marketing
management.   (*Score 1*)
(c) Researchers are regarded as an integral part of the
marketing team – constant dialogue takes place
throughout the organization regarding input needs
and frequency.   (*Score 2*)

The maximum score possible is 20. Very few companies could achieve
such a score. Lower scores can be interpreted as follows:

15–20   **Excellent**
10–14   **Good to very good.**
 5–9   **Fair**
 0–4   **Poor**

5

Product policy and planning

The product or service is the heart of the marketing mix. Without a product there is no chance of satisfying the customer's needs. At the same time it is essential to recall that what the company considers as its product is not necessarily what the customer buys. Peter Drucker summarized this simple notion many years ago by saying: 'Until the customer has derived final utility, there is really no "product"; there are only "raw materials"' (Drucker, 1973).

There are many instances where the customer perceives the product in a totally different light from the way the manufacturer sees its own product. Thus, a company manufacturing drills must understand that the customer actually buys 'holes' or a device that helps to make holes. A company manufacturing ball-bearings and roller-bearings in a large assortment of sizes, alloys and configurations must recognize that the customer buys antifriction devices. Where the customers have no 'friction' problems, they do not need the product and, in Peter Drucker's terms, the product does not even exist.

Every marketer should ask him- or herself, from time to time, the very fundamental question: 'what is my product?' This question represents a subtle shibboleth. The reader may recall the biblical story of the Gileadites who could identify their enemies by asking them to say 'shibboleth'. Whoever responded by saying 'sibboleth' was an enemy and was slain. The inability to pronounce the test word correctly betrayed the person's party, nationality, etc. Similarly, ask a person the simple question 'what is your product?' and you should be able to judge from the answer given the level of understanding and commitment of the interlocutor towards the 'marketing concept' generally, and towards the notion of a product being a 'benefit' or 'utility' to the customer in particular. It is a better test than asking the marketer whether he or she belongs to the Chartered Institute of Marketing, or some other prestigious body to which marketers aspire to belong.

The ideal situation occurs when the market and the customer perceive the product in an identical manner. Examples of the different ways of looking at a product are shown in Table 5.1. All these examples are quite simple. Let us look at some more complicated situations.

A pharmaceuticals company manufactures a number of drugs. By the nature of the industry and its technology, the drugs represent complex chemical compounds. The production and the R & D people would normally define the product in units of the 'wonder compound' that the firm produces. On the other hand, an enlightened marketer would look at the product in terms of the illness or

Table 5.1 The various 'faces' of the product (examples only)

As seen by production people	As seen by R & D	As seen by the customer
Aspirin tablets	A chemical compound	Headache-alleviation tablet
Petrol	A flammable chemical	A liquid which can propel one's car
Rawlplug	A fibre or plastic stick that can be inserted in holes	An aid to fixing things to the wall
Perrier water	Water with certain minerals and a certain volume of bubbles	A socially acceptable drink
Rolex watches – highly engineered, needing a lot of inspection, etc.	A watch with x cogs and y diamonds containing z ounces of gold	Heirloom, social recognition, a badge of wealth
Fertilizers in liquid or solid forms manufactured in casks or bags	Chemicals called ammonium nitrate, etc.	Crop-care material, easy to spread and effective to use
Light bulbs	Incandescent lamps made out of glass with filaments inside a vacuum	Device for creating light efficiently and economically
Insurance policy with a list of terms and easy to sell to as many people as possible	Developing new products with minimum risk to the company	'Product' designed to give the customer maximum security and peace of mind supported by good customer service

condition which the drug seeks to cure or alleviate. Thus the production-orientated manager is likely to boast about the number of units of the antibiotic which the firm has manufactured and sold in a given period; the truly marketing-orientated person would prefer to talk about the number of pneumonia sufferers who were cured by the firm's product. When seeking to measure the firm's market share, he or she will talk not about tonnes, kilos or numbers of tablets but in terms of the true market: namely, the number of pneumonia cases that have occurred in a given period and the company's share of that market.

Normally, the more intricate the product and the more sophisticated the technology, the greater the chasm between the perceptions of the product among the various functions of the firm. The production person feels more comfortable with a perception of the product as seen through technological eyes; the marketer prefers, or should prefer, to look at the product as a cluster of benefits and utilities to the customer. A manufacturer of diesel engines will tend to talk about the number of units, the size of the units and the number of cylinders that have been produced in the course of the year. In this case, 'what is your product?' will inevitably be answered with the statement: 'Diesel engines of 50 horsepower or 75 horsepower configuration.' The same question will be answered by the marketing person as follows: 'We manufacture energy-producing units of a certain design as auxiliary facilities for process plants or ships or hospitals, capable of producing electricity at a cost per unit of x pence', etc. The essence of modern marketing is to respond to the question as if one is the buyer of the product.

It is also important to recognize that the same physical product may represent two or more products in marketing terms. A bicycle can be a cheap and convenient mode of transport for some people; it can also represent an exercising machine for another segment in the market. In technical terms, the product would be more or less the same. Jogging shoes can be viewed as comfortable and safe shoes for athletes who run or jog on hard surfaces. The same shoe, with minor modifications, can represent a high-fashion product among teenagers. Many such examples exist in the marketplace. The significance is that, when one is talking about 'Product life-cycle', one must often be specific as to what 'product' one is referring to, especially when it has a number of alternative uses.

It would now be useful to re-examine the earlier example from the pharmaceuticals industry. Let us imagine that a company called Stanton Chemicals manufactures an antibiotic – Healex. The product can be used effectively in the treatment of a wide range of infections.

If one looks at the product as a technological item, one can trace its life-cycle on the basis of its overall sales and profitability. On the other hand, one can also say that each infection type represents a separate market and that therefore there are as many 'products' as medical indications. On that basis one can plot the life-cycle performance in relation to each indication or sickness. Thus, without getting too involved in the technicalities of a complex industry, one can have a product life-cycle in respect of each identifiable indication, e.g. infections of the throat, ear, lungs, urinary tract, etc. Each indication will have its own 'product' (with or without a different brand name) and each one of these products will have its own 'product life-cycle'. Figure 5.1 illustrates this point in a diagrammatic way.

The situation can be further complicated by saying that the drug used by children in relation to one kind of illness is a different 'product' from the same drug used by adults. Thus, we finish by having a three-dimensional matrix of products. We have drugs, illnesses and segments of potential users. Figure 5.2 summarizes the point: the three-dimensional morphology shows three 'formulae', four indications and two market segments. Altogether $4 \times 3 \times 2 = 24$ subproducts, and in practice each one may have its own life-cycle pattern.

In the next section we shall explore the concept of the product life-cycle and its significance for marketing decisions. The aim so far has been to alert the truly maketing-orientated manager to the fact

		PRODUCTS		
		Formula A	Formula B	Formula C
MARKETS (viz. 'indications')	1				Throat
	2				Ear
	3				Urinary tract
	4				Lungs

Figure 5.1 Three products serving four markets = 12 products in the pharmaceuticals industry

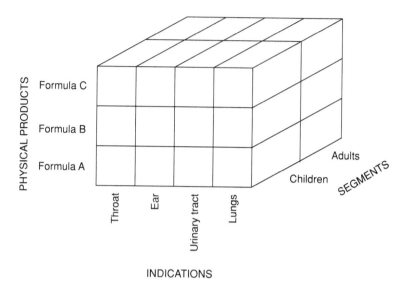

PHYSICAL PRODUCTS

Formula C

Formula B

Formula A

Throat · Ear · Urinary tract · Lungs

INDICATIONS

Children · Adults

SEGMENTS

Figure 5.2 Twenty-four product offerings where three formulae, four indications and two segments exist for a pharmaceuticals company

that the 'product' often has different faces and ideally should be analyzed as an assemblage of benefits and utilities to the customer, rather than as a physical and tactile package produced in a factory. The two perspectives are not always congruent.

The product life-cycle reviewed

The product/service life-cycle is a well-rehearsed concept in most textbooks. The theory suggests that every product or service has a finite life. If one were to monitor sales over a period of time, one would discover that the sales pattern of most products follows a fairly consistent curve, as illustrated in Figure 5.3. Obviously, at the beginning sales are very low; gradually they build up towards a crescendo; finally they start declining. The various phases of the life-cycle and their characteristics are shown in Table 5.2.

The product life-cycle concept is alluring in its simplicity but a difficult notion to apply in practice. The main difficulty is that it is very difficult to anticipate the life-cycle of a product in advance. Very few product managers can diagnose with clarity the precise phase of the life-cycle in which their respective products lie. Through circum-

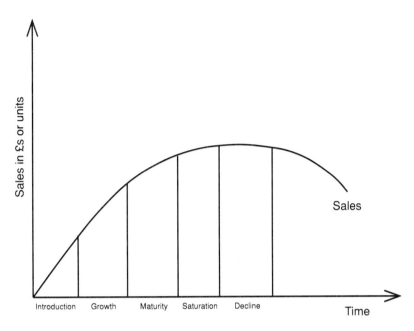

Figure 5.3 Product life-cycle pattern

Table 5.2 Characteristics of the life-cycle phases

Phase of life-cycle	Characteristics
Introduction	Product is new; awareness in the marketplace is low; cost of marketing is quite high; profits are low.
Growth	Assuming that the product has given satisfaction to the first customers who bought it, others follow suit. Sales increase fairly rapidly and the product starts to generate profits. However, competitors notice the success and start planning a competitive offering.
Maturity	The product is reaching its maturity and sales are good, but the battle for market share is about to begin. First signs of pressure on margins can be observed.
Saturation	The market has reached a point at which total sales are not growing any more, the battle for market share is intense and, unless the product is associated with a strong brand loyalty, price becomes a major factor in buying patterns.
Decline	Sales and profits are starting to fall and the future of the product does not look healthy. A remedial strategy (e.g. modifying the product, repositioning, or even deleting the product from the range) is needed.

stantial evidence one can assume that the product is moving from 'growth' to 'maturity'. If, for instance, one notices that a competitor is increasing its advertising budget and/or offering special discounts, one can assume that the growth phase is about to end. These are all tell-tale signals, but they are of doubtful scientific value.

Another problem that may face the marketer who seeks to plot the product sales over time is that the resulting curve may be more a result of mismanagement of the product than a true reflection of market realities. Figure 5.4 illustrates the point.

A company may discover that its own sales are declining, and the marketer may be prepared to assume that the product life-cycle has reached its decline stage. On the other hand, on further investigation, it may be noticed that the sales of the generic product are still increasing. In the life-cycle parlance, the generic product is still in the growth phase. Obviously something has gone wrong. Our marketer is correct in feeling that in terms of his particular product, and the way it has been managed and presented to the market in the past, his product is in decline. However, he must also explore carefully the possibility that he has 'mismanaged' an opportunity. In the diagram, until time T1 both curves are synchronous insofar as they follow the same general pattern. Thereafter something happens to damage the

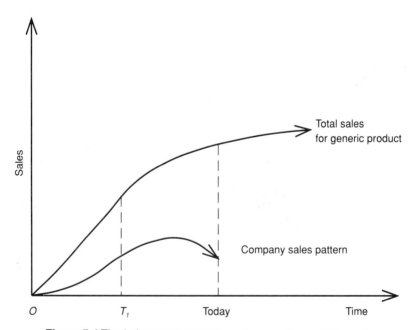

Figure 5.4 The 'mismanagement curve' versus the real life-cycle

prospects of the company's product. Thus, the company's product life-cycle is the result of a 'mismanagement curve' rather than a universal trend.

To the extent that one needs to understand where products are in their life-cycle for planning purposes, the concept is of limited value. On the other hand, there are a few general principles associated with the concept which are of practical importance.

The trend towards shorter life-cycles

All the evidence seems to suggest that product life-cycles are becoming shorter and shorter. This is particularly true in the field of domestic appliances and high-technology products, such as computers and cameras. Table 5.3 shows the product life-cycles of a number of well-known products from the 1950s onwards, and includes estimates for the 1990s (based on responses given by companies manufacturing products in the sectors in question).

Clearly, these figures would disturb any marketer who works for the industries shown in the table. The trend imposes a number of inevitable strategic implications that must be borne in mind when planning a new product policy.

The investment recovery process and the product life-cycle

It is normally accepted that a product is deemed to have been a success when all the investment that has gone into its development and commercialization has been recovered *and* the product is still capable of satisfying members of the consuming public.

A product which has reached its decline phase before the investment that went into its development and exploitation has been recovered is hardly a successful one. This point is illustrated in

Table 5.3 Product life-cycles of well-known products since the 1950s (years)

Product		1950s/60s	1970s/80s	1990s (forecast)
Typewriter	approx.	10–15	3–5	1–2
Accounting machine/ office computer	approx.	10–15	3–5	2–3
Desk/pocket calculator	approx.	10–15	1–3	1
Television set		5–10	3–5	2–3
Stereo equipment		5	2–3	1–2
Cameras		10	3–5	2–3

Figure 5.5. A product must be capable, first and foremost, of earning sufficient funds to recover the full investment that the firm has put into it. Moreover, when we talk about investment we must include not only the cost of design, manufacturing and inventory, but also the full cost of pre-launch marketing projects such as market research, promotion, sampling and physical distribution.

All this means that a product manager must ensure during the planning cycle that the marketing programme is designed to attain a quick investment recovery. There is far less scope in the world of the 1990s to enter the market with a tentative plan. The launch of a product must be carried out in an energetic and creative manner, supported by the full panoply of promotional tools, with the aim of recovering one's investment as quickly as possible. Only when the

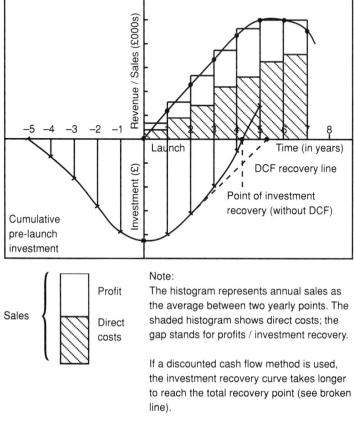

Note:
The histogram represents annual sales as the average between two yearly points. The shaded histogram shows direct costs; the gap stands for profits / investment recovery.

If a discounted cash flow method is used, the investment recovery curve takes longer to reach the total recovery point (see broken line).

Figure 5.5 The investment recovery process and the product life-cycle

investment has been recovered can one start enjoying the fruits of one's effort and talk about returns and success.

International marketing and the investment recovery concept
Linked with the last point, it is true to say that if one has an innovative product one ought to explore from the very beginning the possibility of launching the product in international markets. The logic is simple: the volume that one can attain in international markets is much larger than can be attained in one domestic market. This means that with the right marketing support one can attain more rapidly the kind of volume that will bring the investment recovery within reach while the product life-cycle is still healthy.

International standardization
The debate about whether products should be standardized or differentiated for world markets has been raging for the last decade. 'Standardization or adaptation' and 'globalization or localization' are topics that have attracted considerable interest among academics and businesspeople alike. From a purist marketing viewpoint there is a strong case for saying that a product should be adapted in such a way as to meet the needs and expectations of different cultures and environments. From a commercial perspective, and bearing in mind the importance of achieving a total investment recovery while the product is still in its prime, the case for standardization of products for world markets becomes overwhelming. The quicker the penetration of international markets and the higher the volume, the better chance there is that the investment will be recovered while the product is still in its pre-saturation/decline stage.

The need for a balanced portfolio

The fact that a product has a life-cycle means that an essential part of the marketing task is to ensure that the company does not depend on one product for its success, especially if the product in question starts showing signs of ageing. It is important to remember that product sales performance and profit margins do not follow an identical pattern. In fact, quite often profits start sagging well before the sales peak is reached. If one attempted to plot the product life-cycle and the profit pattern on the same graph, one would often discover that peak profits are reached before the saturation phase. This means that a company that wants to maintain a healthy growth in its profits must address itself to the task of developing new products at regular intervals (see Figure 5.6) or find a way of modifying existing products in order to lengthen their life or cheat old age.

Another problem that arises quite often is when the firm has products which either are of a seasonal nature or have a limited geographical or regional coverage. Thus, a manufacturer of skis and skiing equipment cannot be said to have a balanced portfolio. The skiing season is fairly short and most skiing takes place more or less at the same time of the year. Once the season is over, such a manufacturer has very little to sell if its range consists of skiing products only. Moreover, if snow conditions happen to be very poor in a particular year, the impact upon the business can be disastrous.

Most companies that have been in existence for any length of time have more than one product. They have a range which we can describe as a *portfolio of products*. Some of these products have been in existence for a while and are mature; others are still at their growth stage; yet others are new and need to be fostered with considerable creativity and investment.

An intelligent and effective management of the portfolio of products is an essential part of marketing. In fact, one of the problems that has always plagued corporate and marketing planners is the

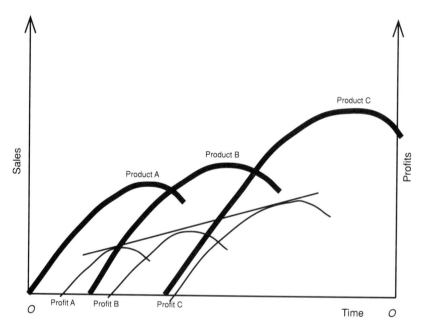

Figure 5.6 Sales and profit patterns design to maintain a company's profitability

difficulty of deciding on an optimum product mix. Historically, a simple methodology based on the *Pareto curve* (or the so-called 20–80 rule) was used. One would identify the 20 per cent of the firm's products which yielded 80 per cent of the company's sales (or profits or some other criterion of performance). The logic of such an analysis was simple: if one could determine which were the company's breadwinners, one knew in which area to concentrate the marketing effort. On the other hand, the products which landed at the bottom of the curve (as illustrated in Figure 5.7) deserved little attention and/or few resources, and in many situations could even be deleted from the range.

Many marketers discovered to their cost that the Pareto analysis suffered from a number of dangerous weaknesses:

- If one drops the 'troublesome' products at the poor end of the curve, one may discover that the portfolio has ceased to be balanced. Customers may simply not order the remaining products without being able to obtain those which were dropped from the range.

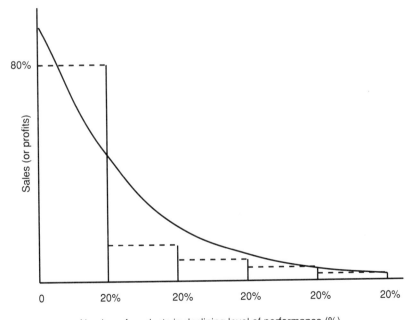

Figure 5.7 A company's product performance on a Pareto curve

- If one drops products from the range without reducing general overheads, one may discover that the whole profit performance suffers.

- The products at the bottom of the curve may well be the new and innovative ones, which will be the breadwinners of the future. Clearly, dropping such products would be folly. In other words, when using the Pareto analysis it is important to recognize that it suffers from a lack of dynamism. All it does is provide us with a static picture of the quantitative relationship between present-day 'winners' and 'losers'. It has no bearing whatsoever on future prospects and developments.

A valuable tool emerged a few years ago in the shape of what we tend to call the *Boston matrix,* inasmuch as it was first developed and used by the Boston Consulting Group of the USA. Its main value was that it helped managers to analyse their product portfolio on a matrix which represented two disparate axes. One axis showed the firm's own performance; first it referred to *market share,* but later this was changed to *relative competitive position.* It was soon recognized that a firm may enjoy a small market share but yet be a dominant force in the marketplace by virtue of enjoying the largest market share among all the competitors. The second axis showed the *market growth rate* (or sometimes the *business growth rate*). This latter dimension was the one which was missing from the Pareto analysis. It referred to the realities of the outside environment in which the firm is operating.

This simple matrix, shown in Figure 5.8, was the beginning of the development of a series of matrices which are known nowadays as *Portfolio management* or *Business Portfolio* or the *Directional policy matrix.* Fuller exploration of these methods is made in Chapter 10 on marketing planning.

Briefly, the Boston matrix is divided into four quadrants. The market share axis is divided into 'high' and 'low' and so is the market or business growth. The theory is that every product and/or activity is capable of being slotted into one of the four boxes. It does not need too much imagination to perceive that, when one talks about 'high' and 'low', one can ascribe well-defined and highly quantifiable criteria to each of the dimensions. Thus 'low' market share may be defined as 'less than 10 per cent' and 'high' as any figure above it. Once again, 'low growth' can be defined as 'up to 10 per cent per annum growth rate' whereas 'low' would be below that figure.

The four quadrants that emerge are 'high/high', indicating products enjoying a high market share in a high-growth market; 'high/low', where a high market share exists in a low-growth market;

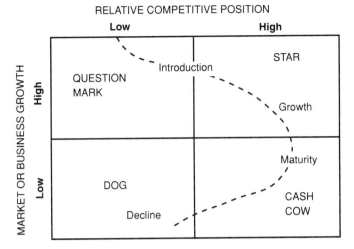

Figure 5.8 The Boston matrix with the product life-cycle superimposed

'low/high', where the market share is low but the market is growing fairly fast; and 'low/low' when both the company's performance and the market growth are low. The Boston Consulting Group chose quaint names for the four quadrants:

'High/high'	'Stars'
'High/low'	'Cash cows'
'Low/high'	'Question marks'[1]
'Low/low'	'Dogs'

The four categories are described and their implications for product management are detailed in Table 5.4.

In an ideal world one's product portfolio should be balanced. It should include a sufficient number of 'cash cows' to generate funds for investing in the 'stars' of today and those of tomorrow (the 'question marks' selected for development). It should contain as few 'dogs' as possible. Unfortunately, for many companies this is an elusive objective. The number of 'stars' that many companies possess is minute, the number of 'cash cows' fairly small, and the number of 'dogs' quite high. The main implication is that, when a company is fortunate enough to have a 'star', it must nurse it along with all the

---

[1] Also known as 'problem children' and 'wildcats', depending on which firm of consultants one talks to. For the purpose of this book we shall refer to this category as 'question marks'.

Table 5.4 Characteristics and implications of the Boston quadrants

Category	Characteristics	Implications
Stars	Innovative products with valuable competitive advantage.	Require heavy marketing/promotional support.
	Growth/early maturity stages of life-cycle.	Margins and profits excellent but often cash hungry.
	High market share	Justify allocation of creative and experienced product/brand personnel. Need careful and constant attention and control. Competitors are vigilant and watching with envy.
Cash cows	Yesterday's successes. Profitable but margins under pressure.	Control of costs must be rigorous.
	Market awareness high.	Advertising budgets must be controlled and emphasis must be on point-of-sale promotion.
	Investment recovery attained or well on the way.	Cash flow positive and must be carefully channelled either to R & D or development of new 'stars'.
Question marks	Market share is low, although growth potential in market is promising. Sometimes true potential is not easy to assess owing to the early stage of the life-cycle.	Need to invest heavily in the products most likely to succeed. Those selected must be promoted aggressively to maximize awareness. Market share must be won in order to create tomorrow's stars.
Dogs	Yesterday's 'cash cows' or products which never succeeded in earning significant market share when the going was good.	Minimum investment in production facilities and promotion. If possible, increase prices to extract maximum payoffs from a lost cause. Drastic pruning of products if resources can be reallocated to more deserving products.

creativity and financial support that it can muster. Neglecting a 'star' is tantamount to commercial suicide.

The skilled marketer must remember that equal attention should not be devoted to all products. The matrix described seeks to highlight the fact that a time allocation depends on the development of a strategy for managing the portfolio. The matrix is one of the aids to identifying the priorities.

Product portfolio management

In attempting to achieve something approaching a balanced port-folio, the marketer must employ a number of different approaches. Sometimes it will be necessary to 'buy' time and squeeze extra life out of ageing products. At other times it will be important to make the product more competitive. Then again, it might become essential to develop some new products or delete existing ones.

Buying time for ageing products

When a product portfolio is in danger of getting out of balance owing to the fact that too many products are approaching maturity simul-taneously, it is necessary to delay the ageing process.

Figure 5.9 shows a product which, if left alone, would follow curve A. At time T_a evidence is available to suggest that sales are likely to

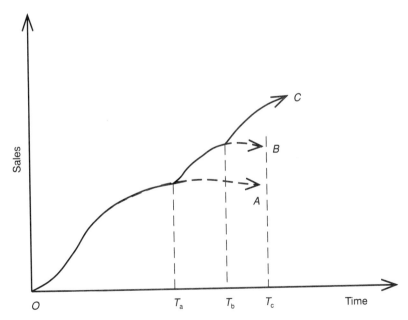

Figure 5.9 Extending the life-cycle

tail off. In response to this challenge, steps can be taken to defy the natural decay pattern and boost sales. The challenge can be met in a number of ways:

- Adding new features and attributes to the product.
- Changing the packaging.
- Changing the way it is advertised and presented.
- Finding new applications in existing markets.
- Finding new markets.
- Building in some added value.
- Special promotions.

By incorporating some of these approaches the original life-cycle curve is displaced by the one shown as B. However, as implied in Figure 5.9, this rejuvenation process will probably need to happen again at time T_b, when further new ideas have to be introduced.

The net effect of these interventions is to extend the useful life of the product from T_a to T_c. This could buy enough time for the next planned product strategy, such as the launching of a new product.

While such a strategy looks fairly straightforward, a number of constraints may reduce the prospects of pursuing such a route. First, one must be sure that there is a genuine opportunity for extending the life of the product. The product may be so close to death that investing in the process of cheating old age may be tantamount to flogging a dead horse.

Second, to the extent that most products at this phase of the life-cycle are 'cash cows', it is not always wise to invest precious resources in rejuvenation tactics which may have limited payoffs. Accepted wisdom demands that only limited investment should take place at this stage. It is unlikely that a massive revamp would recoup the costs during the limited period left for the product.

Developing a competitive position

If extending product life can be seen as the strategy for lengthening the life of a 'cash cow', the development of a competitive position is the recommended strategy for exploiting 'stars' more fully.

A product's competitive position is determined by two factors: (a) the degree of innovation or, as some prefer to call it, 'differentiation' and (b) its relative cost. Cost, of course, is normally determined by volume and productivity. Figure 5.10 illustrates the importance of

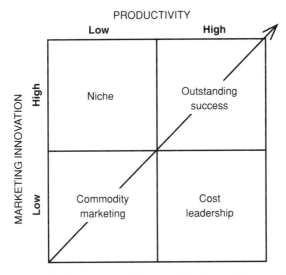

Figure 5.10 Developing a competitive position through innovation and/or productivity

escaping from the quadrant where innovation and productivity are low. Companies operating in that box, the 'commodity' zone, are likely to get into serious trouble sooner or later. The marketer's ultimate aim must be to move towards the 'high'/'high' zone where the firm can enjoy both marketing innovation and cost leadership stemming from high productivity. However, this depends on where the firm's specific strengths lie. If the firm is good at production, it can exploit this by going for volume and developing a lowest-cost advantage. At least it can make up in low prices what it may fail to achieve in differentiation.

On the other hand, the company may find it difficult to fight on a high-volume/cost advantage battlefield owing to size or lack of manufacturing resources. It may opt for the innovation/differenti-ation route through the development of a specialist or niche market position. In effect, the objective here is to become the biggest fish in a smaller pond. That way the marketing company can achieve a large share of a segment rather than of the market as a whole. In seeking to attain a differentiation, one must remember that it is not always essential to change the core product itself. Differentiation can be achieved through assembling innovative intangibles that are of particular appeal to customers. Among such intangibles are image, style, perceived quality and value, social acceptability, the 'feel good' factor and so on. In many situations such intangibles produce more customer satisfaction than the core product itself, and very often at minimal cost.

Figure 5.11 shows that on average the core product usually accounts for something in the order of 80 per cent of the costs and yet makes only about 20 per cent of the impact on customers. The reverse is also true: the product surround or the intangibles with their 20 per cent cost achieve 80 per cent of the impact.

Figure 5.12 provides an illustration of the way that significant players in the watch industry have managed their competitive position in response to an aggressive attack from Seiko of Japan. The industry was dominated for many years by Swiss watch manufacturers. Seiko arrived with a powerful volume and market share objective which gave them a significant cost advantage. The Swiss watch industry got itself into serious disarray. Nonetheless a few companies in that sector managed to survive. The prestigious companies (firms like Rolex and Vacherin Constantin) went for a niche approach by marketing high-quality, expensive heirlooms. This gave them a powerful grip on the 'top of the range' niche. Swatch went for a combination of attractive, fashionable, limited editions coupled with a very low-cost production process. This combination made them into a winning player in the game.

Developing new products

An organization which believes that it need not innovate will eventually stagnate and die. As we saw earlier, any portfolio, no

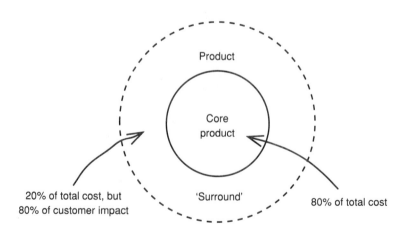

Figure 5.11 Core product versus 'product surround'

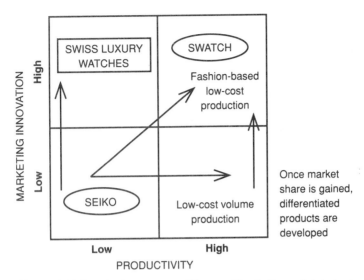

Figure 5.12 Developing a competitive position in the watch industry

matter how good it may be today, must ultimately be overtaken by newer products and technologies.

The Boston matrix makes it clear that new products are worth developing only if highly attractive markets have been identified. Unless there is a large potential for sales revenue, the chances of recouping development costs and eventually moving into profit are significantly reduced.

Every new product development involves the company in a risk of failure. Statistically, more new products fail than succeed. Research has shown that for roughly every 20 products brought to the market, only one is likely to be a complete success. This means that the product development task entails a risk-reduction process. In this connection it is worth remembering that line extension is less risky than a totally new product development. Similarly, a product improvement also carries a lower risk. Figure 5.13 illustrates the levels of risk associated with product strategies.

The main corollary of the aforesaid is that, if one chooses the new product development route as a strategy, extreme care must be taken in passing each proposed product idea through a fine-mesh screening process. However tedious the process may appear, it is an insurance policy against the ever-present risk of failure. The awards to the conscientious are enormous. The penalties to the sloppy marketer may mean ruin.

Figure 5.13 Level of risk associated with product strategies

The new product development process is summarized in Figure 5.14. It assumes from the outset that the marketing team possesses or is capable of generating a bank of new product ideas. Creative thinking techniques should be used to the full in seeking to collect as many product ideas as possible. Bearing in mind that the erosion rate between ideas and potential winners is so heavily biased against the latter, the more ideas one starts with, the better the chance of finding a lower-risk potential product. (For techniques and methods for developing new product ideas, see Majaro (1991b).)

The procedure provided in Figure 5.14 is self-explanatory. The important factor is to make it company-specific. Especially during the screening stage, one must ensure that the various criteria of acceptability match, as fully as possible, the identified strengths and competences of the organization. Moreover, when one defines the list of factors that the product should be congruent with, it is important to remember that some of them may be more significant than others. Therefore the screening procedure may have to introduce a weighting system in order to ensure that the relative values of the various selection criteria are included. An example of such a procedure is illustrated in Figure 5.15.

Once the bank of ideas has been reduced to a few promising ones by means of the screening process, it becomes necessary to test them out in the field and see how target customers react. This is the acid test as to whether the product may gain marketplace acceptance. This customer testing may result in the need to modify the original offering with a view to enhancing its attractiveness to the market.

As a final precaution against the risk element associated with the launching of new products, it is desirable to conduct some test

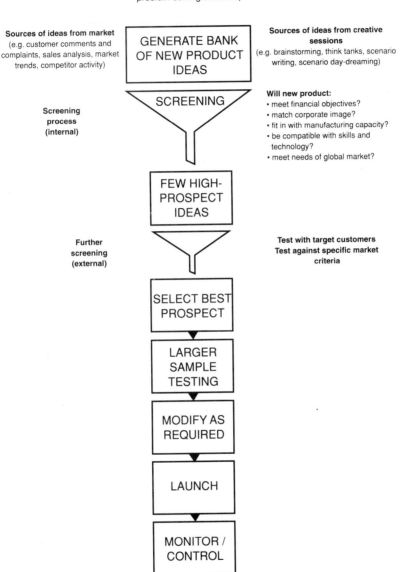

Sources of ideas from within the firm
(e.g. quality circles, creativity circles, new technology, suggestion schemes, creative problem-solving sessions)

Sources of ideas from market
(e.g. customer comments and complaints, sales analysis, market trends, competitor activity)

GENERATE BANK OF NEW PRODUCT IDEAS

Sources of ideas from creative sessions
(e.g. brainstorming, think tanks, scenario writing, scenario day-dreaming)

SCREENING

Screening process (internal)

Will new product:
• meet financial objectives?
• match corporate image?
• fit in with manufacturing capacity?
• be compatible with skills and technology?
• meet needs of global market?

FEW HIGH-PROSPECT IDEAS

Further screening (external)

Test with target customers
Test against specific market criteria

SELECT BEST PROSPECT

LARGER SAMPLE TESTING

MODIFY AS REQUIRED

LAUNCH

MONITOR / CONTROL

Figure 5.14 The new product development process

Criteria	Weight	1	2	3	4	5	6	7	8	9	10	Total
Compatibility with existing range	.10											
Distribution system	.10											
Added value	.20											
Patent	.10											
Image	.15											
Investment recovery	.15											
Capable of global standardization	.20											
Total	1.00											

Figure 5.15 Product screening procedure

marketing with a representative sample of the market or in a representative region. This should provide an additional insight into the most effective method for reaching and satisfying customers.

Deleting old products

Like old soldiers in the patriotic song, some products never die, they only fade away. That is to say, they do not feature in policy decisions but simply drift along. This kind of 'hands off' approach should have no role in a well-managed portfolio. Planning the demise of old products calls for a structured approach. Such products must be judged against three criteria:

- Their ability to earn revenue and profits.
- The support they can provide to the rest of the portfolio.
- The amount of valuable capacity and/or resources they tie up.

The ultimate decision about their future depends on a cost–benefit analysis. During such an analysis one must not forget to calculate the amount of managerial time that may be invested in dealing with problems associated with such 'dog' products. Sad as it may be to drop one's old friends, sentimentality should not play a role in this decision-making process.

Once a decision to delete a product has been made, its demise should be planned with as much attention as with a launch:

- Customers and intermediaries must be informed.
- Field personnel must be communicated with.
- Stocks for a run-down period must be planned.
- Timing of cessation of supply must be agreed upon.
- Spare parts (if appropriate) must be arranged for a decent period.
- Steps to safeguard the firm's image must be considered.

All this represents an important part of an effective marketing effort. Deleting old products calls for as much skill as other marketing activities do.

Branding

In the search for differentiation the establishment of a brand, with all its perceived imagery and the benefits that go with it, can have a major effect on sales. A strong brand brings reassurance to customers by providing a perception of permanence and quality. A brand image cannot be built overnight; it takes a lot of effort and investment to develop. However, once established it can command a premium price owing to the valuable psychological intangibles associated with its name.

Such is the power of branding that in extreme situations customers may adopt the brand as a generic product. The name 'Hoover' is often used by consumers as a synonym for vacuum cleaners. 'Walkman' has almost become a generic word for a personal radio/ stereo. Flattering as it may be to have one's product become a generic name, a brand manager must attempt to avoid such a pitfall. The ideal brand is the one which becomes universally well known but at the same time retains a clear and independent identity.

In many situations corporate names have become brands. IBM represents a powerful corporate identity which doubles up as a brand for its products. The world at large has high expectations of firms like IBM and their products. ICI, Nestlé, Glaxo and many others enjoy a significant corporate image, which in turn provides a strong forum for the development of strong brands.

Figure 5.16 shows how branding can give a firm enhanced sales prospects. A brand represents a unique product, rather than an

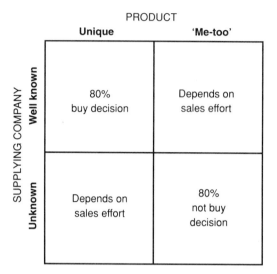

Figure 5.16 'Likelihood to buy' matrix

anonymous, generic 'me-too' product. If, in addition, the supplying company is well known, the combined force of these two strands can be instrumental in buying decisions without the need to rely too much on sales effort. As the diagram shows, other combinations require a higher level of sales activity to win a 'buy decision'. The 'me-too' product from an unknown company faces the greatest inbuilt disadvantage of all.

Establishing a strong brand demands steadfast and costly work. Maintaining its reputation at a high level, once established, is equally demanding. The annals of marketing history are littered with the names of companies that neglected to invest in their brands once they were established. The result is that such brands start to slide towards the commodity end of the market (see Figure 5.17). Pressure on price may be the inevitable consequence.

Although the concept of branding developed mostly in the fast-moving consumer goods field, experienced brand managers are now being recruited into other industries. The banking and financial services world has seen a vast growth in the development of branded products. Airlines, travel companies and industrial goods firms have also recognized the value of brands. However, even the most successful brand will continue to thrive only for as long as it meets customers' expectations. Coca-Cola found to its enormous cost that one cannot fly in the face of such expectations when it decided to

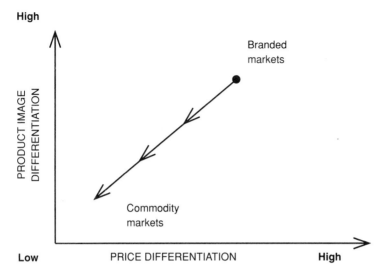

Figure 5.17 Behaviour of neglected brands

'improve' the flavour of its traditional product. Such was the outcry from customers that, regardless of all the expenditure that went into its launch, the new 'Coke' was withdrawn after a short while and the original product reinstated.

PRODUCT MANAGEMENT AUDIT

Score
0 1 2

1. **Does the company develop products in response to identified needs?**

   (a) Most products are developed by the firm's R & D or marketing departments, and when they are ready the sales department is asked to sell them.   (*Score 0*)
   (b) The company attempts to respond to customers' suggestions and/or complaints, and develops products accordingly.   (*Score 1*)
   (c) The marketing department seeks to anticipate needs and develop products in response to such needs.   (*Score 2*)

2. **Has the firm formulated a product strategy?**

(a) No. Products are developed from time to time with little guidance from the firm's mission and corporate objectives.   (*Score 0*)
(b) Yes. The company has laid down overall objectives for its product policy.   (*Score 1*)
(c) The company ensures that its product policy is always consistent with the firm's objectives in a dynamic way.   (*Score 2*)

3. **Do marketing personnel attempt to develop unique features and benefits for its products on a regular basis?**

(a) Only when the products were launched.   (*Score 0*)
(b) Yes, but only when the products start looking 'long in the tooth'.   (*Score 1*)
(c) Management constantly monitors the way products can be improved and their features and benefits augmented ahead of competitors.   (*Score 2*)

4. **Does the company screen product ideas in a systematic way?**

(a) No. Product ideas are looked at only when the firm's products start declining.   (*Score 0*)
(b) Yes. The urge to explore new ideas takes place from time to time.   (*Score 1*)
(c) A system is in place for exploring new product ideas on a regular basis.   (*Score 2*)

5. **Is the product portfolio a balanced one?**

(a) No. The range suffers from obvious imbalances (e.g. seasonal gaps, regional weaknesses).   (*Score 0*)
(b) The range is balanced, but most of the products manifest 'cash cow' characteristics. No 'stars' are on the horizon.   (*Score 1*)
(c) The portfolio is balanced – it has a mix of well-established products as well as new additions to the range.   (*Score 2*)

▶

6. **Does management provide differing marketing support to its products in relation to their life-cycle phases?**

(a) No. Support is always constant as a percentage of anticipated sales volume. *(Score 0)*
(b) Newer products receive more support than older ones. *(Score 1)*
(c) Management has recognized that marketing budgets should be directly related to each product in a dynamic fashion. *(Score 2)*

7. **Is each product's investment recovery monitored?**

(a) No. Such analysis is never considered. *(Score 0)*
(b) Investment recovery is analyzed periodically. No product is deleted if the investment in it has not been recovered. *(Score 1)*
(c) Investment recovery analysis forms an integral part of the whole process of product management, from launch to deletion. *(Score 2)*

8. **Is the notion of 'added value' recognized as part of the process of enriching products?**

(a) No. Product management does not consider added value as an important element in product policy. *(Score 0)*
(b) Added value is considered important, but it does not form part of product screening procedures. *(Score 1)*
(c) Added value is treated as one of the most important elements in product selection and development. *(Score 2)*

9. **Are funds allocated towards developing and supporting brands?**

(a) The firm believes that giving a product a brand in itself guarantees differentiation. *(Score 0)*
(b) Additional promotional resources are allotted to promoting brand awareness, knowledge and liking. *(Score 1)*
(c) The marketers realize that money spent on brand development constitutes an investment likely to

▶

                                                              Score
                                                            0 1 2

strengthen the product position in the
marketplace.   *(Score 2)*

10.   **Does the company have a policy about deleting old
      products?**

      (a) No. Products are kept in the range regardless of
      their impact upon the rest of the portfolio and relative
      costs.   *(Score 0)*
      (b) Products are dropped from time to time, but it
      does not happen in a systematic
      manner.   *(Score 1)*
      (c) Procedures are in existence to monitor product
      performance, and a deletion policy is in
      place.   *(Score 2)*

The maximum score possible is 20. Very few companies could achieve
such a score. Lower scores can be interpreted as follows:

   15–20   **Excellent**
   10–14   **Good to very good.**
    5–9   **Fair**
    0–4   **Poor**

6

Price and pricing policy

Price is one of the crucial elements in the marketing mix. In this context it is a powerful marketing tool which, in the hands of a skilful practitioner, can have an all-pervasive effect on the company's long-term success. Clearly, pricing policy has critical implications for profit. However, at the same time price often entails psychological and behavioural responses. These relate to the perceived quality and value of the product or service, thereby influencing how it can be positioned in the marketplace.

It is important to emphasize at the very outset that price is quantitative and, unlike the other elements of the marketing mix, has the advantage (and sometimes the disadvantage) that it can be changed easily and with immediate effect. It takes time to design and run an advertising campaign or revamp a product range, but the consequence of a pricing decision is rapid.

Such is the importance and complexity of pricing that it demands to be explored in some depth. As we shall see later, there are situations where there is a benefit to the company in increasing prices rather than keeping them at a low and highly competitive level. Pricing decisions cannot be taken in isolation. They must always be taken in full harmony with the firm's strategic environment and the realities of the marketplace. A price which meets the firm's strategic criteria but not the expectations of the market is as wrong as the one that satisfies the customers but fails to meet the commercial needs of the firm.

Supply and demand

The relationship between price and demand

An understanding of the interplay between price and demand is a useful preamble to the whole subject. In practice it is not possible to talk about the demand for anything without specifying or implying a price. The demand at one price level can be totally different from the one which is likely to prevail at some other price. In normal circumstances where demand varies with price it can be assumed that the lower is the price, the greater is the demand. Figure 6.1 seeks to illustrate this relationship.

The steeper the slope of the demand curve (shown here as straight line), the more sensitive is the demand to price. In the example given in Figure 6.1, two products A and B command prices P_a and P_b respectively in order to sell 1,000 units. Analysis shows that in order to increase demand to 2,000 units both products have to be offered at a price P. In this contrived example the price of product A has to fall more than that of product B in order to achieve the same increase in sales. This shows that demand for product A is more price sensitive than that for product B.

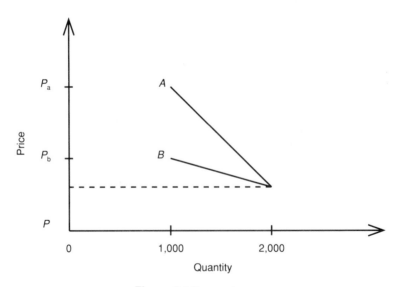

Figure 6.1 Demand curve

Elasticity of demand

While it is useful for the marketer to be aware of the general demand curve, it is even more useful to know the degree of responsiveness of demand to price changes for a particular product or service. In other words, it is important to understand the elasticity of demand.

The elasticity of demand is measured by dividing the proportionate change in demand by the proportionate change in price. If demand changes 12 per cent for a corresponding change in price of only 10 per cent then demand is said to be *elastic*, i.e. changes in price can 'stretch' demand disproportionately. If, on the other hand, demand changes by 8 per cent for a 10 per cent change in price, the demand is clearly less responsive and is deemed to be less elastic. Sometimes, however much one lowers the price, demand does not increase at all. In such situations one can safely say that demand is *inelastic*. If a 10 per cent change in price generates a 10 per cent change in demand then the elasticity is said to be *unity*. It is not unusual for the elasticity to vary at different price ranges on the demand curve.

The significance of all this is probably self-evident. The more inelastic the demand, the less sense it makes for the marketer to entertain using the price weapon to stimulate demand. Not only will there be a poor response to a price reduction in terms of volume sales, but margins and profits will be reduced at a stroke.

A simple example of high elasticity of demand would be the tout who has a few tickets for the finals at Wimbledon. If he offers the tickets at their face value, they will disappear within minutes. On the other hand, he can charge many times the face value for these rare tickets knowing that the heavy demand is such that price is not a deterrent to those who are desperate to see the finals. Somebody will always pay the asking price. If he understands the level of elasticity, he should be able to peg the price so that the tickets will sell at the right speed and provide him with the profit he wants.

Low elasticity of demand can be illustrated by the sales of some food items, such as milk or table salt. Broadly speaking, families have an established pattern of usage. If the price is lowered, they are unlikely to rush out to buy significant extra quantities. In the case of milk there is the extra problem of storing the additional quantities and keeping them fresh. Likewise an increase in price (within an acceptable band) will not stop consumers from buying their traditional daily intake.

Obviously, if the price jumps sharply, thus moving the situation to an entirely different part of the demand curve, buyers of such products as milk may start looking for alternative suppliers or an acceptable substitute. What happens here is the entry of a new factor into the equation: the level of supply.

The effect of supply and demand on price

Just as lower prices tend to stimulate demand in most markets, so higher prices tend to encourage suppliers to produce more. The attraction is obvious: the more items that one can make and sell at higher prices, the greater are the prospects of obtaining higher margins. The supply curve therefore approximates to the one shown in Figure 6.2.

Supply and demand have an effect on price in the following way: price tends to gravitate towards the level at which supply and demand are matched (see Figure 6.3). Furthermore, an increase in demand or a decrease in supply will lead to a rise in price, whereas a fall in demand or an increase in supply will lead to a fall in price, as illustrated in Figure 6.4.

All of the issues about pricing discussed so far are based on classical economic theory. For them to be strictly accurate there are two qualifying conditions:

• There has to be a *perfect market*, i.e. a market where there is only one price for the same quality of similar goods and where there is competition between many buyers and sellers.

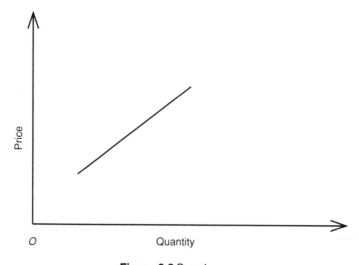

Figure 6.2 Supply curve

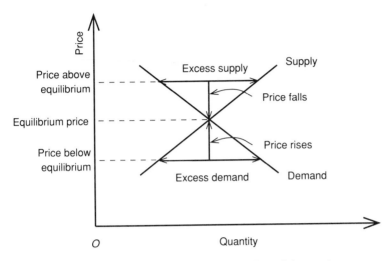

Figure 6.3 Price determined by supply and demand

- There has to be *perfect competition.* For this to happen all suppliers must be selling exactly the same kind of product, there must be many buyers and sellers, and there must be freedom of entry into the market so that newcomers can add to the supply.

Experience tells us that such perfect markets and competition rarely exist. One obvious exception is where a single supplier dominates the market – the monopoly. Another is where only a few suppliers compete – an oligopoly.

Pricing in a monopoly

The monopolist has a virtually clear field in which to set prices, especially if entry is difficult for new suppliers. While it is relatively easy for the monopoly supplier to control output, thus in effect controlling demand and hence prices, this does not always happen in practice.

One reason for this is that the monopolist is generally less concerned about price, and more concerned about overall profits. It therefore becomes attractive to manufacture at a level which ensures that unit costs are at their lowest. As long as this quantity of output does not flood the market and offers a prospect of holding prices at a

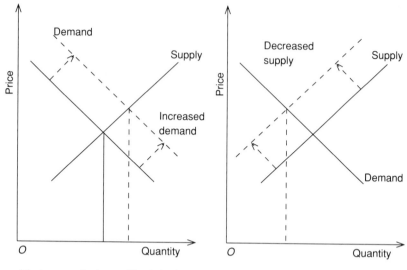

(a) Increase in demand leads to rise in price and increase in quantity supplied

(b) Decrease in supply leads to rise in price and reduction in demand

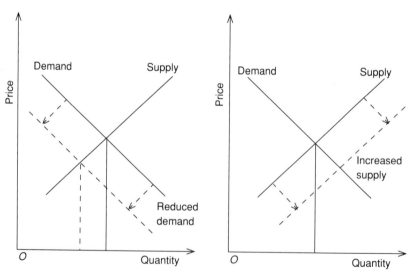

(c) Decrease in demand leads to fall in price and reduction in quantity supplied

(d) Increase in supply leads to fall in price and increase in demand

Figure 6.4 Effect of increases and decreases in supply and demand

reasonably high level, then clearly the greatest possible margins will be achieved.

Another restraint on the apparently unlimited freedom of the monopolist is a political one: in other words, what is deemed to be against the interests of the state or sections of its people. Examples of this dimension can be seen operating in the newly privatized public utilities in the UK. British Gas in particular has been singled out as making unjustifiably high profits at the expense of the consumer. Exactly how the issue will be resolved is yet to be seen, but a warning shot has been fired across the company's bows, and it would be foolhardy for the company to ignore it.

Pricing in an oligopoly

It is well recognized that members of an oligopoly acting in concert would in effect be a monopoly. Indeed, competition legislation both in national markets and in the European Community has been designed to prevent such a situation occurring to the detriment of the consumers. It is unlawful for powerful suppliers to collude in a way which could manipulate supplies or prices. The antitrust legislation in the USA is particularly vigilant in this regard, and the penalties for those who seek to evade such laws are severe.

The petroleum industry with its few giant companies is a prime example of an oligopoly. The best policy for a company to adopt in these circumstances is to shadow its competitors: it is unlikely to be in the interest of any individual member of the oligopoly to rock the collective boat and, for instance, start a price war. Thus, a cosy sort of interdependence develops. This materializes in prices edging towards the highest level at which it is possible to achieve a sustainable demand, and at the same time one at which the companies can achieve some reasonable economies of scale in their production.

Different ways of looking at price

We have been considering price mainly from the suppliers' viewpoint. However, this is not a wholly realistic position to take because clearly the customer also has a perspective on price. The supplier who overlooks the fact that customers vote with their feet, or rather with their money, is forgetting one of the fundamental truths of business.

The way a supplier/manufacturer views price can differ tremendously from the way the customer views it, as Figure 6.5 shows. The manufacturer, because of his/her intimate involvement with the product, tends to focus on volumes, costs and margins. The manufacturer knows that it is commercial suicide (generally speaking) to sell things for less than they cost to make. The customer, on the other hand, could not care less about these issues. He/she sees price as a comparative yardstick in making a purchase decision between competing products. To the customer, price conveys 'affordability' and benefits. If the twain do not meet there will not be a sale.

It will be apparent that pricing has to take into account a number of different factors, and we will now consider these in more detail.

Pricing and costs

Inevitably, any discussion about pricing always seems to raise the issue about the role that costs should play in determining price. Traditionally, many manufacturers would calculate their costs for making a product and then add a margin for profit in order to arrive at a price. Such is the grip of *cost-plus pricing* that many companies

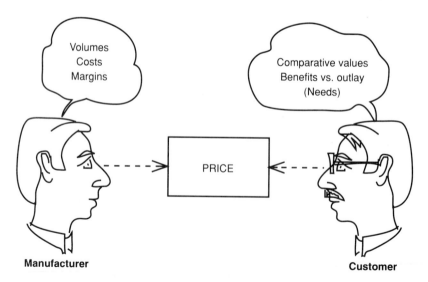

Figure 6.5 Different perceptions of price

still use this procedure. While there is an element of financial logic behind this form of pricing, in reality it can be criticized on several counts.

The first criticism is a fairly obvious one. The cost-plus formula might finish up with an unacceptably high price which no customer would entertain. Equally disastrous would be the situation where this approach puts the product on the market at a price way below that of competitors, thereby throwing away potential sales revenues and profits.

Another objection centres on the fact that, although costing systems are on the whole rational, the vexed question about how indirect costs (overheads) are allocated can be quite arbitrary. These can be loaded on a product in a number of different ways, and each formula can lead to a markedly different cost.

The third criticism arises because it is recognized that costs can vary depending upon the quantity of product made. The break-even chart in Figure 6.6 illustrates this.

Before a single product can be made there has to be an investment in facilities such as factory, heating and lighting as well as plant and machinery. This is the fixed element of cost and is quite independent of the throughput. However, each product will use up materials and labour. The scale of these variables is directly proportional to output, and varies according to the production level.

In the example above, the sales revenue (price × units) generated by producing Q_a units is just enough to meet the fixed costs (point

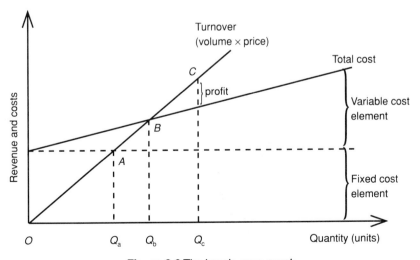

Figure 6.6 The break-even graph

A). An increase in unit sales to Q_b ensures that the total costs are met (point *B*, the break-even point). Further increases in output once past the break-even point provide an ever-increasing profit margin. Q_c on the graph is just one possible outcome.

However, all of this discussion relates to one particular price. What would happen if a company either increased or reduced its price? In Figure 6.7 we can see that for a given price *P*, the break-even point is reached at quantity *Q*. If the price is increased to P_h then costs are recovered quicker, and the break-even point moves to 2, which is reached with a quantity Q_h. Likewise, lower the price and a greater quantity needs to be sold.

Clearly, the implication of all this is for the company to charge as much as it can and thereby reap the rewards of profit at the lowest level of output. Attractive though this might be, as we saw earlier the producer does not have the freedom of choice that a simple diagram might suggest. The laws of supply and demand tend to limit the pricing option to a particular range. What is important is that the volume of production and revenue is sufficient to pass the break-even point. To this extent pricing and costs are tied together in a critical way. Yet, as these graphs convey, once production can be geared to levels beyond the break-even point, cost is an ever-diminishing factor in the pricing equation.

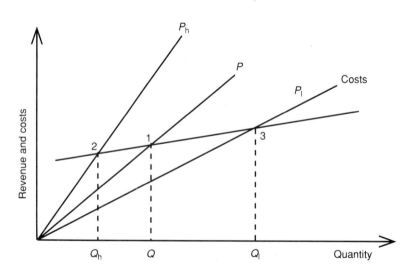

Figure 6.7 Effect of pricing on the break-even point

Price and the product life-cycle

The product life-cycle is another method of showing supply and demand at work, but this time over a long period. In Chapter 5 we saw the shape that a typical life-cycle takes. It will be recalled that a product follows a number of stages: introduction, growth, maturity, saturation and decline. Obviously a different pricing philosophy is normally applied during each of these stages. Pricing policy for mature products cannot be the same as for new ones or those enjoying rapid growth.

In general terms one can ascribe the following pricing characteristics to the various stages of the life-cycle.

Introduction

Here the product is new, perhaps little known in the market or viewed with some mistrust because of its originality. Whatever the reason, sales are invariably at a low level while a few customers, especially the 'innovators', are willing to test the product and establish whether it is likely to meet their expectations. One can pursue one of two strategies:

- Apply a relatively high price. The 'innovators' are less price sensitive than subsequent generations of buyers.
- Offer special promotional discounts in order to tempt customers to give the product a trial, and thereby stimulate demand.

Growth

This is a good time in the life of a product. Customers must feel that they receive value for money and the price must reflect such a perception. At the same time the marketer must remember that the growth stage is likely to mirror a wider recognition of the acceptability of the product in the marketplace. Just like wasps to a jampot, other manufacturers are attracted to areas of growth. Therefore the marketer must be very vigilant and make sure that the price is competitive and the firm's market share can be maintained and defended. This is also the moment to start planning for a cluster of 'intangibles' which can enrich the core product and impart to it some competitive advantage, thus reducing the pressure on the price.

Maturity

At the maturity stage the company must think less about winning growth and increasing market share because such aims are less feasible. Instead it should use its pricing policy for defensive purposes and ensure that it continues to hold to those segments of the business which are still profitable.

This is the point at which non-price competitive advantages must be pursued with the utmost vigour and creativity. Alternatively, if the firm's strategists come to the conclusion that the product is reaching its 'cash cow' stage and its days are numbered, the firm could start milking the product in the most productive and efficient way with a view to using the cash flow for developing new and better products. In other words, the pricing policy must be linked to the role that the firm ascribes to the product within the whole portfolio of products and not in splendid isolation. It must be remembered that a product seldom lives on its own.

Saturation

At the next phase sales remain virtually stable, or begin to show the slight decline which heralds the onset of the final phase. Here the pricing policy cannot be defined without a clear view as to the company's policy on the future of the product and its importance within the range. Moreover, it is difficult to develop a pricing strategy without incorporating full input from the firm's R & D department. In other words, if such analysis indicates that a replacement product is in the pipeline, the attitude to price will depend on the product's ability to maintain a strong foothold in the business. If no such innovation is likely, the pricing policy may be based on a final and cost-effective exploitation of the 'cash cow' payback.

Decline

Here sales start to tumble until they reach a level where the company decides that the product is no longer viable and withdraws it. Withdrawing a product also calls for 'de-marketing' skills. Customers who are still loyal to an ageing product do not wish to be let down by having their supplies stopped. Pricing policy is unlikely to help an easy withdrawal from the market.

One must always remember that upsetting customers at this stage can have long-term effects on image and general satisfaction. Many a marketer has regretted the day that he decided to withdraw a product in a peremptory way just because it appeared to be at the decline stage of its life-cycle. The promotional mix must be resorted to in a creative manner when one wants to delete a declining product but still satisfy the few loyal customers who are prepared to buy it.

In summary, in developing a pricing policy throughout the life-cycle different considerations apply at each stage of the cycle. The essence of a sound pricing policy is that a high level of integration between price and marketing/product strategy must be applied at all times. Normally the level of integration becomes vitally important during the maturity/saturation and decline phases. The degree of 'milking' may in the end be determined by whether or not the company needs to buy time until a new product is available to take the place of the old one. As emphasized earlier, pricing cannot always be considered for just one product in isolation.

It is useful to remember that key success factors of the marketing process follow a pattern of evolution during the life of a company. This applies to all subactivities, starting with marketing planning and marketing research and finishing with marketing control. A different logic is applied to each task during the various stages of the company's evolution. This is particularly true in the case of pricing and the firm's orientation towards pricing policy. The firm's approach during its pioneering stage is totally different from its attitude towards pricing during its mature era.

One can describe the stages of evolution of a firm in many ways but the following seems cogent:

- Primitive.
- Elementary.
- Mature.
- Enlightened.

The firm's pricing orientation during these stages is summarized in Figure 6.8 (overleaf).

The product portfolio

Ideally a company will have more than one product. Moreover, each of these products will be at a stage of its life-cycle which protects the total sales revenue against the dangers experienced by single-product companies. The total portfolio would look something like Figure 6.9.

STAGES OF EVOLUTION			
Primitive	Elementary	Mature	Enlightened
Cost-based pricing	Competition-based pricing	Perceived value-for-money pricing	Added-value component pricing

PRICING PHILOSOPHY

Figure 6.8 Pricing orientation and stages of evolution

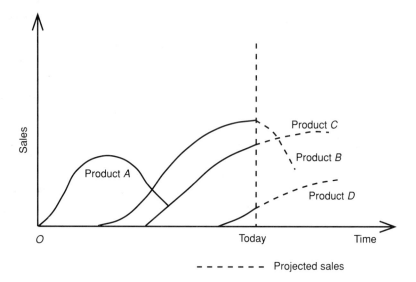

Figure 6.9 Product portfolio

The range of products is dynamic. Products come, grow and die over time. At any particular moment each might be at a different stage of its life-cycle. For example, in the diagram product B is in decline and product D is in its introduction phase. This would not be a very promising portfolio were it not for product C, which is still in its growth stage, albeit projected as nearing its end.

In order to manage the product range effectively and thereby to optimize sales revenue, pricing must take a holistic view. In the above example it might be necessary to price product D very competitively in order to launch it quickly into a position where it can make up for the decline of product B and eventually take over from product C as the growth product. Once again there is a strong case for formulating an approach to the firm's pricing which relates the whole process to the realities of the product portfolio and not to each product on its own. This point is often overlooked by marketers and needs to be watched with scrupulous care.

Price and the customer perspective

When we looked at the demand graph we saw that the general rule 'the higher the price, the lower the demand' operated. This is because in every purchase the customer is weighing up the cost of that transaction against the benefits that accrue as a result of buying the product or service. As the price gets higher, it becomes less and less likely that the 'cost' of the benefit stays as attractive and the result is that demand falls. Therefore it is important for marketers to have an understanding of the benefits their customers are looking for, and to establish how much they are prepared to pay for acquiring those benefits.

It must be remembered, however, that benefits are different from advantages, as the following example shows. Imagine that you want to buy a new car. You walk into a showroom and fairly soon enter into a discussion with a salesman. He puts forward a most persuasive case for one of the models – you hear that it is the most economical car on the road, it requires virtually no maintenance, it comes in a wide range of colours and specifications, it has the largest boot size in its class, and it has a safety record second to none. All of these things are clearly advantages in the car's favour.

Yet if your own objective in buying a car is to have a vehicle which can leave everything else standing, then all the features he has offered to you are not benefits within your own frame of reference. They simply cannot satisfy your personal craving for life in the fast lane. If a particular vehicle held the promise of meeting this criterion then the chances are that you would happily find the extra cash to buy your dream car.

Many manufacturers and suppliers of services appear not to recognize the differences between advantages and benefits. As a result they get their pricing (and advertising) wrong. However, it does not have to be this way as the following case study shows.

CASE STUDY
Yummy Convenience Foods Ltd

This hypothetical company has invented a new convenience meal. It is experienced enough to know that offering it on the market at a similar price to other convenience foods might not necessarily be the best strategy to follow. It knows that its new product offers these advantages:

- It cooks in less time.
- It is nutritionally balanced.
- It offers a larger portion than the competition.
- It contains no additives.
- It is low calorie.

In order to find out how these might be evaluated as benefits, the company needs to carry out some research with typical customers for this product. After perhaps eliciting from them how various customers think 'Yummy' foods compare with 'Stodgo', their biggest competitor, the research gets down to basics.

Customers are asked a series of questions about what is important to them. For example:

'Is it more important to you that this food cooks quicker or that it is low calorie?'

'Is large portion size more important than the fact it contains no additives?'

By using this approach, which is called *conjoint analysis*, the company can analyze the results and establish exactly what benefits the customers seek. Furthermore, with suitably designed research it becomes possible to put a monetary value on what these benefits are worth: this is generally termed *price equivalence*.

According to the results of this type of analysis, Yummy Foods can more accurately position its new product against competing foods, and thereby exploit and develop its potential for adding customer benefit. For example, if it finds 'portion size' and 'cooking time' to be the prime customer benefits, it can position the product on the type of map shown in Figure 6.10. Such a visual representation can illustrate how and where Yummy can differentiate its product and price it accordingly.

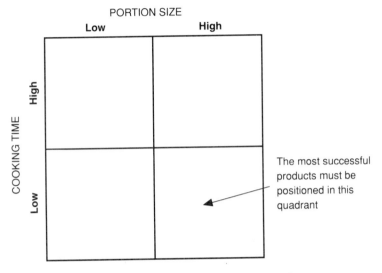

Figure 6.10 Product positioning benefits

Another example of how the conjoint analysis technique can be used in relation to an industrial product will help to illustrate its value. The example refers to the pricing of a software system. In this case the following attributes of the product might be important to the buyer:

- Ease with which the new system can be introduced.
- User training is provided.
- Fast-response back-up service should anything go wrong.
- Potential to be extended.
- State-of-the-art technology.
- Supplier's reputation.

A panel of customers could be asked to imagine they were supplied with a total package including all the above items, for £x. Then they are asked: if a price increase became necessary, which attribute would they rather eliminate instead of paying a higher price? The attributes are jettisoned one at a time so that the customers' perception of value is rated from least to most important. Only the most important attribute remains at the end.

Useful though this information is, it has to be remembered that while a customer claims that, say, the supplier's reputation is a significant attribute, the supplier in question might have a relatively poor reputation in the industry. Thus the supplier needs to use the criteria rating of customers in two ways:

- As valuable information in its own right.
- As a yardstick against which to judge one's own performance and that of competitors.

Only where the supplier outscores the competition in key attributes is there really the true potential for extracting a higher price (Figure 6.11).

In the diagram, minimal disruption is the most valued attribute. If the software supplier can show that its approach is less disruptive than that of competitors then this is indeed an area which can justify a premium price. Similarly, training is the least important attribute. Even if our software supplier outstripped all competition and provided super deluxe training, it is doubtful if this would justify a price increase. In this case, training does not appear to be highly valued by customers.

A word of warning should accompany this type of analysis, and this concerns the choice of the customer panel. They must be chosen with care and represent the 'typical' person who champions the buying decision. If this does not happen, the attribute trade-off could

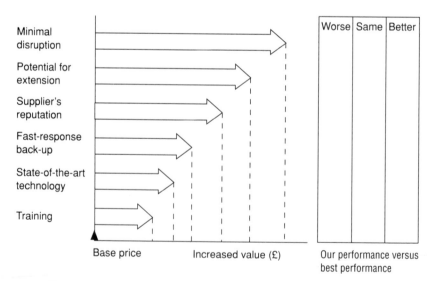

Figure 6.11 Buyer's perception of system attributes (example only)

be skewed and rendered useless. For example, if the panel were all computer wizards then state-of-the-art technology might have the most appeal. In contrast to this, if human resources people were predominant, training might be awarded a disproportionately high score.

Conjoint analysis can produce some useful information for the marketer over and above influencing pricing:

- Where important attributes are valued low by customers, marketing communications could be used to 're-educate' the clientele and change their perceptions.

- The analysis provides a basis for upgrading particular attributes or building in new ones.

- This approach could lead to an improved method of seg-mentation, i.e. around those customers who value attributes in which the company leads the field.

Pricing and image

While price can often contribute to the image of a product, it is impossible to sustain an image if the product is not worthy of it. Generally speaking, the more a product or service can be differen-tiated from its competition, the more successfully price can be used to enhance this differentiation.

In Figure 6.12 anything falling into quadrant A is something of a surprise. It can only occur if perhaps the product is in short supply or the customers are ill-informed in terms of understanding what they are paying for the product. The product's inherent lack of differen-tiation cannot otherwise justify a high price.

Quadrant B is a sustainable proposition and is what one might expect with branded products.

Quadrant C represents 'me too' products which can command little price differentiation. It is here that many commodity items will be found.

Anything in quadrant D does not appear to make commercial sense. The product is highly differentiated and yet offered at a low price. Clearly, this can represent a true waste in the sense of throwing away potential earnings. The only justification might be if the company's strategy is deliberately to determine a low price in order to establish a large share of the market.

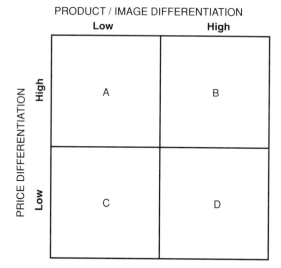

Figure 6.12 Price and product image

Such a diagram helps to explain why, for example, an expensive perfume with its distinctive fragrance and image can command such a high price, whereas something like a bag of nails has to be sold cheaply. Indeed, such is human psychology that people would probably steer clear of an ostensibly prestigious product offered at a ridiculously low price. Something in our psyche warns us that the product is probably substandard and not worth the risk.

The use of discounts

No chapter on pricing would be complete without some reference to the use of discounts. In theory a discount is offered as a reward to a customer or intermediary for buying larger quantities, buying out of season, or paying promptly. In this sense, a discount is a tactical weapon to encourage throughput, level out seasonal production inbalances, or stimulate cash flow.

For these reasons discounts ought to be considered very carefully in terms of what they are trying to achieve, and the level at which they should be set in order to be 'motivational'. Unfortunately, discount structures have too often evolved as custom and practice, and have little bearing on the company's overall product strategy.

Without such careful consideration discounting might prove to be an extremely successful method of throwing away potential sales revenue.

Summary

In this chapter pricing has been looked at from a number of different angles. We started by considering supply and demand, and the elasticity of demand. We looked at pricing in the special cases of a monopoly and oligopoly. We saw that price can be viewed differently by the manufacturer and the customer.

Whereas the manufacturer tends to think of price mainly in terms of costs and margins, the customer is more concerned with perceived value, in terms of how the product delivers benefits. From this we concluded that pricing had to take into account a number of different factors, such as the position on the product life-cycle, the overall product portfolio, customer benefit analysis and even the product's image.

Taken together all of these things conspire to make pricing something of an amalgam of art and science. However, Figure 6.13 can perhaps help to simplify the process of fixing a realistic price. The 'priceometer' shown in the diagram enables the pricing situation to be measured. It initially records the average price charged by competing products. Thereafter the reading moves either upwards or downwards according to the following factors.

Upward forces

- Short supply.
- Exclusivity/image.
- Highly differentiated from competing products.
- Decision to 'milk' product regardless of its future.
- High costs to be met.

Downward forces

- Lack of differentiation.
- Strategy to capture market share.
- Product used as a loss leader (e.g. to sell more profitable ones) in the range.

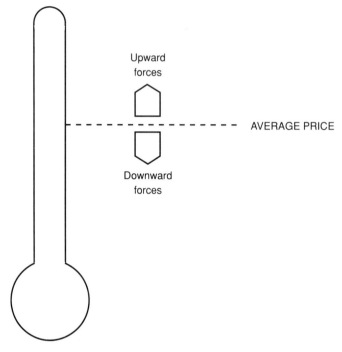

Figure 6.13 The pricing 'thermometer': the priceometer

● Oversupply situation.

The scale on the priceometer is in £s, but each company may decide to select its figures in whichever unit is the most appropriate to its own circumstances, thus customizing it for its own purposes.

PRICING POLICY AUDIT

Score
0 1 2

1. **Does the company have a sound pricing policy?**

   (a) Essentially prices are based on a cost-plus
   policy.   (*Score 0*)
   (b) Prices are based on shadowing competitive
   policy.   (*Score 1*)
   (c) A pricing policy exists as part of the firm's overall
   marketing and corporate strategy.   (*Score 2*)

2. **Does the firm think of customers and their needs
   when fixing the price?**

   (a) No. Prices are based upon the costings system
   only.   (*Score 0*)
   (b) An attempt is made to find out what the customer
   is prepared to pay.   (*Score 1*)
   (c) A full analysis of the 'value of the benefits'
   (tangible and intangible) to customers is made before
   prices are fixed.   (*Score 2*)

3. **Is an attempt made to integrate pricing policy with the
   marketing mix?**

   (a) No. Prices are determined in isolation from the
   rest of the mix.   (*Score 0*)
   (b) Partial integration with the mix is considered from
   time to time.   (*Score 1*)
   (c) The role of price in the mix is under constant
   review.   (*Score 2*)

4. **How flexible is the firm's pricing policy?**

   (a) Once prices have been determined the firm
   adheres rigidly to them.   (*Score 0*)
   (b) An attempt to identify mistakes and respond to
   them is made from time to time.   (*Score 1*)
   (c) The firm seeks to ensure that its information
   system provides a dynamic feedback of market
   attitude to its pricing policy, and it plans a response to
   such an input.   (*Score 2*)

▶

5. **Does the firm actively seek to understand the level of price elasticity that exists in relation to its products?**

    (a) No. Such information is only gleaned from past experience.　　　　　　*(Score 0)*
    (b) Somehow. However, such information is not incorporated into the pricing strategy until it becomes absolutely necessary.　　　　　　*(Score 1)*
    (c) Yes. It forms a significant basis for formulating the firm's pricing policy.　　　　　　*(Score 2)*

6. **Does the firm's pricing policy pay attention to the existence of various segments in the market?**

    (a) No. Everybody pays the same.　　*(Score 0)*
    (b) Yes. The company has a policy of charging different prices for different segments.　　　　　　*(Score 1)*
    (c) Yes. Not only do the prices respond to the existence of segments, but the whole mix is analyzed and, if appropriate, differentiated.　　*(Score 2)*

7. **Has the company formulated criteria for making price adjustments?**

    (a) No. Prices are changed simply to improve margins and profits.　　　　　　*(Score 0)*
    (b) Prices are adjusted for inflation. Some investigation as to whether the customer is willing to pay more is also made.　　　　　　*(Score 1)*
    (c) A system for establishing the right price within the product life-cycle is in place at all times.　　　　　　*(Score 2)*

8. **Does the company use discounts?**

    (a) Discounts are given in accordance with the traditions of the trade/business and the level of pressure placed by customers.　　*(Score 0)*
    (b) Yes, depending on traditions of the trade coupled with the firm's own pricing policy.　　*(Score 1)*
    (c) Yes. Discounts form an integral part of the firm's marketing and pricing strategy and have been formulated following a full analysis of customers' expectations.　　　　　　*(Score 2)*

▶

Score
0 1 2

9. **Whose responsibility is it to fix prices?**

    (a) Accountants only.   *(Score 0)*
    (b) The boss.   *(Score 1)*
    (c) The marketing department with a wide functional
    participation.   *(Score 2)*

10. **How often does the firm monitor its pricing performance?**

    (a) Never.   *(Score 0)*
    (b) Once a year.   *(Score 1)*
    (c) Continuously.   *(Score 2)*

The maximum score possible is 20. Very few companies could achieve such a score. Lower scores can be interpreted as follows:

15–20   **Excellent**
10–14   **Good to very good.**
 5–9   **Fair**
 0–4   **Poor**

7

The promotional mix

In this chapter we will explore the meaning and role of the promotional mix in marketing. In fact, we are concerned now with the process of planning and controlling a mix within a mix. Confusion is often created as a result of some textbooks referring to this mix as the 'marketing communications mix'. The important point to remember is that, whichever term one chooses to use, one is talking about a whole panoply of tools and not only one activity. The overall aim of the promotional mix is to communicate a range of messages to the customers and/or the channels of distribution with the ultimate aim of ensuring that the product is sold, is consumed and creates satisfaction.

As a preamble to the whole discussion the communication process should be explored briefly. Figure 7.1 describes how the sender of a message has to encode it in such a way that the ultimate receiver is able to decode it. The message has to be transmitted via a message

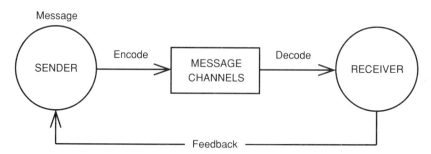

Figure 7.1 The communication process

channel which is effective and within the receiver's sensual vicinity (ears, eyes, smell, touch). The process is completed by the sender soliciting some feedback with a view to finding out whether the message has reached its destination in the manner that the sender hoped. Thus the characteristics of the communication process entail a number of 'players' and/or mechanisms (Table 7.1)

Communication takes place in all walks of life and in all areas of human endeavour. Indeed, communication takes place throughout the animal world. We humans do not always understand animal messages because we seldom know how to decode them. An aircraft pilot communicates with other aeroplanes or the control tower by transmitting messages in a recognized pilots' language which he knows the receivers can easily decode. The pilot has at his disposal channels of communication which put him within communication earshot of his interlocutors. Moreover, a system of feedback is normally in operation, enabling him to judge whether the message has been received and understood.

Marketers resort to a similar pattern of communication. They have messages; they encode them; they transmit them through the channels available to them; and they attempt to ensure through a system of feedback that the encoded messages were properly decoded. This description of the communication process or the promotional mix could not be simpler. Yet there are many nuances attached to it and there is a lot that can go wrong when it is applied in practice.

The major problems associated with communication effectiveness are inherent in the process itself:

Table 7.1 Characteristics of the communication process

Parties to the process	Points to watch
Sender	Must have clear objectives as to what he/she seeks to communicate. Must gain an insight into what the receiver is capable of understanding and decoding, and his/her willingness to listen.
Message	Must represent correctly what the sender wants to communicate and what the receiver is capable of decoding.
Receiver	Must be within 'earshot' of the communication. Must be willing to listen to or observe the message.
Message channels	If there is a choice, preference must be given to the most effective message channel. There is no point using an inefficient system when better and cheaper ones exist.
Feedback	This is an essential culmination to the communication cycle. The sender must establish that the message has been accurately received and understood.

- The sender is not always clear about what he or she wants to communicate.

- The message is encoded into a message which the receiver is not able to decode correctly. At that point the message is likely to be misconstrued.

- Interference with the transmission reduces the quality of the communication (Figure 7.2). Interference diverts the receiver's attention elsewhere. For instance, a very creative whole-page advertisement in the national press may miss its audience as a result of a dramatic piece of news that attracts a lot of attention on the same day.

Promotional channels

Marketers have at their disposal a number of channels through which they can communicate with whomever they need to. The main channels are as follows:

- Advertising.
- Sales promotion.
- Publicity and public relations.

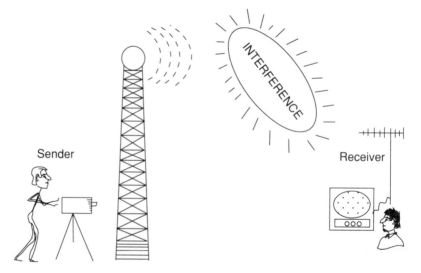

Figure 7.2 The role of 'interference' in the quality of communication

- Direct marketing.
- Personal selling.

Each one of these channels has its advantages and disadvantages, and its relevance and effectiveness have to be analyzed in relation to a given set of circumstances. Indeed, in some situations all five channels can be used simultaneously with great effect.

A brief definition of the five communication channels is appropriate:

- **Advertising:** Advertising is any paid form of non-personal communication of products, services or ideas placed in one or more of the commercially available media by an identified sponsor.

- **Sales promotion:** Sales promotion activities, also known as 'below-the-line' activities, represent non-media campaigns such as demonstrations, sampling, displays, shows, exhibitions, price deals, contests and self-liquidating premiums.

- **Publicity:** This is the process of stimulating a favourable mention in the media of significant news items about the firm, its products and its activities without actually paying for it. Publicity is often achieved as a result of public relations activities.

- **Direct marketing:** This is communication through the mail, telecommunication system, or direct response advertising between the company and its customers and/or prospects based on careful targeting of individuals listed in a databank.

- **Personal selling:** This is face-to-face communication with one or more prospective buyers, deciders, users and/or influencers with the aim of moving the prospect towards a purchase or a decision.

Personal selling will be described fully in Chapter 9.

Promotion objectives

A modern enterprise rarely fails to measure the effectiveness of its human resources. Similarly, it is quite normal for a company to analyze carefully the productivity of its manufacturing process. Yet one comes across many companies that do not measure the results of their promotional and advertising expenditure. 'I know that half of my advertising budget is wasted, but I do not know which half' is a comment ascribed to Lord Leverhulme, the founder of Unilever, and summarizes the dilemma that faces marketers. The main problem is that many marketers start with inadequately formulated objectives. Without clear objectives there is no way that one can measure results in a meaningful way.

For many years a controversy raged among promotion and advertising experts. Two opposing schools of thought enriched the literature with conflicting philosophies. The first averred that advertising and promotion can be judged only by the sales that they have achieved, while the second supported the concept that the promotional mix seeks to attain a whole range of clearly defined communication objectives. Advertising and promotion succeed, according to the former school of thought, on the basis of the level of sales achieved. According to the latter, it depends on how well predetermined information and attitudes have been communicated and at what cost. The former is often referred to as *action communication*; the latter is called *DAGMAR* communication. DAGMAR is an acronym for 'defining advertising goals – measuring advertising response/ results'.

The controversy was somewhat futile inasmuch as both philosophies are right in certain circumstances. The action communication applies when the promotional campaign is designed to sell the product and nothing else. For instance, an advertisement which invites people to send a coupon with a cheque or credit-card details is clearly action orientated. Depending on the number of coupons received, one can gauge whether the campaign was successful or not. On the other hand, where advertising is used to alleviate 'cognitive dissonance' (post-purchase doubt, in simple language) the DAG-MAR school carries the day. Similarly, a campaign seeking to create 'primary demand', say for wool or steel or aluminium in their generic forms on behalf of a whole industry, in order to increase general interest in the excellent properties of the product, irrespective of specific brands, cannot be measured in sales terms. The time-lag between the campaign and the possible purchase of a specific brand ('selective demand') is simply too long. DAGMAR wins again.

One can list many examples of both action-type and DAGMAR-type campaigns. They are both valid and each has a role to play in the marketing programme. The important point to remember is that, broadly speaking, action campaigns are easier to measure. Sales are quantitative and counting orders is much easier than measuring an increase in 'awareness'. On the other hand, marketers must always remember that the underlying philosophy of DAGMAR is that clear objectives must be defined in advance, since then the probability of being able to grapple with the task of measurement is greatly increased. Thus, the essence of an effective promotional mix is the clarity of purpose and objectives which underlie it. The clearer the objectives, the easier it will be to measure the subsequent results.

Over the years a number of behavioural models have emerged to demonstrate what promotional mix seeks to achieve. Two simple models will be described.

One model is referred to as the *AIDA framework*. Each letter represents a behavioural state of mind on the part of the customer:

A = Attention
I = Interest
D = Desire
A = Action

The implication is obvious: customers are unlikely to purchase a product until they have gone through the logical process of first becoming aware of the product; then becoming interested in it; then having a desire to own it; and finally acting upon it. It is an attractive concept in its simplicity, but it ignores some of the intermediate subtleties of the way customers really behave in response to advertising or other promotional campaigns.

Another model developed by Lavidge and Steiner (1961) and adapted slightly for this chapter is illustrated in Figure 7.3. The main aim of the adaptation is to correlate the shift in communication objectives to the various stages of the product life-cycle. Clearly, as the product is ageing, the emphasis is changing from awareness creation to other tools of the mix, thus helping to bring the customer nearer to the point-of-sale venue.

Having briefly explored two communication models, it is important to remind the reader that more detailed objectives can be ascribed to every promotional campaign. A checklist for evaluating promotional objectives is provided in Figure 7.4 (see p. 125). While the list is not comprehensive, it takes care of most situations. A marketer is well advised to cast an eye over these objectives when preparing a promotional programme. At the end of the exercise one can quickly identify the items which are particularly important and weave them into the promotional campaign or the promotional brief. This can be a great aid to promotional planning.

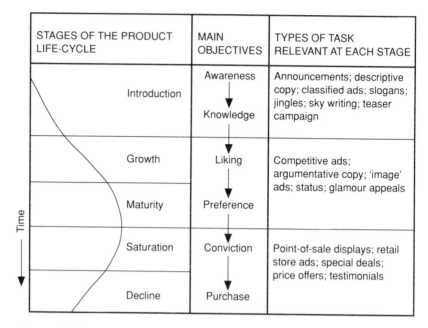

STAGES OF THE PRODUCT LIFE-CYCLE		MAIN OBJECTIVES	TYPES OF TASK RELEVANT AT EACH STAGE
	Introduction	Awareness ↓ Knowledge	Announcements; descriptive copy; classified ads; slogans; jingles; sky writing; teaser campaign
	Growth	Liking	Competitive ads; argumentative copy; 'image' ads; status; glamour appeals
	Maturity	Preference	
	Saturation	Conviction	Point-of-sale displays; retail store ads; special deals; price offers; testimonials
	Decline	Purchase	

Figure 7.3 The main objectives of communication at the various stages of the product life-cycle (adapted from the Lavidge and Steiner model)

Advertising

Advertising is inevitably the 'loudest' ingredient in the promotional mix. It stares at us from television screens and/or the media in general. It is difficult to ignore. Outsiders to the marketing fraternity often regard advertising as synonymous with marketing. They overlook the fact that advertising is just one element in the promotional mix, and that the latter is one element in the marketing mix. Like a good chef who can mix his ingredients to produce a mouth-watering dish, so can the master marketer, through a creative and intelligent use of components, devise a competition-beating recipe. However, in both instances it is essential to know precisely the influencing stimuli that make the customer react positively to what is being offered.

Knowing the target audience

In the case of marketing the influencing process can be compared to a

	Scale of importance				
	0	1	2	3	4

Scoring: 4 = very important; 3 = fairly important; 2 = less important; 1 = not important; 0 = irrelevant

1. Perform the complete selling function (action advertising/promotion)

2. Close sales to prospects already partly sold through past promotional efforts

3. Announce special reasons for 'buying now' (price, premium, etc.)

4. Remind to buy

5. Tie in with some special buying event

6. Stimulate impulse buying

7. Create awareness of the existence of the product and brand and their features and benefits

8. Stimulate a 'brand image' or a favourable emotional disposition towards the brand

9. Provide information about the superior features of the product

10. Counteract competitive claims

11. Correct false impressions, misinformation and other obstacles to sales

12. Develop familiarity and easy recognition of trademark and/or packaging

13. Build confidence in company and its brand for the long term

14. Develop increased demand with a view to placing the company in a stronger position *vis-à-vis* its distributors

15. Place advertiser in a better position to select preferred distributors or dealers

16. Secure universal distribution

▶

	Scale of importance				
	0	1	2	3	4

17. Establish a strong platform from which to launch new brands or products

18. Establish brand loyalty which will, in turn, help the company to open up new markets (geographical or segment orientated)

19. Maintain customers' loyalty against the inroads of competition

20. Convert users of competitive brands to advertiser's brand

21. Stimulate people to specify advertiser's brand instead of asking for product by generic name

22. Convert non-users of a product type into users of company's product and/or brand

23. Turn occasional or sporadic customers into steady customers

24. Increase consumption among present users by advertising new uses of the product

25. Increase consumption among present users by persuading them to buy larger sizes or multiple units

26. Persuade prospects to ask for descriptive literature, enter a contest

27. Persuade prospects to visit a showroom and ask for a demonstration

28. Invite prospects to sample the product

29. Help the sales force to open new accounts

30. Help the sales force to get larger orders from middlemen

31. Help salespeople to get preferred display space

32. Provide salespeople with an entrée to potential clients

▶

	Scale of importance				
	0	1	2	3	4
33. Build a morale of company personnel					
34. Impress the trade generally					
35. Inform customers 'where to buy'					
36. Inform customers 'how to use' the product					
37. Inform customers of new models, features, packaging, prices, special terms and policies (e.g. guarantees). Specify details					
38. Develop confidence and goodwill among customers and potential customers					
39. Develop confidence in the trade (e.g. among distributors, dealers, retail sales personnel)					
40. Develop confidence among employees and potential employees					
41. Develop confidence among the financial community					
42. Develop confidence and goodwill among the public at large					
43. Build a different image as a result of a repositioning strategy.					
44. Promulgate a family resemblance of a diversified range of products					
45. Develop a corporate citizenship					
46. Promote an image of growth, progress and technical leadership					

Figure 7.4 Checklist for evaluating promotional objectives

game of snakes and ladders. The marketer's task is to try to move customers up the behavioural ladders, which in turn lead to the next platform of influence. At the same time the customer is subjected to negative stimuli that act as 'snakes' to lower his or her readiness to buy the product. The concept is illustrated in Figure 7.5.

Until marketers understand fully their target customers they will not be in a position to encourage them to move up the behavioural

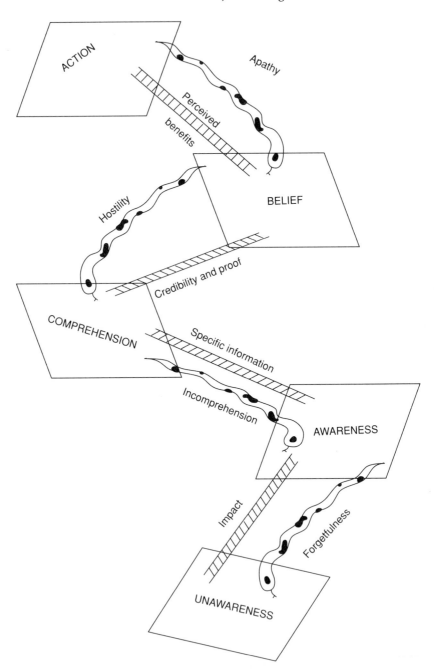

Figure 7.5 The influencing 'snakes and ladders'

ladders; nor will they be able to neutralize the forces pushing customers downwards. Lack of knowledge about customers and their motivational stimuli is one of the major barriers towards propelling customers upwards in the snakes and ladders game.

Clearly, one of the important elements in the game is the choice of media through which to communicate. Thus, if a bank wishes to encourage young people to open accounts, the choice of media can act as a snake or a ladder depending on its appropriateness in the eyes of the target audience. Research undertaken recently by one of the banks in precisely such a situation has indeed brought to light a number of problems:

- Young prospects did not fully understand what the bank was offering. In other words, they failed to 'decode' the message that was being communicated.

- They gained the impression that a lot more money was needed to make their custom attractive to the bank. In fact this was not the case.

- The traditional image of the bank was at variance with the fashionable dress and hairstyles of the potential customers targeted upon. They in turn were somewhat uncomfortable about being seen in the branches of such a bank.

Each one of these responses acted as a 'snake', making the campaign less and less effective. In order to overcome these negative stimuli a commercial was produced with the specific task of addressing them. Since the audiences at cinemas were closest to the age profile of the target customers, the cinema was chosen as the communication channel. Using this advertising outlet ensured not only that the right customers were targeted, but also that there was none of the wasted cost overspill that wider coverage in such media as television or national papers would inevitably incur. Remembering the DAGMAR concept, the campaign was monitored against the opening of new accounts in the 18–22 age bracket. By this measure the campaign was found to be highly successful.

Life-style coupled with socioeconomic factors can provide valuable information about customers in terms of what newspapers they read, which TV channels they watch and whether or not they travel by public transport and might be susceptible to scanning billboards. Moreover, travelling habits can highlight whether commercial radio listening habits can make radio advertising a valuable medium. A wealth of information is provided by the media owners and/or excellent publications such as BRAD (British Rates and Data). The information is there: the marketer must collect it and analyse its implications as part of the task of understanding the customers and their behavioural patterns.

Selecting the best media

Selecting the media for reaching the target customers in the most cost-effective way is a prime task for those responsible for the promotional effort. A few important factors must be taken into account.

Comparative cost

The marketer is often faced by a plethora of advertising media from which to select the communication channel. The pages of BRAD offer an embarrassingly large choice of options. In such circumstances the final choice must be influenced by the relative cost effectiveness of each medium. As a simple yardstick one can talk about 'the cost of reaching 1,000 viewers, listeners or readers'.

Using this measure one may find that advertising in a selected number of regional newspapers, whose advertising rates may be lower than the national press, is more effective. Similarly, a billboard campaign can in certain circumstances be much more cost effective than radio advertising.

Characteristics of the medium

This refers to the physical possibilities that the medium provides. Here we are concerned with such factors as its geographical coverage, its frequency of publication and hence the ability to repeat or reinforce the advertising message, its potential for sound, colour and movement (some are even experimenting with smell), and its ability to reach special segments.

Generally speaking, the more senses to which a message can appeal, the greater its impact on the receiver. However, again cost can be a limiting factor when it comes to choosing the medium. An all-singing, all-dancing, two-minute television extravaganza may be exactly what is required, but the cost may be prohibitive in relation to the objectives set.

The atmosphere

This refers to the image that the medium conveys. Obviously, the marketer wishes to choose a medium which is compatible with the nature of the product. A serious, high-quality product will need a medium which is seen to carry a sense of gravitas. A popular, 'jazzy' product will need to be communicated in a congruent medium.

Thus, while it is quite appropriate for a local window-cleaner to place leaflets through letter-boxes, the same is not true for a company offering an expensive and high-quality service. Conversely, it would not make sense for the window-cleaner to advertise in a glossy magazine.

From this brief look at advertising the key points to remember are as follows:

- Be clear about what you are trying to convey.
- Know why you want to convey such a message.
- Know to whom the message is addressed.
- Speak in the customer's 'language'.
- Choose the most appropriate medium.
- Decide the best time to make contact.
- Measure results.

On the surface these are seven logical and seemingly simple steps. However, we have already seen that in reality some hard decisions have to be taken before one knows which course of action is likely to provide optimum results. The situation is further complicated inasmuch as one has to pay heed to what competitors are doing in this regard. They are also jostling for customers' attention and by doing so distract them from listening to our message. It is not enough to grab customers' attention; the marketer must also endeavour to keep it long enough to make an impact.

Promotions

Promotion activities tend to be short term in duration and aims, and are normally devised to solve particular communication problems. A promotion is a featured offer to a defined audience within a specific time limit. The offer, in whatever form it is made, is something over and above that which would normally be associated with the 'package' of benefits which comes with the product or service in normal circumstances.

Typically, sales promotion is designed to stimulate customers to behave in a way which is more congruent with the company's plans. For example, if certain parts of the product range are proving to be slow moving, promotion could be designed to remedy the situation. Similarly, promotion in the shape of samples may be used to encourage a trial purchase. Other types of promotion may seek to outmanoeuvre a competitor, encourage repeat purchase or level out seasonally skewed demand patterns. These are the more overt types of sales promotion aimed at customers.

Behind the scenes the company may alternatively, or in tandem, offer similar types of incentive to their intermediaries or to their own sales force. Thus, promotions are not necessarily just concerned with volume sales increases, but can be designed to encourage any part of the marketing channel to buy earlier, more frequently, larger quantities and different pack sizes, to pay earlier and so on. As long as the marketer recognizes that sales promotions are not a substitute for selling and will only bring about short-term changes, they can prove a useful tactical weapon.

However, although promotions are of a short-term and tactical nature, this does not mean that they should be treated in isolation and in a spasmodic way. They need to be planned and integrated with the company's other marketing activities in such a way that their impact is maximized. Equally, there is no reason why a promotional activity cannot build on the momentum of its pre-decessors.

To avoid sales promotions failing through inadequate planning, the basic principles applicable to all other marketing activities should be followed:

- Clear objectives must be ascribed to the campaign.
- The most effective way of attaining these objectives must be thought through and selected.
- There should be some pre-testing in order to check that the proposed method is likely to attain the desired results.
- The promotional programme should proceed in the light of the pre-test experience.
- Results must be evaluated at the end of the exercise.

Types of promotional offers

Space does not permit a detailed discussion of all the different types of activity that fall under the heading of promotions. Nonetheless as customers and consumers most people have had personal experience of sales promotions activities of one kind or another.

'Special offers', the typical manifestation of promotional campaigns, can take the form of monetary incentives or the provision of free goods and services. Moreover, such incentives can be offered directly or indirectly. Direct monetary inducements take the form of lower prices or special credit terms. Indirect offers normally take the form of coupons or labels which can be exchanged for cash or a cash equivalent. Similarly goods can be offered as part of a promotional campaign, once again on a direct or indirect basis. For example, a free bowl with every six tins of cat food is a direct offer. Providing the customer with a free tin once six labels have been assembled is the indirect equivalent.

Through experimentation, coupled with careful control procedures, the marketer can identify the approach which evokes maximum response from customers and produces the best results in a given set of circumstances.

Direct marketing

Developments in information technology have made it possible for companies to assemble a wealth of data about their customers and prospects. Marketers have recognized the power that such databanks have in terms of interactive communication. The company can simply 'talk' to its customers as individuals, rather than communicating with them in an anonymous fashion through the mass media.

Mail order companies were the first to recognize the value of reaching people in their homes and generating business via letters and/or sales catalogues. Over the years the borderline between effective personal communication and what is seen by the customer as 'junk mail' has forced the direct marketing industry to develop methods and procedures for improving the image and effectiveness of the process. It is not enough just to personalize a letter and to sprinkle the customer's name over the text a few times. Direct marketing in its modern form is much more sophisticated than this.

Direct marketing can be defined as marketing communication that establishes and capitalizes upon a direct relationship between the company and its customers and prospects *as individuals*. It uses a number of techniques either singly or in combination. These include direct mail, telemarketing, direct selling and digital marketing (the use of electronic media similar to teletext). The last of these methods is not used extensively in the UK but can be seen a fair amount on satellite television programmes. There is little doubt that, as technology advances and the audiences for satellites increase, this method will become much more widespread.

Of all the methods mentioned, telemarketing is the fastest growing in terms of expenditure. Overall, it is interesting to note that in 1990 it was estimated that 13 per cent of the total media advertising in the UK was spent on direct response advertising.

The key to success in the direct marketing game is to have a databank of prospects that is as accurately targeted as possible. This means that a company may need to experiment with possible sources of data as illustrated in Figure 7.6.

At first sight promotions and competitions may appear to be unusual ways of gaining prospects. However, if the entry form for a competition, or the promotion claim procedure, invites participants to volunteer relevant information about themselves or their circumstances, then clearly the company may reap rich rewards for their future communication strategy.

Complaints about the personal intrusion of direct marketing are often voiced. Research has shown that recipients of direct mail find it acceptable under the following circumstances:

- When it comes from companies with which they have done business before or have had earlier contact.

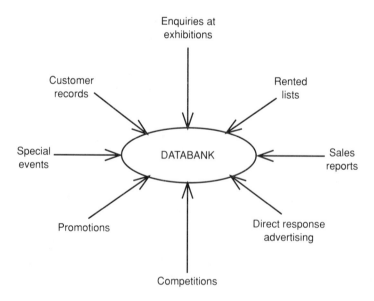

Figure 7.6 Sources for updating the databank

- When it is relevant to their specific needs.
- When it is unambiguous about its purpose.
- When they know how any information they provide will be used.
- When they feel that they have some control over what they receive.

In contrast people regard direct mail as an invasion of privacy, a waste of resources or a nuisance in these circumstances:

- When personalization is phoney and patronizing.
- When there are mixed messages (e.g. the bank tells you that you are overdrawn and in the same envelope invites you to insure your life with it).
- When it pressurizes or threatens the reader with unpleasant consequences.
- When it involves the recipient in too much work or cost (e.g. having to complete a tedious questionnaire or return a bulky parcel).

Preparing the communication plan

Although we have looked at advertising, sales promotion and direct marketing as separate activities, in practice they must be integrated not only with each other, but also with all the other ingredients of the mix, including sales activity. The starting point is the overall marketing plan with its objectives and strategy for a particular market segment. The process illustrated in Figure 7.7 must be thoroughly pursued. Each programme of communication should provide answers to the following questions:

- Who is the target audience?
- What is scheduled to happen?
- How is the activity to be organized?
- When will it take place?
- What special organizational support is required?
- What response or results are expected?
- How will they be measured?
- What will it cost in relation to the anticipated benefits?

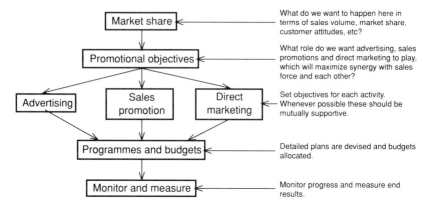

Figure 7.7 Preparing the communication plan: a schematic approach

In summary, as was emphasized throughout this chapter, the success of any planning in the area of promotion depends upon a clear definition of one's objectives and a full understanding of customers' behaviour and their responses to the various stimuli presented to them. Without these ingredients the whole promotional programme is likely to be ill-conceived and the measurement of results of dubious quality.

PROMOTIONAL MIX AUDIT

Score
0 1 2

1. **Does the company have a clearly defined promotional plan?**

    (a) No. Money is spent on promotion/advertising when resources allow.   (*Score 0*)
    (b) Yes. A percentage of sales turnover is allocated towards promotion.   (*Score 1*)
    (c) Yes. We have a set of promotion/advertising objectives related to the marketing plan. Full integration between marketing and promotion plans is constantly sought.   (*Score 2*)

Score
0 1 2

2. **How often are promotional objectives and strategy reviewed?**

   (a) Rarely.   *(Score 0)*
   (b) Sometimes.   *(Score 1)*
   (c) Regularly, as part of our control
   procedures.   *(Score 2)*

3. **How does the firm determine its promotional budgets?**

   (a) A fixed sum is chosen by management once a year
   on the basis of affordability.   *(Score 0)*
   (b) We shadow competitors' expenditure and choose
   a figure based on this analysis.   *(Score 1)*
   (c) Having defined our promotional objectives we
   determine the tasks that need to be carried out and
   allocate the appropriate resources.   *(Score 2)*

4. **Does the firm attempt to measure the results of its promotional/advertising expenditure?**

   (a) No. We do not believe that it can be
   done.   *(Score 0)*
   (b) Occasionally. We try but find that the cost of such
   measurement outweighs the benefit of the whole
   exercise.   *(Score 1)*
   (c) Yes. We allocate a specific budget towards
   measurement procedures. We find that with clear
   objectives measurement becomes
   easier.   *(Score 2)*

5. **When selecting specific tools from the promotional mix, does the company attempt to evaluate their relative effectiveness?**

   (a) No. We choose the component that we know best
   and that worked for us in the past.   *(Score 0)*
   (b) Yes. We try to identify the tool in the mix that is
   likely to work best.   *(Score 1)*
   (c) We try to relate the tools available to us to each
   product and its life-cycle and determine the optimum
   mix in the circumstances.   *(Score 2)*

6. **How far does the company rely on its advertising agency to prepare an advertising plan?**

    (a) We rely on them entirely. They must earn their money. *(Score 0)*
    (b) We tell them what to do. We know the facts better than them. *(Score 1)*
    (c) We work closely together in order to debate the best strategy, choice of media and creative content of the campaign. We respect their professionalism and they value our involvement. *(Score 2)*

7. **At what level are promotional decisions taken?**

    (a) All decisions are taken by the finance director inasmuch as money is involved. *(Score 0)*
    (b) We have an advertising manager who takes such decisions alone. *(Score 1)*
    (c) We have a communications manager who discusses all the details of the advertising/promotion programme with brand/product managers, the marketing director and, when appropriate, top management. A thorough debate takes place with all 'stakeholders'. *(Score 2)*

8. **Does the firm experiment with new communication ideas?**

    (a) No. The process is complicated enough without attempting new methods. *(Score 0)*
    (b) We wait for others to take the initiative in this regard. If they are successful we follow suit. *(Score 1)*
    (c) We are always interested in new ideas for communicating with the marketplace. *(Score 2)*

9. **How is the promotional mix viewed by the firm's management?**

    (a) As a waste of money. *(Score 0)*
    (b) As a necessary evil. If we could achieve communication with customers without spending so much money, it would be wonderful. *(Score 1)*
    (c) As an essential and valuable communication and/or dialogue with customers. Altogether it is viewed as a long-term investment. *(Score 2)*

▶

Score
0 1 2

10. **To what extent does the company seek to foster its corporate image as an aid to marketing??**

(a) Corporate image is not considered of importance when marketing products.   (*Score 0*)
(b) Corporate image is regarded as important, but resources are allocated towards it only when the firm is having a good time.   (*Score 1*)
(c) The firm's image is treated as an integral part of the firm's communication strategy, and resources are allocated towards its enhancement when promotional plans are being prepared.   (*Score 2*)

The maximum score possible is 20. Very few companies could achieve such a score. Lower scores can be interpreted as follows:

15–20 **Excellent**
10–14 **Good to very good.**
 5–9 **Fair**
 0–4 **Poor**

8

Distribution and logistics

Ask most managers what they understand distribution to be about, and they will come up with descriptions of lorries rushing up and down motorways – the physical transportation of goods. Certainly that is one aspect of distribution and logistics, but in this chapter we will consider it as the 'place' element of the four Ps in the marketing mix. Seen in this context, distribution becomes a much wider issue and is concerned with finding the best outlets for the customer to receive the product or service, and with maintaining supplies so that those who want to buy are able to do so. The overall aim is to provide the customer with optimum satisfaction in relation to what economists call the utility of place and the utility of time.

Selecting the most appropriate channel for output to reach the customer is a decision of great strategic importance. It is a decision which helps to drive the subsequent logistics system and provides the customer satisfaction envisaged by the marketing process. From the company's viewpoint, choice of the wrong channel can push up distribution costs alarmingly, whereas choice of the right channel can provide the company with a competitive edge.

Surprisingly, although distribution and logistics can be a critical area of the company's marketing activity, for many organizations it has been something of a Cinderella activity. Somehow it does not seem to have the glamorous image associated with advertising and brand management. Nevertheless it is quite possible for distribution and logistics to cost almost as much as advertising and selling (see Figure 8.1). For this reason it is a marketing activity well worth putting under the microscope.

In this chapter we shall look at the various channel options open to

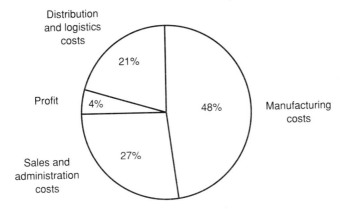

Figure 8.1 An example of one company's apportionment of product costs

the marketer and how to select the best one. We will then look at the logistics that underpin the problem of getting the right product to the right place and at the right time. It is also important to look at the area of customer service, and finally at some of the innovations that are taking place in distribution at large.

Marketing channels

There are a number of different channels open to the marketer, as Figure 8.2 shows. He or she could deal directly with customers, reach them via wholesalers, agents or retailers, use mail order as a channel or employ any combination of these. When the customer buys direct from the manufacturer the channel is described as a *short* one. When a large number of intermediaries is involved the channel is referred to as *long*.

Should it be decided to use some form of intermediary, a new set of challenges arises as to how these might be chosen and motivated to work hard in the interests of the supplier and the customer.

Let us refer back to Yummy Foods, the example that appeared in Chapter 6 on pricing. How might the company best reach its customers? It has several possible ways of getting its new convenience meals to the dining table:

- It could open a shop at the factory and invite customers to buy from it direct. This could limit its sales tremendously inasmuch

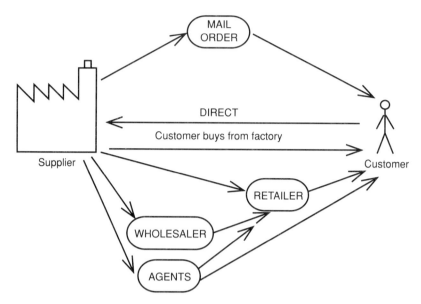

Figure 8.2 Possible marketing channels

as it would not provide the customers with 'utility of time and place'.

- It could open a chain of its own shops. This may prove extremely expensive owing to the cost of establishing the retail infrastructure.
- It could sell through retailers, but which ones? Health food shops could be compatible with the healthy image it is trying to generate. Supermarkets might offer the biggest throughput of customers. Freezer centres are places to which seekers of convenience foods might first turn.
- It could sell its food to the catering trade, either direct or through cash and carry wholesalers, but this might require different packaging sizes and presentation.

What should the company do? Yummy Foods, like any other supplier, should think long and hard about its target customers, their needs and expectations. The decision must be based on customers' preference in this regard and not only on what suits the supplier. The implication here is that manufacturers need to know a good deal about their customers, not only in terms of their needs, but also in terms of their buying patterns and preferences. If it were found that customers preferred to have their Yummy meals delivered to their homes, this option would have to be given very serious consideration.

At the end of the day, the final choice will be governed by two factors:

- **Market considerations:** Customer preferences, their geographical spread, socioeconomic circumstances and so on must be clearly understood and analyzed.

- **The capabilities and requirements of the suppliers:** Here suppliers must inventory their own strengths and weaknesses and list their requirements for the most efficient and cost-effective distribution system. At the same time they must recognize that it is not always possible to select the optimum channel because of a lack of resources or the costs involved. Moreover, in some cases the desired channel simply does not exist.

As in the case of marketing as a whole, the distribution dilemma is one of finding the best way of matching the company to the needs of its customers in a way that is likely to satisfy both parties to the maximum.

The choice of intermediaries

If a decision is taken to use a channel intermediary then ideally there should be a marriage of interest. The manufacturer needs to make the arrangement work just as much as the intermediary, for both have much to gain and a lot to lose if things turn sour. Both parties must have a considerable amount to offer to each other as a basis for a harmonious collaboration.

The manufacturer can provide:

- Know-how.
- Financial assistance/preferential purchasing.
- Administrative procedures and controls.
- Training.
- Credit and other incentives.
- Geographical exclusivity.

- Advertising and promotional campaigns.
- Continuing supplies.

For its part the intermediary can provide:

- Local stockholding.
- Local knowledge, contacts and market coverage.
- Staffing (in terms of quality and numbers).
- Performance standards.
- Financial commitment.
- Display and merchandising.
- Service at agreed levels.

Essentially the manufacturer needs to feel that the intermediary is trustworthy and someone with whom it is possible to establish a productive working relationship. Of course, there are some basic criteria to take into account:

- Creditworthiness.
- The right projected image.
- The geographical location in the context of the overall marketing strategy.
- Compatibility of inventory and customer service.
- A successful track record.

The essential point to remember is that mutual respect and trust must exist between the marketing company and its intermediaries.

Power in the distribution channel

The foregoing text has indicated that mutual interest should be the cement that holds together the manufacturer and intermediary. While this is certainly true, the bargaining power of the parties concerned might be weighted more on one side than the other. Indeed, the issue about who has the power can be fundamental to how the channel is selected and managed.

Figure 8.3(a) shows a channel where the manufacturer carries the most 'clout'. An example of this would be the car industry, where the

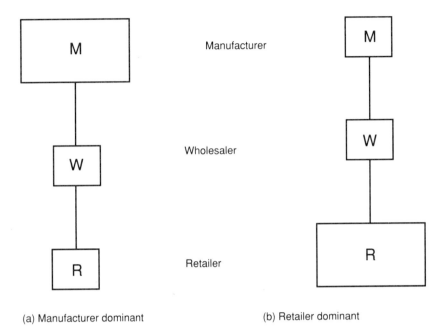

(a) Manufacturer dominant   (b) Retailer dominant

Figure 8.3 Patterns of channel power

few giants tend to dictate to tied distributors what they can and cannot do. Until recent government intervention, a similar pattern existed with the brewers and their numerous public houses. It is interesting to note that, wherever a manufacturer carries excessive power, the legal system tends to step in with a view to curbing what is liable to be a restrictive practice with adverse impact upon the customer's interest.

On the other hand, Figure 8.3(b) shows a situation where the retailer has the balance of power. For example, retailing giants such as Marks & Spencer can dictate to their suppliers what to deliver and to what quality. They can even lay down conditions about the manufacturing environment of their suppliers in pursuit of high-quality merchandise.

For some marketers winning channel leadership might be just as legitimate a goal as winning market share. Indeed, achieving the former might prove to be an enabling objective to reaching the latter. Clearly, those organizations which achieve this position of leadership can set the conditions, standards and tempo of activity to their own advantage, and to the discomfort of their competitors.

Channel motivation

Looking at the market channel from the manufacturer's viewpoint, two broad motivation strategies are possible in order to stimulate throughput, as shown in Figure 8.4.

In broad terms, the manufacturer can adopt a *push* strategy. In this case the manufacturer will sell hard down the channel by offering attractive inducements to all intermediaries, all of which will be geared to maximizing the quantity sold.

An alternative strategy will be to focus on the customers and use advertising and promotions to generate demand, thereby developing a *pull* mechanism which 'draws' goods through the channel.

Most commonly, manufacturers do not rely solely on one of these approaches, but use a combination, the balance of which is selected to optimize their distribution objectives. The exact nature of the way the manufacturer tries to stimulate movement in the channel is summarized in Figure 8.5. The challenge is to attempt to maintain a high level of motivation throughout the channel system over a long period and not just at launch or during spasmodic spurts of activity. This calls for a certain amount of experimentation and the need to resort to fresh ideas whenever existing practices cease to provide the appropriate motivational stimulus to members of the channel.

As we have seen, incentives can be offered to channel intermediaries or the customers in order to create movement, whether by push or pull. Incentives fall into three categories:

- **Money incentives:** These can take the form of reduced prices, quantity discounts, easy terms, free credit, money prizes for competitions and money-equivalent incentives such as coupons or vouchers.

- **Goods incentives:** These can be free gifts, trial offers, premium offers (e.g. 3 for the price of 2), trade-in or part-exchange, vouchers or coupons for goods, and competitions with goods and prizes.

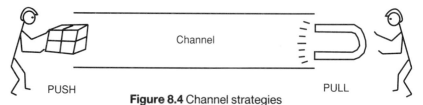

Figure 8.4 Channel strategies

NATURE OF INCENTIVES

	Money	Goods	Services
Wholesalers			
Retailers			
Customers			

ADDRESSES

Figure 8.5 Summary of incentives

- **Service incentives:** These include guarantees, free training, demonstrations, exhibitions, admission to special events, group participation events, free consultancy, reciprocal trading, vouchers, coupons and competitions with service-type rewards.

All of these motivational methods cost money, sometimes large amounts. On the other hand, what many manufacturers overlook is that it costs nothing to motivate intermediaries by making them feel important, listening to ideas they put forward and staying in regular contact, not only when things go wrong. This last point is often raised, especially by export agents who complain, 'The only time we hear from the manufacturer is when he comes over to us complaining about something.'

The logistics of distribution

There are five areas of distribution which need to be considered from the logistics viewpoint – it is in these areas that all the costs are hidden.

Physical distribution

This is the aspect of distribution which most readily springs to mind. The company needs to consider how it will physically transport its product to the next stage of the channel, so that it arrives on time and in the best possible condition.

Whereas in the past it was fairly common for companies to use their own lorries and vans, the cost of running their own vehicles often became prohibitive, especially if they were moving only partial loads. The development and growth of efficient specialist carriers and hauliers has made the use of one's own transport system less attractive. Today the manufacturer is faced with a wide range of options involving land, sea and air, at standard or express service levels. Some carriers even specialize in specific areas such as refrigerated foods, hanging garments and computers.

The physical distribution choice is about establishing a balance between costs and meeting the customer's requirements. Thus, the cheapest solution is not always the best one. This is why growers in the Channel Islands are prepared to air-freight flowers and tomatoes to the mainland UK to ensure that their produce arrives 'freshly picked'. Without such obvious visual appeal these products would be less competitive.

Facilities

In order to ensure that products reach the right place and at the right time, companies have to invest in facilities for holding and fanning out stocks. These might take the form of a warehouse at the factory or, if this cannot provide the appropriate geographical coverage, a number of distribution depots strategically placed near high-density markets.

Of course, the use of intermediaries may go some way towards providing local stockholding. At the same time one must realize that it is not always an attractive proposition for, say, a merchant to be saddled with high quantities of stock. The company must therefore decide in the interest of providing the right levels of customer service whether distribution can be managed centrally or if additional and expensive facilities need to be brought into play.

Inventory

Holding stock, whether at the factory, in depots or at intermediaries, is not without its attendant costs. It always represents tied-up capital, and in addition there are the space and overhead costs associated with the storage area. The concept of every customer being able to buy any product or service exactly when he or she wants it is clearly laudable, but in practice it is quite meaningless. The cost of holding an inventory (or in the case of a service, people on standby) at a level which can provide 100 per cent customer satisfaction will be prohibitive for most companies.

Furthermore, as Figure 8.6 shows, the implications of striving for that 'little bit extra' in providing customer satisfaction can have a disproportionate impact on investment in the inventory. In the diagram it can be seen that stepping up the service level from 98 per cent to 100 per cent requires an inventory investment increase from Y to Z. From the same investment at lower levels of service (X to Y) the company could expect to improve customer satisfaction from around 83 per cent to 98 per cent. Reality tells us that there has to be a level of inventory above which it becomes excessively costly to attempt a very marginal improvement.

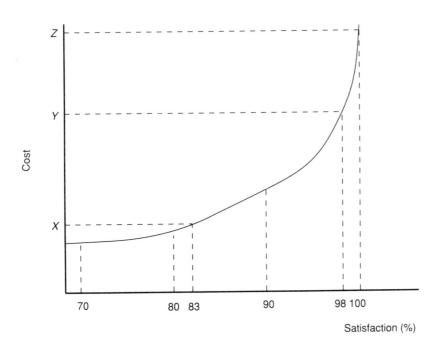

Figure 8.6 Inventory vs customer service level

Unitization

This aspect of distribution logistics concerns the way goods are packaged and assembled for handling. The objective for the manufacturer is to provide the product in such a way as to minimize subsequent handling and storage costs. Thus, for instance, a pallet load may be a suitable format for some products, whereas for others a container load may be better. It all depends upon the ultimate destination and the handling facilities which are available.

An illustration showing how unitization can be grossly mismanaged concerns a fertilizer producer. At the factory it was found that the most cost-effective packaging system was the production of individual 50 kg bags, shrink-wrapped on pallets. This kind of packaging facilitated movement of goods using fork-lift trucks and allowed easy stacking in the warehouse. Unfortunately, the customers, who were farmers, did not always possess fork-lift trucks, and even if they did they could not be taken into the fields where fertilizers needed to be spread. As a result farmhands had to manhandle the bags of fertilizer in order to move them. Not only was this very tiring, but it was also adding a cost to the process of spreading fertilizers. Not surprisingly, their loyalty switched to another producer who provided fertilizer in semi-bulk 'bags' capable of being handled by using an arm on a tractor.

Communications

Accompanying the flow of products in the distribution channel is also a flow of information. This can be in the form of order processing, invoicing, demand forecasting and even customer returns. The more efficient and even user-friendly such communications are, the more they will contribute to overall customer service. Conversely, if such communications are sloppy and ill-devised they can result in mistakes, delays and duplication of effort – all of which can be costly, both in financial terms and in causing customer antagonism.

Customer service

In the foregoing section there was repeated reference to customer service, together with the suggestion that all aspects of the distribution logistics are traded off against some notional service level. But what exactly is customer service, and how might it be measured?

It has been found that companies can have widely varying views about what constitutes customer service. For some it is a cosmetic gloss on their business. They believe it is enough for their staff to be encouraged to fix their customers with a phoney smile and to utter the phrase 'Have a nice day'. Others realize that customer service is more than a cheap gimmick. For them it is fundamental to success and they are constantly striving to improve their standards. They see customer service as involving the following elements:

- Consistency and reliability of delivery.
- Availability (when the customer wants the product or service).
- Quality of the goods/service.
- Accuracy of transactions.
- The time it takes to process an order.
- The quality of after-sales care.

It follows from this that customer service components and standards may vary from one marketing situation to another. For example, a manufacturer of automotive components will have to ensure that its delivery record is exemplary otherwise the production lines will grind to a halt. Similarly, a passenger transport company strives to get its customers to their destination on time. In contrast, a customer-orientated dentist will aim to minimize pain and produce long-lasting oral hygiene as part of his or her service satisfaction to patients.

Customer service benchmarking

Because it is difficult to talk about customer service in absolute terms, many companies are beginning to use the technique of benchmarking. To do this they follow a series of steps:

1. A list is made of all the pertinent customer service factors associated with the particular product, service or type of business.
2. These are graded in terms of their importance to the customer.
3. Similarly, each of these elements of customer service is graded in terms of its perceived performance compared with current best practice in the industry.

Note: Both of these dimensions of importance and perceived performance are often best measured by independent researchers who are free of the bias that might creep in if company personnel make the assessments. A 1–9 point scale can produce clear results.

4. This information is then plotted on a matrix as shown in Figure 8.7. A number or code letter is used to identify each item of customer service.

This technique enables one to see at a glance where an investment in customer service is providing value in the customer's eyes. The area in Figure 8.7 shaded as overkill denotes where the company's peformance is extremely high, but in areas little valued by the customer. Energy is better directed elsewhere. In contrast to this, the underperformance area shows where items are important to the customer but the company performs badly. Clearly, actions must be taken if elements of customer service fall into this part of the matrix.

The 'target area' denotes where importance to customers and performance are in line. This is probably the best customer service recipe that the company can put together.

Developing a customer service culture

It is one thing for top management to agree that customer service must be improved, and quite another for it to happen on the ground.

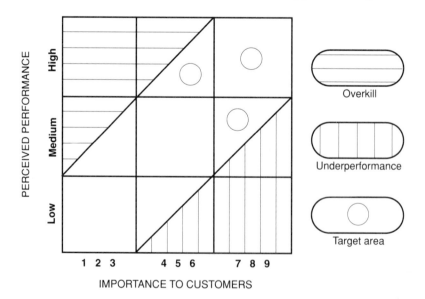

Figure 8.7 Customer service matrix

Figure 8.8 helps to explain why. Like an iceberg, much of the organization is kept hidden from the customer's sight. All that is seen are some of the 'surface' phenomena. However, what happens on the surface of the organization is very often a manifestation of the underlying systems and procedures. If any of these are changed, the firm's perceived behaviour is likely to change as well.

In turn the systems and procedures are sustained by the underlying corporate values. If they are not, then they should not have been acceptable in the first place. Thus, the shared values of an organization have a profound effect on all aspects of the firm and its behaviour, including its approach to the management of its distribution system and customer service. What happens, for example, if a manager rescues a contract that is going wrong by pulling out all the stops on behalf of the customer, but in the process overspends his budget? Is he seen as a hero (keeping the customer satisfied) or as a villain (wasting money)?

If, deep down, customers are perceived as ignorant, awkward characters who do not really know what they want and just cause problems, then it is hard to imagine real customer service ever being provided. At best people will learn a few routines designed to improve customer transactions, but they will be hollow and sooner or later discovered for what they really are.

To develop a customer service culture requires a genuine desire to change and provide real service *throughout the organization*. It is argued that all jobs, because they have an output, have a 'customer'. Thus the typist's customer is the person whose draft scribble he/she has translated; the maintenance engineer's customer is the machine operator who wants trouble-free production; and so on. If everyone

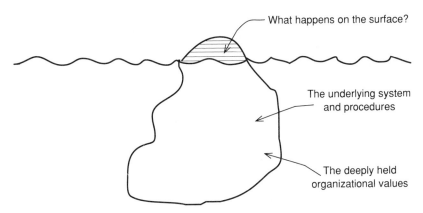

Figure 8.8 The organizational 'iceberg'

tries to provide the right quality service to his or her 'customers' internally, it follows quite logically that the 'external' customers will be similarly well treated, regardless of the level at which they make contact with the supplying organization.

This approach was used by British Airways when it attempted to change its culture, from a bureaucratic state-owned carrier into 'the world's favourite airline'. Not only was this a much talked about campaign at the time, it also proved to be very successful in terms of changing attitudes towards customers.

To set the right culture for customer service is a relentless task. It is part educational and part evangelical. However, as customers become more sophisticated in their expectations and as their choice becomes wider, companies ignore the service element at their peril.

Developments in Distribution

The widening use of computers and the growing sophistication of their programs is making inventory control a much easier task than formerly. At the push of a button the level and location of stocks can be made available to the market. Bar coding and the use of electronic point-of-sale systems at supermarket checkouts ensures that new inventory levels can be recorded and activated at the moment an item is sold.

Another relatively new development is the way that some carriers are providing a 'total package' to the manufacturer – or, for that matter, the retailer. They will provide transport and drivers in the supplier's livery, have their own depots – if necessary with refrigerated facilities – and 'pick and mix' bulk loads into specific smaller drops. Some are now taking over responsibility for inventory management, linking their computer systems with those of the manufacturer. Moreover, some carriers are now operating on a global basis and have their own fleet of aircraft, the size of which exceeds those of some national airlines.

With astute management, specialist carriers can maintain high levels of vehicle loading and economies of scale denied to most production companies. By using their services the manufacturer can control more effectively many aspects of the logistics system without reducing customer service levels.

DISTRIBUTION AND LOGISTICS POLICY AUDIT

Score
0 1 2

1. **Does the company have a sound distribution and logistics policy?**

   (a) No. We do what we believe our customers want us to do.   *(Score 0)*
   (b) Yes. We have analyzed fully the economics of the various options open to us.   *(Score 1)*
   (c) Our distribution policy is fully integrated with our marketing strategy, the cost effectiveness of the channel chosen and full consideration of our customers and their expectations and needs.   *(Score 2)*

2. **The effectiveness of the distribution system is to a large extent reflected in the way it is managed. How is it managed in your firm?**

   (a) No one has an overall responsibility for distribution and logistics.   *(Score 1)*
   (b) Someone is responsible for distribution but tends to operate in isolation from marketing personnel.   *(Score 1)*
   (c) Distribution and logistics are managed in an integrated fashion with the rest of the marketing mix.   *(Score 2)*

3. **How are channels of distribution selected?**

   (a) Largely in an arbitrary manner. The system has evolved over the years.   *(Score 0)*
   (b) On the basis of establishing a good relationship with reputable firms.   *(Score 1)*
   (c) Following a deep analysis of target markets and the preferences of customers in these segments.   *(Score 2)*

4. **What are the criteria used in selecting intermediaries?**

   (a) Rather vague and ill-defined.   *(Score 0)*
   (b) Based on quantitative information about facilities, staff, location, creditworthiness, etc.   *(Score 1)*
   (c) Based on quantitative information and qualitative

criteria which reflect on compatibility and a
potentially good working
relationship. *(Score 2)*

5. **Does the company have targets and standards of performance for intermediaries?**

(a) No. We simply hope that they will
perform. *(Score 0)*
(b) Yes. We give them targets. *(Score 1)*
(c) We discuss and agree targets. These match market analysis. We monitor their performance and provide support where necessary. *(Score 2)*

6. **Does the company seek to compare its transport and unitization methods with its main competitors??**

(a) No. What the competitors are doing is their own
business. *(Score 0)*
(b) Spasmodically and not in depth. *(Score 1)*
(c) The firm monitors competitive practices continuously with the aim of offering a superior and customer-friendly service. *(Score 2)*

7. **Are the firm's delivery system and procedures compatible with customers' acceptance systems and procedures?**

(a) No. This is not considered our
problem. *(Score 0)*
(b) They match reasonably well. *(Score 1)*
(c) We have ensured that there is a high compatibility in most cases. *(Score 2)*

8. **How does the firm consider its inventory level and how is it controlled?**

(a) We have no specific policy in this regard.
Everything we produce goes into
stock. *(Score 0)*
(b) Inventory is controlled by the available space or overall costs. *(Score 1)*
(c) An inventory policy is in place seeking to provide a known and calculated level of customer service. *(Score 2)*

9. **How does the company respond to complaints about deliveries, shortages or damage in transit?**

(a) We handle each complaint in the best way we can on an *ad hoc* basis.   (*Score 0*)
(b) Complaints are analyzed and acted upon in a systematic way.   (*Score 1*)
(c) We have a system of responding to complaints and ensuring that they never occur again. We strive for a zero-fault system.   (*Score 2*)

10. **Does the company use the 'benchmarking' technique, or a similar method, for evaluating the relevance and value of service elements to customers?**

(a) No. We know nothing about it.   (*Score 0*)
(b) We try to identify underperforming areas in an unstructured way.   (*Score 1*)
(c) We constantly seek to determine the service areas which customers perceive as particularly useful, and build them into our distribution service strategy.   (*Score 2*)

The maximum score possible is 20. Very few companies could achieve such a score. Lower scores can be interpreted as follows:

15–20   Excellent
10–14   Good to very good.
 5–9   Fair
 0–4   Poor

9

Selling

Selling is a vital component in the marketing effort. The fact that so many textbooks talk about the four Ps concept because of its mnemonic elegance conceals the importance of selling in the mix. Indeed, in many companies, selling is by far the most potent instrument for attaining results.

The sales force: its role and objectives

The sales force is one of the most precious resources of a firm. It takes many years to build and develop, and an effective sales organization is the envy of any competitor. However, it must be emphasized that the sales force can be effective only where the other ingredients of the marketing mix are sound. To expect salespeople to become more productive in isolation is hardly fair. Each ingredient of the mix must be placed under the microscope in order that its productivity may be improved. The product itself, the pricing policy, the promotional mix (advertising, sales promotion and the publicity effort) and the distribution system all have an indispensable contribution to make to the overall success of the marketing programme.

The sales force is the infantry that has to visit customers and/or channels of distribution to impart information and knowledge (as is the case with medical representatives), actually obtain orders from specific customers, or ensure that existing customers are happy with the firm and its service. A host of other objectives may be ascribed to the firm's selling effort. Later on we shall explore the kinds of objective that can be given to salespeople and the basis upon which they should be determined.

The role and objectives of the firm's selling effort can be specified only after the initial steps in the planning process have been taken. It is impractical to define the objectives of the sales force and its various constituents without having defined the objectives of the marketing effort as a whole, and also the objectives of the other ingredients of the mix. Moreover, before defining the objectives of the sales force and determining the way in which it should be organized and developed, the strategies and resources of competitors must be studied and understood. It is imprudent to develop a reliable working plan for the sales force without understanding competitors' strengths as well as their weaknesses.

The need for objectives

In a well-managed and productive sales force one must specify objectives for the overall effort, for the regions (if the force is organized geographically) and for each individual. The salespeople are entitled to know what level of performance and productivity is expected of them. The attainment of objectives not only represents a tool for measuring results, it also offers a very potent motivational stimulus to the individual performer. Therefore, the practice that some sales managers indulge in of giving salespeople enormous and unattainable targets in order to 'keep them on their toes' is hardly a clever thing to do. The danger of such a strategy is twofold: the sales people can get totally demotivated when they see that their objectives are incapable of attainment in spite of hard work; and even more serious is the fact that the firm's plans may get into total disarray as a result of inflated published sales budgets.

In defining the objectives of the sales force, one must remember that three major conditions must be fulfilled if they are to represent an effective standard of performance.

- **Measurability:** Ideally, salespeople should be able to finish a day's work and evaluate their own level of attainment in accordance with the standards ascribed to them. Thus, if the objectives are specified in terms of units sold, it can easily be determined if the day or week's quota has been met, depending on the nature of the business.

- **Relevance:** The objectives given to salespeople must be relevant and appropriate to their job. If they are selling aeroplanes, the

'number of calls a day' is a totally irrelevant standard of performance. The first principle of effective sales management is to
identify and define the most relevant success factors for the
selling task. Being relevant and not measurable is as bad as being
measurable and not relevant. Both conditions must be considered
and met.

● **Fairness:** In an organization seeking to conduct its affairs in a
supportive and decent manner, it is important that objectives
given to individual members of the team are fair and capable of
being attained by well-trained and hard-working people. Where
these objectives are overstated in relation to the area of operational performance, one might as well double, treble or quad-
ruple them. Unfairness in this regard is synonymous with the
nonexistence of standards of performance.

As an aid to reflecting upon and selecting the most appropriate
criteria of performance for a sales force, Figure 9.1 sets out a list of
options. The list is not comprehensive and other items can be added
to it. However, the person responsible for deciding upon the most
appropriate set of performance criteria in a given set of circumstances should run through this list, and attempt to evaluate each
item on a simple screening device provided at the right-hand side of
the form. Any item that earns a high score (say 3 or 4), after a
thorough discussion with everybody concerned, will probably need
to be incorporated in the salespeople's terms of reference and
measurement of performance system.

The changing role of selling

It is appropriate to review briefly the nature and scope of selling and
also to explore the changes that this function is undergoing in a
modern marketing environment. A full understanding of these
changes may help to discover methods of improving the productivity
of the selling effort. The words 'to sell' cover a great variety of
activities ranging from the salesperson who actually delivers the
product (e.g. a milkman) to the salesperson who sells a sophisticated
'turnkey' nuclear power plant. They both sell, yet they are as
different as chalk and cheese. Between these two extremes one
encounters a wide range of activities known as selling, varying
enormously in level of complexity and scope. Nonetheless, as we
shall see later, they all have something in common: namely, an
effective 'selling' skill. A milkman could not sell a computer, not

	Relevance				
	0	1	2	3	4

Scoring: 4 = very relevant; 3 = relevant
2 = fairly relevant; 1 = not very relevant;
0 = irrelevant

I   MEASURES OF ACHIEVEMENT

(A)   Objectives utilizing volume of sales

1. Sales volume by salesperson by value

2. Sales volume by salesperson by units

3. Sales volume by salesperson by
    number of customers

4. Sales volume by salesperson to new
    accounts and old accounts – ratio
    clearly prescribed

5. Number of sales related to number of
    calls

**(B)   Objectives utilizing market and/or
customer penetration**

1. New accounts secured

2. Number of customers sold to
    compared with number of customers
    assigned

3. Number of customers sold to
    compared with number of customers
    in area

4. Accounts lost

5. Share of market achieved in area

6. Towns sold or not sold to

7. Number of customers served among
    the 20% who represent 80% of the
    business in the area

(C)   Objectives utilizing margins

1. Gross margin or contribution secured
    (especially where salespeople
    exercise some discretion in quoting
    prices)

2. Amounts of high- and low-gross-
    margin products sold

	Relevance				
	0	1	2	3	4

3. Gross margins secured per call

4. Gross margins secured per day (week, month) in relation to salesperson's costs

(D) Objectives utilizing expenses

1. Salary (or salary plus expenses or total emoluments) related to sales or to number of units sold

2. Salary + travel expenses + a proportion of overheads (directly related to selling effort) related to sales or to number of units sold

3. Sales cost: sales ratio

4. Cost per day

5. Cost per call

II MEASURES OF ACTIVITIES

(A) Daily calls

(B) Days worked

(C) General demeanour, tact, judgment, etc.

(D) Planning work

(E) Conduct of interviews

(F) Number of quotations

(G) Use of sales aids and/or equipment

(H) Procurement of prospect lists

Figure 9.1 Standards of performance for members of a sales force: an evaluation procedure

because he lacks the skill but because he does not possess the appropriate knowledge of the product, the technology and the information industry.

Salespeople fall into a number of distinct groupings:

- **Salespeople who deliver the product** (milk, fuel, papers, etc.).

They need to spend very little time on communicating or persuading. The customer is almost pre-sold. The main effort is to provide a punctual, cheerful, friendly face at all times.

- **Salespeople who function in a well-defined marketplace** (shops, travel agents, offices, government departments). The role of selling here is to ensure that the customer's needs are fulfilled quickly, efficiently and with a smile. In certain circumstances, skill can be applied to ensure that a deal does take place and that the customer does not leave empty-handed (e.g. a car salesperson).
- **Salespeople who are expected to build goodwill or impart knowledge** (e.g. the medical representative). The salesperson's task here is first to make sure that the customer agrees to see him or her, and second to make an effective presentation which is instructive, interesting and meets the needs of the recipient.

- **Salespeople who sell on the basis of excellent technical knowledge**. They are expected to sell and in fact to obtain orders, but seek to achieve these goals through a well-informed counselling service. They almost act as consultants to their client companies. Obviously, to be able to do so they need considerable knowledge, and must be equipped with excellent sales aids. While their productivity can be measured in terms of results, it depends to a great extent upon the productivity of the training methods invested in them, and the quality of the tools placed at their disposal (e.g. sales aids, specifications, promotional handouts).

- **Salespeople who sell tangible products to the ultimate consumer** (e.g. washing machines, vacuum cleaners, encyclopaedias). They must be creatively persuasive and very often must attempt to strike a sale in a single session.

- **Salespeople who sell intangible products** (e.g. insurance, banking). Sellers of such products must possess thorough product knowledge, yet must know how to communicate this knowledge in terms that the customer is able to understand. Many sales in this area are lost for the simple reason that the customer is incapable of decoding the messages transmitted by the salesperson and/or the firm's literature.

This is a fairly comprehensive list of selling activities. Each has its problems and each needs its own skills and knowledge. Yet they all have a common requirement: the ability to communicate in an effective and empathetic way with a customer or group of customers who have needs, tangible and intangible, and who want them fulfilled in an efficient and honest way. Within such a well-defined framework, people who sell diesel engines well should be able to perform an admirable selling job in a local grocery. This is not meant as an insult. On the contrary, it is meant as a compliment to a person who knows how to relate to and communicate with fellow human beings.

The role of salespeople, especially in the more advanced technological industries and/or service organizations, is undergoing a radical change. It is suggested that 'salesmanship' in the 1960s meant 'tellmanship'. The job of salespeople was simply to knock on doors and tell customers about 'our wonderful product'. The customers felt honoured by the opportunity to buy the offered product.

In the more competitive world of the 1970s selling graduated to its proper role. 'Selling' meant communicating details of the product and its benefits and unique selling points, persuading, dealing with objections and striking a deal – a more challenging and creative task.

The 1980s saw the emergence of the concept of *counselling*. Salespeople virtually became consultants – walking *Which* reports. In trying to sell their product they needed to communicate to the customer the cost–benefit relationship of using that product as against competitive offerings. The aim was to assist the customer in taking wise, cost-beneficial, result-orientated decisions. This meant that the quality of the sales technique hinged on the quality of the information that the firm's marketing department was able to impart to the salesperson. Many firms equipped their sales forces with tools that enabled them to communicate reliable and up-to-date information to their customers about the wisdom of a certain course of action. Obviously, the credibility of such counselling activities depended on the quality of the advice offered, the methodologies used in reaching the various conclusions, and also the standing of the firm and its image in the marketplace.

The challenge for the 1990s is referred to as *joining*. 'To sell' means 'to join'. The winner in the competitive marketplace of the 1990s will be the selling organization that recognizes that a relationship with the customer is not a hit-and-run affair. Selling entails a long-term relationship with one's clients. This relationship can be expressed in the following spirit: 'The client may not require my products or services this year or next, but one day he is bound to return to the market. I must be ready for him, and if I invest in this special relationship I shall be the first supplier he will approach when the time comes. Meanwhile I shall make a point of keeping myself up to date with his problems and opportunities, and developments in his marketing environment. I shall endeavour to be as knowledgeable about the goings-on in his marketplace as he is.'

This may be a tall order. Nonetheless the rewards may be substantial. Obviously, productivity in this kind of challenging selling environment is very different from just counting daily calls, measuring the number of units sold, or measuring the level of expenses per call. In this new environment a salesperson will become an 'account executive' with a long-term relationship with the client, and the *quality* of his or her work will assume as important a role as the *quantity* of his or her short-term achievements.

Improving the productivity of the sales force

A sales force is a precious and expensive resource. When one adds all the direct and indirect costs associated with recruiting, employing, training and managing a salesperson, one is entitled to pose the questions: 'are we getting an adequate return on each member of the sales team?' and 'can we improve the productivity of the sales force?'

The aim here is to explore a number of areas in which marketing-orientated companies can help the sales force to act and perform in a more productive manner.

Identifying the 'perfect customer'

One of the weaknesses of asking salespeople to carry out a number of calls per period is the danger that one tends to concentrate on the quantity rather than the quality of calls. It is more sensible to target one's effort on a smaller number of 'better' calls. Let us imagine that salespeople know that customers or prospects in their patch fall into four categories:

A = Excellent
B = Good
C = Fair
D = Poor

At this point they can plan their marketing day in a more effective way by allocating more time and effort upon A or B customers, some time on the Cs, and little or none on the Ds. This means that the call rate can be better targeted on promising prospects and little time is wasted on contacts which are less likely to yield results.

The preparation of a 'hit' list designating levels of attractiveness to potential customers can be a powerful spur to productivity in the selling effort. In the case of industrial products one can use the Standard Industrial Classification (SIC) as the basis for categorization of customers. This is particularly valuable if research has established which group or class in the classification offers promising pickings.

Not every business can take its aim on an SIC-based target. Other classifications may be more compatible with the firm's needs and must be considered. A few important principles must be borne in mind:

- Very few firms can afford to target their sales force on every potential customer, large and small. Some selectivity is essential, especially if one aspires to be more productive and run the sales force as a tight and effective crew.

- What is an opportunity for firm A is not necessarily an opportunity for firm B. With this important thought in mind, the planner can identify the targets that should be avoided. By doing so one avoids spending valuable selling energy on customers that competitors are in a far better position of penetrating.

- In classifying customers into typologies one can use a large number of criteria:

    - Size of firm and/or its consumption level.
    - Segments that potential customers serve.
    - The nature of the firm's products, technologies and production processes.
    - The personality of the decision-makers and/or their motivational stimuli (e.g. wanting to buy from large firms or from small firms only).
    - The geographical location of the customers.
    - Levels of expenditure on specific areas (e.g. 'Our ideal customer is the one who spends 8 per cent of his turnover on R & D' or 'Our ability to sell to firms spending over 7 per cent on physical distribution seems somehow favourable').
    - Personal foibles of members of the decision-making unit.

Many other criteria can be identified and considered. It calls for a painstaking analysis of a considerable amount of data. However, if one can emerge at the end of this exercise with a profile of the 'perfect' and 'next to perfect' customer or group of customers, one has a dramatic aid to a more productive and more effective selling organization.

Understanding the customer's decision-making unit

A salesperson seldom sells to one individual. He or she has to deal with a number of stakeholders. As we saw earlier in this book, one normally talks about 'deciders', 'buyers', 'influencers', 'users' and 'gatekeepers'. Each one of these has a role to play: sometimes supportive and sometimes obstructional. A good salesperson must understand the way the 'unit' functions, and the respective roles of each member thereof.

The situation is further complicated by the fact that in large firms there are many members in the decision-making unit. Each one of them needs to be communicated with in some form or another, and it is impractical, inefficient and often positively imprudent for the salesperson to contact them all. One uses other ingredients of the marketing mix to communicate with the less important or less accessible members of the unit: for example, through literature, direct mailings, exhibitions and conferences. This is an excellent example of an exercise in the integration of the marketer's promotional mix. A large number of people in a customer's organization must be communicated with and the following objectives must be set:

- The total communication programme must be achieved in the most cost-beneficial way.
- Every member of the decision-making unit must receive the right amount of information: not too much and not too little.
- All the bits communicated must be integrated into a cohesive 'package'.
- The sales force must concentrate its efforts on the most important and decisive members of the customer's buying team.

In a 'business-to-business' marketing environment salespeople could benefit from the following steps:

(1) Assembling a dossier about every one of the more promising customers: Such a dossier should contain a number of items:

- Annual reports and published accounts.
- A scrapbook of published material about the firm.

- The company's literature and product specifications.
- Organization charts.
- A 'who's who?' of personnel in the organization.
- Ideally, comparison of the firm's performance with that of its competitors.

If the dossier is complete and up to date the salesperson is addressing a customer about which his or her knowledge level is so high that a true partnership can be forged.

(2) Preparing a comprehensive list of members of the decision-making unit (DMU) and, together with the other subdepartments of marketing, designing an integrated communication programme. The theory here is that the company has at its disposal a number of communication tools, including selling techniques. However, it is important that each member of the DMU is targeted in the most productive and cost-beneficial way. Salespeople are a scarce resource, and their effort should be concentrated on those members of the DMU upon whom they can have maximum impact.

Figure 9.2 illustrates a method for preparing an integrated communication programme with members of the DMU. Evidently, one can afford to undertake such detailed analysis only in situations in which the marketer has a fairly small number of large potential accounts. One cannot expect to carry out such an exercise where the marketplace consists of thousands of customers or more. Nevertheless, it is surprising how many firms do not bother to collate the most rudimentary information about their client company, even where the total catchment market consists of no more than a couple of dozen firms.

Capitalizing upon internal information

Many firms do not appreciate what wealth of intelligence is scattered around the organization. This is often particularly true of decentralized organizations operating on a multinational scale.

A story about a large British company, operating in the field of engineering, electrical equipment and turnkey projects, demonstrates the kind of missed opportunities that can occur. Five senior sales personnel representing different subsidiaries of the same company went on a selling trip to the same destination in the Middle East without any of them knowing about the others. Two met on the plane, two of the others bumped into each other in the hotel. All five

Members of the DMU	Communication tools to be applied					
	Trade press	Technical press	Sales staff	Direct mail	Exhibition	Other (specify)
INTERNAL						
Managing director						
Marketing director						
Production director						
Finance director						
R & D director						
Other board members						
Buying officer						
Chief engineer						
Quality controller						
User of the product						
Others (specify)						
EXTERNAL						
Consultants						
Financial advisers						
Advertising Agents						
P.R. Agencies						
Designers						
Others (specify)						
Scoring: 4 = very important; 3 = important; 2 = fairly important; 1 = worth considering; 0 = irrelevant						

Figure 9.2 An integrated communication programme with members of the customer's decision-making unit

possessed some important knowledge about the marketplace, but the synergy between their respective bits of intelligence could have yielded enormous strength to all five. A simple system for collating and cross-fertilizing internal information and 'who knows what?' in a company can be of great benefit to all members of the sales force.

In many organizations a sales force consists of a significant number of people. They spend a considerable portion of their working day with customers. To that extent they can represent the 'eyes and ears' of the firm they work for. It is inevitable that among all these people someone knows something which can be of great benefit to the others. It is the job of an effective manager to develop a system capable of catching the gems which normally get lost. The traditional reporting system which most salespeople have to complete should contain a section soliciting data about snippets of information which the salesperson believes might be of value to other members of the sales force.

Learning from the 'star' performers

A sales force consists of a myriad of personalities. With all the training in the world one cannot expect to achieve total homogeneity of behaviour, attitudes and performance. It is simply contrary to human nature. The team normally consists of high-flyers at the one extreme and 'sloggers' at the other. The former are enthusiastic, creative and effective. The latter may work hard, but results do not come easily to them.

By analyzing the level of performance of individual salespeople, one can designate the top 10 per cent as the 'stars'; the next 20 per cent as 'good'; the next 30 per cent as 'adequates'; and the bottom 40 per cent as 'problem children' (see Figure 9.3).

Once the sales force has been categorized into clearly defined groups based on their performance quality, one can ask a simple question: 'what does the "star" do which is so different from the others?'

If one could identify in some detail how the 'star' behaves in front of a customer, the way he or she communicates the message, plans and manages time, uses sales aids, etc., one would know how to

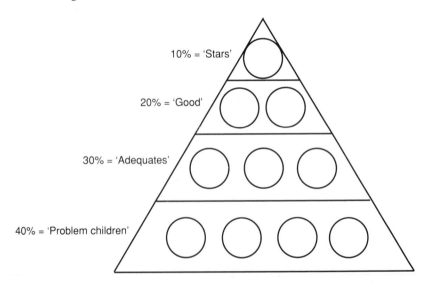

Figure 9.3 Members of the sales force stratified by their overall effectiveness

develop new training methods for the rest of the force. An insight would be gained into the selling and buying environment, and this should help in discovering areas in which productivity can be improved.

Sales force size

Ideally, a sales force should not be too large or too small. If it is too large, it incurs unnecessary costs. If it is too small, it may not be capable of covering the marketplace effectively with a resultant loss of sales. Somewhere along the line there is a size which is capable of achieving optimum performance. The ability to pinpoint this size is a most valuable tool in the productivity game.

A few obvious principles may help in determining the optimum sales force size:

- *Some* increase in sales volume can always result from the addition of a sales person. Nevertheless, a salesperson who costs, say, £30,000 per annum and who generates an annual volume of £100,000 with a gross margin of 30 per cent has just about covered his or her cost. If one adds all the indirect costs (car expenses, administrative costs, etc.) the person's value to the firm is in some doubt.

- Sales volume hardly ever increases in a linear relationship to an increased number of sales personnel. Life would be very cosy for sales managers if they knew that an increase of 30 per cent in the sales force would generate a 30 per cent increase in sales volume. Unfortunately, the practical reality is less helpful. The 'law of diminishing returns' sets in at a certain point, and the addition of salespeople after that generates an ever-decreasing sales volume.

- The law of diminishing returns is reached by different sales forces at different rates. Some firms can afford to increase their sales forces for quite a while before diminishing returns start taking their toll. Others find that the diseconomy of increasing one's sales force occurs at a fairly early stage.

  One of the tasks of sales managers is to try to understand the relationship that exists between growth in sales force size and sales volume in their own selling environments. It is absolutely impossible to extrapolate from one marketing environment to another.

- In designing territories for individual salespeople, one must strive to give each one of them a territory of equal potential. Thus, if the market is estimated to be worth £100 million and one employs 100 salespeople, the country should be divided, as far as is possible, into 100 territories worth a potential of £1 million each. Obviously, many factors such as mix of accounts in the territory, geographical structure and economic developments must be taken into consideration. However, one must attempt to give every salesperson a comparable challenge.

- The minute the cost of every additional salesperson is not matched by commensurate profits (gross margin minus direct costs) one ceases to increase the size of the force. This is, of course, based on the assumption that the existing sales force is efficient and is operating at a fairly acceptable level of productivity. It is also assumed that the rest of the marketing mix is reasonably effective.

The salesperson's 'profit and loss account'

Most salespeople realize that they represent a cost and that their efforts must yield a result. They also recognize that the output must exceed the input. How far they are actually aware of the quantitative details depends on the firm for which they work, and the style of management that prevails therein. In some firms the data are blurred. The salesperson knows only very vaguely what cost he or she represents, and knows even less what net revenue his or her sales have generated. In other firms the data are comprehensive, open and well tabulated.

Equipped with the appropriate data regarding cost, margins and selling time required, it is possible to work out a simple profit and loss account for each customer, group of customers, typology of customers, segments, etc. This kind of calculation can be worked out on the basis of historical data and also as part of the firm's planning process, in which case the information will be based on forecasts and estimates.

Table 9.1 shows a profit and loss account for five customers. For each customer the figures show sales, contribution, marketing costs and selling costs, net contribution towards profit and overheads, and percentage of contribution in relation to sales. The figures are self-explanatory. They show which customer yields the best return in

Table 9.1 Profit and loss accounts for five customers: a comparative study

	Customer				
	A	B	C	D	E
Sales during year	£1,800,000	£1,300,000	£1,450,000	£1,700,000	£2,400,000
Cost of goods supplied as % of sales	70%	70%	67.5%	72.5%	75%
Cost of goods in £s	£1,260,000	£910,000	£978,750	£1,232,250	£1,800,000
Contribution	£540,000	£390,000	£471,250	£467,500	£600,000
Marketing costs (direct costs + allocation of total marketing overheads)	£90,000	£65,000	£72,500	£85,000	£120,000
Cost of finance (based on credit given to each customer)	£45,000	£16,250	£27,200	£21,250	£90,000
Selling costs	£22,000	£12,000	£15,000	£7,500	£30,000
Total marketing, selling and finance costs	£157,000	£93,250	£114,700	£113,750	£240,000
Net contribution	£383,000	£296,750	£356,550	£353,750	£360,000
Percentages of sales	21.28%	22.8%	24.59%	20.8%	15%

terms of contribution as a percentage of sales: namely, customer C, who yields 24.5 per cent. This is the result of a combination of factors: low production costs, relatively low credit terms and also low selling costs. In the productivity pecking order it is the most attractive customer, although in absolute terms other customers generate higher contributions (A and E have higher contributions, yet E is the least productive in relation to the effort invested therein.)

Another example is shown in Table 9.2. Here the analysis is based on the profit and loss account of three products which the sales force have to sell. The analysis shows the prices of the three products, their relative costs, contributions, marketing costs and selling costs, contribution per unit as a percentage of the selling price per unit, and the efficiency of the selling effort as a ratio between net contribution and cost of selling per unit. The higher the figure, the more productive it is in relation to the selling task.

Table 9.2 Net contribution made by three products (an example)

	Product A	Product B	Product C
Price per unit	£600	£800	£1,450
Cost of sales	68%	71%	72%
Contribution	£192	£232	£406
Marketing costs per unit	£48	£64	£72
Selling costs per unit	£42	£80	£72.5
Total marketing and selling costs	£90	£144	£144.5
Net contribution	£102	£88	£261.5
Percentage of sales	17%	11%	18%
Contribution: selling costs	$\frac{102}{42} = 2.43$	$\frac{88}{80} = 1.1$	$\frac{261.50}{72.50} = 3.61$

Other combinations and permutations can be worked out in respect of other cost elements and/or other divisions of the marketing/selling activities of the firm. The aim of these examples is to illustrate how an analysis of the costs that go into generating a sale can help to increase understanding of relative productivity in a multiproduct, multicustomer environment.

In summary, it is worth remembering that selling must yield results which justify its costs. This applies to every ingredient of the mix, and the essence of effective marketing is to ensure that the cost/benefit is constantly kept under measurement and control.

SALES MANAGEMENT AUDIT

Score
0 1 2

1. **Does the company have a sound selling policy?**

   (a) We believe that good selling is the most important element in any business. *(Score 0)*
   (b) We know that selling is vital for success, but we also understand that other elements of the mix are important. *(Score 1)*
   (c) Our selling policy is fully integrated with marketing strategy. Moreover, we attempt to identify the kind of selling approach which customers can relate to and appreciate. *(Score 2)*

▶

2. **Is selling treated as part of marketing management?**

(a) No. Selling and marketing are regarded as totally
different functions.   (*Score 0*)
(b) The two functions work closely together, but we
recognize that 'selling' is the function that gets us
results.   (*Score 1*)
(c) Selling is an integral part of the marketing mix and
to that extent it comes under marketing
management.   (*Score 2*)

3. **How is the size of the sales force determined?**

(a) As many salespeople as we can
afford.   (*Score 0*)
(b) By dividing planned sales volume by expected
sales per person we calculate the number of people
needed.   (*Score 1*)
(c) The marketing plan provides detailed computation
of call rate × average sales per call × salespeople
needed to achieve sales.   (*Score 2*)

4. **Does the company provide each salesperson with
clear standards of performance?**

(a) No. We expect each member of the team to work
hard.   (*Score 0*)
(b) Yes. Each salesperson is given annual sales
targets.   (*Score 1*)
(c) Each person receives a detailed set of objectives,
both quantitative and qualitative, reflecting the
estimated results for his or her area.   (*Score 2*)

5. **Does the company attempt to compare its selling
methods with those of its main competitors?**

(a) No. We believe that our sales force is the
best.   (*Score 0*)
(b) Yes. Whenever we recruit a salesperson who has
worked for competitors we try to find out how they
operate.   (*Score 1*)
(c) We monitor competitors' practices, sales aids,
training, motivational stimuli, creativity, etc., at all
times. Part of our salespeople's job is to observe and
report.   (*Score 2*)

6. **Are members of the sales force trained?**

(a) We believe that the most effective training method is learning on the job by 'doing' things.   (*Score 0*)

(b) Sales personnel are trained by those who have been in the field for a while.   (*Score 1*)

(c) We have a structured training system, run partly by internal trainers and partly by external specialists. Each person is exposed to a series of programmes during his or her career. Moreover, the system is updated in the light of changing needs.   (*Score 2*)

7. **How are members of the sales force motivated?**

(a) They know that their job depends on the way they work and results.   (*Score 0*)

(b) On reaching a certain level of sales they can start earning extra commission.   (*Score 1*)

(c) Each salesperson is motivated by financial and non-financial stimuli which form part of the selling plan and relate to targeted sales in each area. Such targets are measurable, relevant and deemed to be fair.   (*Score 2*)

8. **Does the sales force have a system for communicating ideas and pieces of intelligence from the field?**

(a) No. If a salesperson wants to communicate something of interest he or she can inform the boss.   (*Score 0*)

(b) We welcome useful snippets of information from the marketplace.   (*Score 1*)

(c) We have a system for collating and screening ideas and pieces of intelligence communicated by members of the sales team. Written procedures are in existence.   (*Score 2*)

9. **Are sales personnel briefed about targeting procedures in relation to potential customers' 'attractiveness' levels?**

(a) No. Sales personnel are judged by the number of calls a day they make and their conversion rate only.   (*Score 0*)

(b) Yes. Sales personnel are told that when they
encounter what they consider a good prospect, they
should concentrate their time on
them.   (*Score 1*)
(c) Salespeople are given an 'Identikit' which enables
them to target their sales effort on those conforming to
the typology of the best prospects.   (*Score 2*)

**10.   Does sales management undertake 'profit and loss'
procedures?**

(a) No. It is impossible to carry out such a control
system.   (*Score 0*)
(b) Yes. Such an analysis is carried out for the sales
force as a whole.   (*Score 1*)
(c) Yes. We attempt to control 'profit and loss' in
relation to the selling effort both of salespeople and
customers. Everybody recognizes that 'output must
exceed input'. We encourage sales personnel to
undertake such an analysis
themselves.   (*Score 2*)

The maximum score possible is 20. Very few companies could achieve
such a score. Lower scores can be interpreted as follows:

15–20 **Excellent**
10–14 **Good to very good.**
  5–9 **Fair**
  0–4 **Poor**

10

Marketing planning

Marketing has been described as the locomotive which pulls all the other departmental carriages along. If this graphic metaphor can be extended, then the marketing plan can be likened to the rails on which the train runs. Without a structure which provides direction, marketing will never arrive at its chosen destination. The marketing plan not only helps to keep the marketing effort on the right track but also provides a framework for the whole corporate plan. At least this is the case in a firm that has chosen to run its affairs in a marketing-orientated fashion.

Regrettably, important though marketing planning is, few companies seem to manage to get the process right. Various research studies have shown that only 15–20 per cent of British companies have marketing plans worthy of the name. Many companies rely on allied processes such as sales forecasts and budgetary control procedures and call them marketing plans. While such approaches sometimes work in the short term (because any sort of planning is generally better than none at all), they often fail to provide the appropriate integration of all the elements of the marketing mix into a meaningful whole, which is the prime task of marketing planning.

Clearly, there will always be fortunate companies that, more by luck than judgment, achieve success without pursuing a disciplined marketing planning cycle. Unhappily for the rest of us, planning is an essential process to ensure that opportunities are identified and exploited, and that risks are avoided.

Benefits of marketing planning

Planning offers many benefits and these must be understood and sought:

- Planning helps to coordinate activities which can facilitate or impede the attainment of objectives over time.
- It forces management to reflect upon the future in a systematic way.
- Corporate resources can be better balanced in relation to identified market opportunities.
- The chance of identifying possible developments in the marketplace is greatly enhanced.
- Internal communication can be improved and the risk of conflict reduced among functions and/or hierarchical levels.
- A greater preparedness to accommodate change can be stimulated.
- A plan provides a framework for a continuing review of operations.

In spite of these benefits, many companies fail to apply themselves to the task of developing an effective planning cycle. The trouble is that, although the process is fairly straightforward, many managers are intimidated by the cerebral process which is envisaged by the planning subroutines. There is too much 'thinking' associated with the process, and managers on the whole prefer 'doing' activities. The latter yield immediate results, while planning conjures in people's mind too much intellectual reflection and analysis.

It is important to emphasize at the outset that, if planning is to become a potent instrument of managerial effectiveness, it must be regarded as part of the firm's cluster of shared values and must reflect a corporate attitude and organizational ethos. The notion that planning is a means to a safer and more innovative future must pervade the whole organization and not be the prerogative of a small number of elitist individuals attached to top management. In other words, planning must be part of the firm's climate, and the value of the process to future success must be universally accepted by all those who have a contribution to make to the firm's direction. Altogether the successful introduction of an effective planning system depends on the recognition of the various barriers that can impede the process (see Figure 10.1).

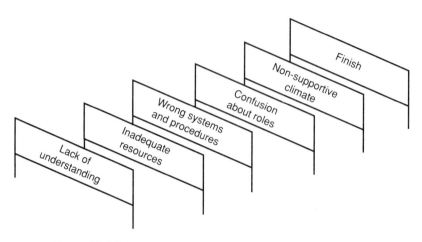

Figure 10.1 Barriers to an effective marketing planning process

Like a hurdler the marketer has to be able to surmount these obstacles to reach the winning tape. Yet unlike his or her athletic counterpart on the track, the marketer will find that these barriers are not always of the same height. Moreover, the height of each barrier may differ from company to company. Indeed, at times the height of the barrier is so high that jumping over it may be virtually impossible! Obviously in such circumstances the planning cycle will cease to be helpful to the firm's overall future welfare.

Understanding the process

Confusion surrounding the planning process generally arises from three main areas:

- The way marketing planning should relate to the corporate plan.
- The steps that should be pursued in preparing a plan.
- The individuals who should be responsible for producing the plan.

A few brief comments about each of these areas should help to provide a practical focus to the whole process.

The context for marketing planning

The boundaries of marketing planning are more or less prescribed by the corporate objectives, as expressed in the corporate plan. At the same time it is important to understand that marketing 'input' has a significant role to play in the assembly of the corporate plan. The relationship is iterative and interdependent. In fact the whole planning edifice operates in a hierarchical fashion, as shown in Figure 10.2.

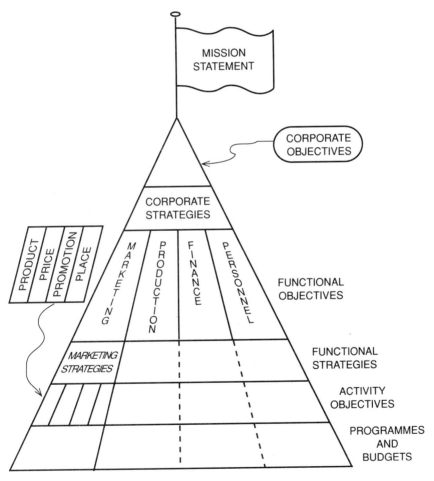

Figure 10.2 The planning hierarchy

The mission statement

This is the 'banner' under which the whole firm operates. It serves to remind everyone about the company's purpose and long-term vision. It states top management's view as to what business the firm believes it is in or ought to be in for the next few years. Having such a document is not merely some piece of intellectual sophistry – it provides the compass that helps company personnel to steer their route towards the attainment of the firm's aims.

In practice the mission statement should be brief and phrased in clear and unambiguous terms. Ideally it should encompass the following:

- **The role or contribution that the organization is seeking to provide:** For example, is the firm assuming the role of a profit-maker, service-provider, opportunity-seeker, innovator or lowest-cost operator, or a judicious combination of some of these characteristics?

- **Business definition:** This should preferably be stated in terms of the benefits that are provided to the customers or the needs that are satisfied, as opposed to being couched in terms of what the company makes. Thus a ball-bearing manufacturer should talk in terms of 'anti-friction' systems rather than 'ball or roller bearings'.

  In stating the firm's perception as to the business it believes it ought to be in, full cognisance of the threats and/or opportunities affecting the future ought to be considered and analyzed.

- **Distinctive competences:** These are the special skills, capabilities and strengths which have contributed directly to the success that the company has enjoyed to date. However, if these skills or capabilities are equally descriptive of competitors, then clearly they are not distinctive and will need to be reconsidered.

- **Indications for the future:** This represents a declaration of faith on the part of the top management. It is something of a value statement for the company. It indicates what the company *will do*, *might do* or *will never do* in the future.

Once agreed by senior management, the mission statement should be capable of resolving potential conflicts on many issues. For example, the development of new products or a new business direction should become a clear and logical corollary of the mission. Room for doubt or confusion should be lowered to a minimum.

Corporate objectives

An objective is a measurable achievement which the company by its actions pursues. Generally this is expressed in terms of profits and/or returns on investment, inasmuch as these are norms understood not only by managers but also by shareholders and the owners of the business. To that extent they represent the accepted measures of effectiveness for most organizations and are therefore the overriding objectives to which all other activities are subordinated.

On the other hand, it has been known for firms to pursue, certainly in the medium term, growth objectives regardless of profits with a view to attaining a dominant position for the longer term. Obviously, such an objective will dominate everything the firm does during such a phase, including the whole approach to its marketing effort.

Corporate strategies

'How' an objective is to be achieved is a question of strategy. The subtle difference between objective and strategy is often missed by managers, with the result that the logic of the process becomes blurred. Thus, if an objective is to achieve a given level of profitability, the strategy question is which is the most effective way of achieving it. A number of strategic options spring to mind:

- The effective exploitation of products and markets (marketing).
- A more effective use of existing facilities (production and logistics).
- Improved labour utilization through training and development (personnel).
- A more economic use of funding (finance).

Many other options can be identified and considered. A combination of functional strategies can be coalesced with a view to developing the most promising strategic plan for attaining the firm's objectives. The important point to remember is that what is seen from the top as a strategy eventually becomes a functional objective. Thus, if the strategic level selects product development as a strategic route for achieving corporate objectives, this becomes a functional objective for those responsible for introducing new products.

This is the basis upon which the whole logic of the hierarchy of objectives becomes such a powerful instrument of effective planning. What is a strategy for one person becomes an objective to the next person in the pyramid. If we stick with marketing and thereby confine ourselves to the overall theme of this book, we can see that corporate strategy regarding products and markets clearly influences the next level down in the planning hierarchy: namely, the marketing objectives. And marketing strategies themselves indicate objectives for marketing subactivities such as advertising, pricing, distribution and selling.

Any marketing activity should be capable of being traced up through the planning hierarchy so that its practical contribution to achieving the corporate objectives can be seen. Indeed, all objectives and strategies should be capable of being traced in a logical and direct sequence both upwards and downwards. This is a protocol which is too important to be ignored if the planning cycle is to represent the firm's model for success.

In summary, the 'corporate plan' is the schedule of all the activities which together are directed to achieve the 'corporate objectives'. In contrast, the 'marketing plan' is concerned only with those activities which are designed to achieve the 'marketing objectives'. Obviously, the marketing plan represents a sizeable chunk of the corporate plan.

The marketing planning process

Regardless of the terminology they use, most marketing practitioners agree that the planning process involves a number of steps which are more or less universally accepted. These are described in Figure 10.3.

Marketing audit
This is the 'input-gathering' stage, which seeks to collect and collate information relating to pertinent issues affecting the company's internal and external environments.

SWOT analysis
The marketing audit is distilled so that the major strengths, weaknesses, opportunities and threats can be identified. Most readers will be aware that SWOT represents the initial letters of these four areas of concern to planners.

Assumptions
Some basic assumptions have to be made about the company and its environment in order to provide some anchor points for the marketing plan. For example, assumptions regarding the political stability of the firm's main export market have to be made unless strong evidence to the contrary is at hand. The important point to remember is that as few assumptions as possible should be made, and that they should be based on the most reliable and up-to-date information.

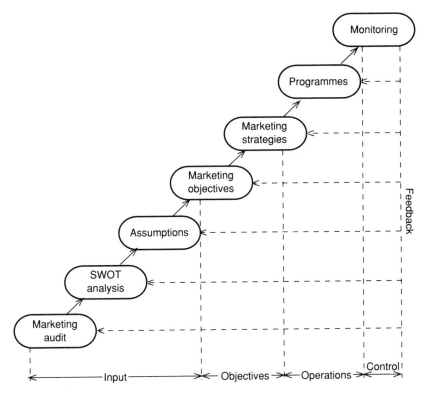

Figure 10.3 The marketing planning process

Marketing objectives

If the foregoing steps are pursued with thoroughness, coupled with an intelligent appraisal of the firm's overall objectives, the marketing objectives should become almost self-evident. Essentially, we are concerned here with a set of objectives which state clearly, and in quantitative terms, which products go to which markets or sub-markets.

Marketing strategies

At this point the plan should specify the strategies which have been selected as the most likely ones to achieve the objectives. Moreover, these should relate to the role which each ingredient of the marketing mix is likely to play in the whole task.

Detailed programmes

Detailed programmes of work should now be developed for each of the marketing activities which contribute to the marketing strategy.

These programmes should allocate responsibilities, timings and costs.

Monitoring procedures

A mechanism for monitoring, at regular intervals, the attainment of key results areas is an essential part of the whole cycle. This mechanism, with its supportive procedures, should seek to provide the appropriate feedback upon which corrective measures can be taken.

While the monitoring and review mechanism should be capable of providing feedback to all the stages described, its main role is to control the detailed programmes of work and the strategic route chosen. This is not to say that the marketing objectives area is sacrosanct and should never be reviewed during the planning period. Nevertheless this should happen only in extreme situations and in the face of overwhelming evidence that the objectives are wrong or that circumstances have made them unattainable. Otherwise 'moving the goalposts' frequently will make a mockery of the planning process and damage its credibility beyond repair.

It is also worth remembering that, although the planning process is essentially linear, it has to be operated with some degree of flexibility. Instead of grinding on in a mechanistic way, one must be prepared to backtrack if necessary. For example, the marketing objectives which first emerge might not be in the right order of magnitude. This will necessitate taking a fresh and critical look at the audit and SWOT analysis to check if something important has been overlooked.

At the end of the day, each component of the process must sit comfortably and rationally with all the others. For convenience and ease of communication, a planning model has been described which appears to consist of discrete steps. Yet understanding the inter-relationship among all these steps is an essential element in the preparation of a well-structured plan.

Finally, when considering the marketing planning process it is useful to recall that the final plans seldom include the detailed analyses and thinking involved in their preparation. One seldom lists all the elements of strength which one has identified, although considerable reflection time should have gone into their identification. Figure 10.4 provides a summary of the contents of a sound marketing plan.

REMEMBER
MARKETING PLAN CONTAINS:

• Mission statement

• Financial summary of
what it seeks to achieve

• Market overview

• SWOT analysis

• Assumptions

• Marketing objectives

• Marketing strategies

• Programmes (with
forecasts and budgets)

Figure 10.4 Contents of the marketing plan

Who should produce the plan?

For many organizations this presents a thorny problem. Instinctively, they know that the more people who are involved in the planning process, the more likely they all are to feel committed to the resulting plans. At the same time, busy managers are often too involved in day-to-day issues to be able to devote adequate time to the detailed assembly of reliable and well-considered input. The inevitable result is that plans often pay no more than lip-service to the planning task.

Some companies set up a special marketing planning department with the aim of overcoming this problem. This can work well as long as those responsible for the preparation of the plans do not work in complete isolation. Plans emanating from a team of people working in an ivory-tower atmosphere cannot earn the support and commitment of those who operate at the sharp end of the marketplace. Such plans are often treated with cynicism, if not ridicule.

In fact there is no easy answer to the question of who should be responsible for the production of marketing plans. There are too many variables in terms of individual company sizes, complexity of product ranges and so on to be able to provide a single recommendation.

In a small company with a fairly homogeneous range of products, the chief executive is likely to be the person who assumes the responsibility for all aspects of the planning process. Conversely, in a complex multinational and multiproduct organization, planning is beyond the capability of one individual.

Companies should develop their own recipe to resolve the dilemma as to who should assume the responsibility for masterminding an effective planning cycle. Nonetheless there are some general principles that most organizations ought to consider in this regard:

- The planning process must be seen as an extension of top management's responsibility. In other words, whoever is responsible for the actual assembly of data and the detailed preparation of plans should be regarded as a direct delegatee of senior management and have their full support.

- It must be remembered at all times that line managers and those in daily contact with markets and customers possess a wealth of marketing information. It is essential to capture this by involving such people in the marketing audit process, even if it can only be done by resorting to questionnaires and checklists.

- As a direct corollary of the previous point, the marketing planner could appropriately be seen as the coordinator and analyst of organizational data.

- The person (or department) responsible for the planning process must carry some gravitas in the organization. A person of insufficiently high standing would not be able to attain cooperation and influence company policy decisions.

- Whoever produces the plans must be capable of using analytical tools such as forecasting techniques, statistical methods and gap analysis.

Aids to marketing planning

A brief description of a number of the 'tools' available to the marketing planner is appropriate at this juncture.

Scenario writing and scenario day-dreaming

The planner is essentially concerned about the future. His or her role is to prepare a plan which seeks to match the firm's capabilities with future opportunities. This means that part of the planner's task is to assemble a *vision* representing the environment in which the firm will be operating at a certain point in the future. The logical sequence underlying the planning process is described in Figure 10.5.

Talking, thinking and dreaming about the future can act as powerful stimulants to identifying future opportunities (or potential threats). The sheer process of 'gazing over the fence' of present-day reality into the unknown can have a most salutary effect upon management's future vistas. The accuracy of the scenario is almost secondary. The most important feature of the exercise is that those responsible for developing a vision approach the task with an open mind and reflect upon the future without extrapolating from the past or the present.

Scenario writing

As the term implies, scenario writing usually produces a document describing a logical, albeit imaginary, sequence starting from the present (or any other given moment in time) and ending at a future point, listing the step-by-step evolution of likely events. A well-conceived document of this nature helps to forecast events which can offer the firm opportunities for exploitation or identify threats to be avoided. A scenario which alerts a car manufacturer to the vision that

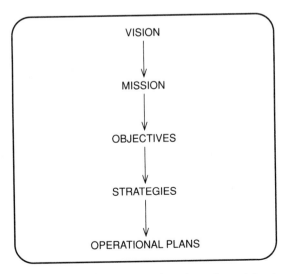

Figure 10.5 The logical sequence underlying plans: from vision to operational plans

within a decade all European countries will prescribe anti-pollution systems means that this manufacturer stands a better chance of incorporating such a factor in its marketing plans than the one which waits for such a contingency to occur. The former can be proactive, while the latter can only be reactive and, inevitably, less prepared to exploit such an insight. The former can develop a competitive advantage over the latter.

In practical terms, the scenario-writing team gets together in order to reflect upon events that are likely to take place in some distant future and consider the impact, favourable or otherwise, which such events will have on the strategic direction of the firm. Ideally, the team should consist of people who possess some expertise in specific areas, such as economics, environment, media, logistics. The aim is to bring together such knowledge and opinions into a cohesive vision and place it in a written document.

Scenario day-dreaming

Scenario day-dreaming seeks to undertake the same task but over a shorter period, and the visioning process takes place verbally. It is like a brainstorming session but relates to the team's imaging of the world at a given date in the future, say the year 2000. Each member of the planning team is allocated a factor for exploration, such as economic trends, politics, ecology or the availability of mineral resources (if appropriate). Topics for reflection should preferably be allocated in accordance with people's specific knowledge and/or expertise. The discussions must be centred around the concept that the group has catapulted all its attention to a point in the future. In other words, they must feel that 'today is January 2000 and this is what is happening in the world around us'. The use of the future tense must be avoided at all cost. A scribe records the main issues that will have emerged, and through an iterative process the vision is refined and the implications for the company are explored in some depth.

The collective knowledge and wisdom of members of the team should help to coalesce a plausible scenario of the future. If one remembers that the most important point about planning is the process itself rather than the outcome, a scenario day-dreaming exercise can provide a most potent aid to planning generally and to marketing planning in particular.

Gap analysis

Gap analysis is a simple technique designed to judge whether

existing marketing practices and programmes are likely to be sufficient to match the expectations of the firm for the future. It is
illustrated in Figure 10.6.

Let us assume that the company operates with a strategic planning
cycle of three years. The target revenue envisaged by the corporate
objectives (shown in Figure 10.6 as target revenue) is more ambitious
than the forecast revenue emanating from the analysis of current
marketing strategies. Forecast revenue falls far short of target
revenue, thus highlighting a gap. How can the gap be bridged?

The aim of the exercise is to explore ways of lowering or bridging
the gap. In the first instance, the marketer can try to 'tighten' the
various elements that contribute to results:

- **Improving productivity:** This entails analyzing the productivity
  of each element of the mix. Thus, making the sales force more
  productive, generally reducing costs, increasing the price, etc.,
  may help to reduce the gap.

- **Market penetration:** This simply means taking steps to increase
  market share or the overall usage of the product. Clearly, such
  activities will have the net effect of increasing sales revenue to a
  revised forecast which, although showing an improvement, may

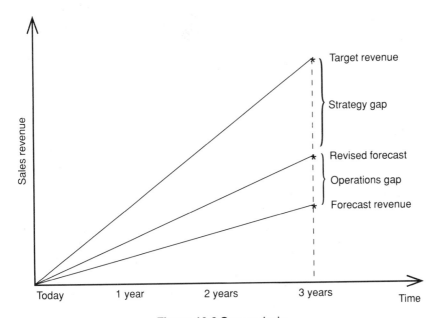

Figure 10.6 Gap analysis

still fall short of the target. Other strategies may have to be resorted to if the gap is to be completely bridged.

- **Market extension:** This entails finding new user groups/segments or expanding geographically into new territories and/or countries.

- **Developing new products:** In many situations new product development may be the only way in which the planning gap can be bridged.

- **Diversification:** Here one refers to a combination of new product(s) for entirely new market(s). In fact the company is attempting here to enter into a difficult strategic area inasmuch as it is indulging in the development of a new product and at the same time offering it to markets about which it possesses little knowledge.

A judicious exploration of these various routes may help to reduce the gap between forecast and target. However, one must be realistic enough to recognize that even after pulling out all the stops the new forecast may fall short of target. At that point one must be prepared to ask whether the target prescribed by the corporate objectives is realistic or simply a figment of somebody's imagination. The result may be that the original target has to be scaled downwards. The whole method is designed to highlight the gap and see how it can be bridged in the most effective manner.

Ansoff matrix

Following the description of the gap analysis method, it is appropriate to mention the so-called Ansoff matrix, named after Igor Ansoff who first formulated it in his book on corporate strategy (Ansoff, 1965). It is a valuable framework for exploring market strategies and is illustrated in Figure 10.7.

It can be gleaned from this matrix that the top left-hand quadrant represents existing products offered to existing markets. To that extent it is a 'safe' sector to be operating in. The firm is familiar with the details of the product and knows its markets. All its learning and experience has been derived in this area. The shading suggests that the further the company moves away from this quadrant, the higher is the risk involved. Indeed, as was suggested earlier, the bottom right-hand quadrant – new products to new markets (diversification)

PRODUCTS

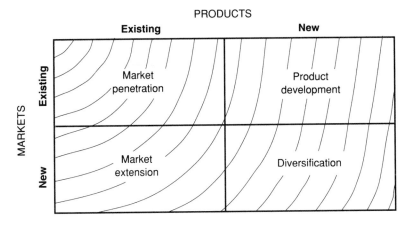

Figure 10.7 The Ansoff matrix

– represents a huge step into the unknown and is clearly the riskiest possible combination.

The cautious marketer will look to achieve much of the company's corporate ambitions by focusing on marketing objectives which involve existing products and existing markets. Only when all possibilities here have been exhausted will he or she look further afield, using SWOT analysis. If the organization is strong technically and in product design, it may consider the new product development route as the safest to pursue. Conversely, if the company has a strong reputation and finds that its skills enable it to open up new markets relatively easily, it will opt for the market extension route.

Market segmentation

A company may decide to gain a competitive advantage by opting out of the mass market and concentrating its main effort on a group of customers who have some common identity. Thus, instead of communicating with all customers in the marketplace, the company tailors its approach and marketing mix specifically to meet the needs of particular segments. It is appropriate to explore this topic as one of the aids to planning insofar as it is during the planning stage that decisions pertaining to segmentation are taken.

There are many ways in which markets can be segmented. It is a fertile ground for creativity and marketing success, particularly if based on the identification of an imaginative segmentation policy that no competitor has have thought of. Broadly speaking, bases for segmentation fall into a number of obvious categories.

Segmentation on the basis of buying behaviour ('what the customer buys')

For instance, customers may be characterized by the following:

- Purchasing frequency.
- Order size, in terms of either volume or value (heavy users as against light users).
- Place of purchase.
- Prices paid.
- Buying through the range.
- The physical attributes of the product (e.g. passion for design).
- Wishing to buy innovative products when they first appear on the market (known as 'innovators'), or conversely preferring to buy older and well-established products ('laggards').

Although these represent fairly elementary ways of segmenting markets, they can provide some degree of differentiation and a more 'customized' approach to a well-defined group of individuals who respond to certain behavioural stimuli.

Segmentation on the basis of customer motivation ('why the customer buys a specific product')

This form of segmentation seeks to group customers according to their reasons for buying. The following may be of interest to the planner.

- Benefits sought.
- Perception of the reliability of the supplying company.
- Perception of price/value.
- Social cachet.
- Longevity of products in use.

Here the marketer must acquire considerable knowledge about the motivational stimuli of existing and prospective customers.

Segmentation on the basis of customers' typology ('who the customer is')

Here are some examples:

- Socioeconomic groupings (e.g. in the UK, the A, B, C1, C2, D and E classification).

- Life-style, real or aspirational.
- Demographics.
- Cultures, ethnic groupings, religion, etc.
- Membership of special interest groups or clubs.

Companies may use a combination of these three broad approaches with a view to selecting the most appropriate segmentation basis for development. Whatever basis one chooses, it is always important to remember a number of preconditions for a successful segmentation policy:

- The segment under scrutiny must be large enough to offer the company an adequate return on the marketing effort involved.
- It must be sufficiently distinct as an entity from all other parts of the market.
- It must be accessible in the sense that suitable channels of distribution exist and the infrastructure for communication is also available.
- It must be durable. A segment which is here today and gone tomorrow is of dubious value to the marketer.

If any of these conditions cannot be met, the choice of a segment may prove costly and should be avoided. Moreover, segmentation is a very alluring strategy and marketers often fall into the trap of oversegmenting their marketing programmes. This can easily raise the spectre of the company trying to be too many things to too many groups of customers, thus diluting the marketing effort beyond the point of being effective. Indeed, some companies that went over-board on segmentation in the past have more recently started to 'desegment' their markets by aggregating two or three smaller segments into a larger one. This in turn helps to meet the conditions outlined earlier regarding segment size.

Mapping and positioning

Mapping is a technique designed to place the whole competitive scene on one diagram, thus highlighting: (a) crowded areas to be avoided and (b) empty or thinly populated zones which can be exploited profitably. The method can be best described through two examples.

Figure 10.8 illustrates a 'map', ascribed originally to BMW, showing all car models placed on a matrix. The horizontal axis shows the

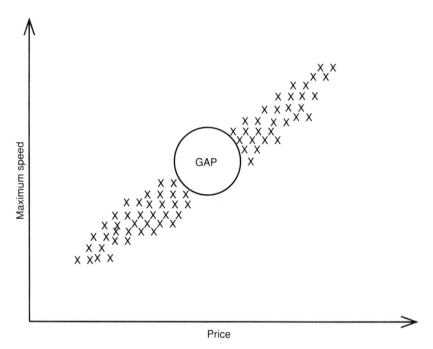

Figure 10.8 Mapping in the car industry (for illustration purposes only)

model's price; the vertical axis shows the car's performance (expressed in maximum speed). The final map highlights the fact that somewhere in the middle there was a glaring 'hole'. This is where BMA *positioned* its product development strategy.

Figure 10.9 illustrates a 'map' of cigarettes in the German market (the details do not necessarily represent correct and up-to-date data: it is purely an illustration). Instead of a matrix the picture is shown on a cross. While the horizontal line shows age stratification ('young' and 'old'), which is capable of quantification, the vertical line provides qualitative customer perception ('luxury' and 'cheap'). The various brands are shown in the appropriate positions on the chart.

The result of such an exercise can provide the marketer with a very powerful basis upon which to formulate a positioning plan. To move a brand from one position to another, the whole mix needs to come into play and over a period of time. Thus the product and its packaging may have to be refurbished, advertising and promotion given a different image, and so on.

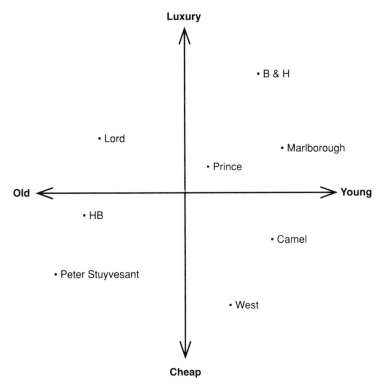

Figure 10.9 Mapping of cigarettes in the German market (illustration only – positions shown are not necessarily correct today)

Critical success factor analysis

Every business must identify the critical factors which contribute to its success. This principle applies to whatever business one is in, be it selling ice-cream or marketing computers. The more a business meets these success factors in comparison with competitors, the more successful it will be. This method is useful in identifying the most significant strengths and weaknesses during SWOT analysis. Normally one should apply this kind of analysis to each market segment in which one is operating.

Let us explore a simple example from the ice-cream distribution business. Mario sells ices from a van on the sea-front of a popular holiday resort. His biggest competitor is Marco, who operates from a similar van about 100 yards away. Mario understands the essence of marketing and reflects upon the value of critical success factors. He has come to the conclusion that success in his business depends on excelling in a number of areas. Moreover, he has checked that his assumptions are correct by talking to his customers about them. Table 10.1 (below) summarizes the position.

Mario listed all these factors and scored both for himself and for Marco out of 10 for each item. Since Marco could be very surly at times, Mario outscored him on 'friendly service'. Similarly, Mario prided himself on keeping his van sparkling clean at all times, whereas Marco's often looked as if it could do with a good scrub. On price both were equally competitive, but Marco scored on having a wider range of products.

At a glance Mario can see his strengths and weaknesses and how they contribute to his overall success. As a result he plans to increase the range he carries and thereby extend his lead over Marco.

This kind of simple analysis can work in most businesses. Furthermore, it can be made even more effective by weighting the key success factors according to their perceived importance and multiplying the 'raw scores' in a way that represents more accurately the realities of the business world.

Product life-cycle analysis

The product life-cycle and its implications were discussed in Chapter 5. It is evident that a thorough analysis of where existing products stand in relation to their life-cycle is an important aid to planning and can provide useful insights into the kind of strategies that could be adopted. Any attempt at predicting how the life-cycle is about to unfold can provide the marketer with a valuable scenario of how opportunities and/or threats are likely to present themselves during the planning period. Altogether product life-cycle analysis offers an excellent input to the SWOT analysis.

Table 10.1 Critical success factor analysis

Critical success factors	Mario	Marco
Friendly service	9	7
Hygienic appearance	9	6
Competitive prices	10	10
Wide range of ices and lollies	7	9
Total	35	32

Market share analysis

Market share is acknowledged by most companies to be a valuable indication of performance in the competitive marketplace. It is normally recognized that the company that enjoys the highest market share in a given sector of business is likely to be the most successful one.

On the face of it, market share is a very simple concept. A manufacturer of bicycles sells 50,000 units in a market consisting of around 500,000 a year. Its market share is rightly said to be 10 per cent. Let us imagine that further investigation indicates that over the last few years the company's market share has in fact increased from 7 per cent. All this augurs well for the future provided the external market looks equally promising. However, a number of valid questions can be asked regarding the market share analysis:

- How is the market share being measured – in terms of money, units sold, share of cyclists in the country, or some other measure?

- What is our share of bicycles for adults, men, women and children? We may be strong in one segment but not in others.

- What is our share of bicycles sold in various channels of distribution? We may be strong in department stores but weak in specialized shops.

- What is our share of the various motivational subgroups? Some people buy bicycles for racing; others for transport; yet others purely for exercise. Our market share may be very different among such subgroups.

In order for market share analysis to be a truly meaningful aid to planning, the marketer should attempt to measure it in a number of ways. In fact measuring market share is one of the most potent tools of diagnostic analysis that the marketer possesses. If used correctly, it can alert the creative marketer to areas of weakness in the marketing programme.

Let us cast our minds back to the bicycle manufacturer. Let us imagine that further analysis shows the following figures:

Market share in terms of units sold	10%
Market share in terms of sales revenue	8%
Market share of men's bicycles	7.5%
Market share of women's bicycles	12%

It does not require enormous imagination to work out a number of obvious diagnostic conclusions: average prices are lower than those of competitors; sales of bicycles to women are better than to men. Additional analysis may yield other insights. Hopefully, the company was aware of these facts. Otherwise it should be grateful to the market share analysis inasmuch as it has helped to identify weaknesses and strengths in the system.

The example given was a very simple one. More complicated studies can be undertaken by creative diagnosticians. They can ring the changes in a variety of ways, measure market shares in accordance with a myriad of unusual, albeit logical parameters, and manipulate the results with a view to identifying relevant strengths and/or weaknesses in marketing variables. Indeed, in some cases marketing results can be improved while ostensibly reducing market share.

Business portfolio analysis

In Chapter 5 a number of techniques known collectively as the *business portfolio methods* were explored. Notably we looked at the Boston matrix and the directional policy matrix. All these methods are of great value during the planning process. Essentially, they are all based on the notion that a matrix is a valuable tool for comparing two disparate but very significant dimensions. Thus, when the Boston matrix looks at market share on one axis and market growth on the other, the product falling into the 'high'/'high' quadrant is obviously the winner, and ought to be supported with vigour and a generous allocation of resources.

The important point to remember is that the technique is simple and flexible. There is no reason why the two axes cannot be changed to suit the requirements of each planner. A number of illustrations will show how valuable portfolio methods can be in a number of situations.

Figure 10.10 illustrates a matrix designed to identify the most attractive segments from a myriad of options on offer.

Figure 10.11 provides a similar system for choosing the best countries for marketing development from among a large number of countries.

Figure 10.12 shows how the matrix can be used as a predictive device for highlighting current and future positions. The sales revenue of each product is plotted on the matrix, represented by a circle whose area is roughly in proportion to the size of the revenue. Forecasts are then made for each product three years hence, and

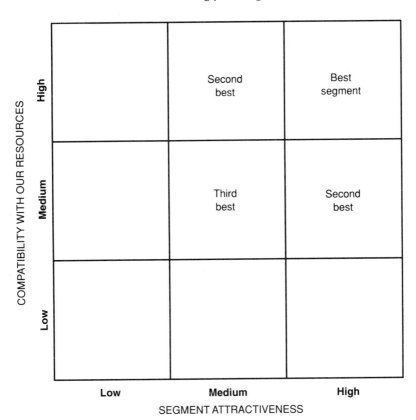

Figure 10.10 Matrix for screening the most attractive segment for development

these are also plotted. The example seeks to show that while products C and D are 'cash cows' today, they are forecast to fall away leaving a gap in this quadrant. Product A is well on the way to becoming a 'star' and product B is still growing. While the portfolio looks quite well balanced today, it looks like getting out of control in the future unless it is managed more astutely.

Formulating marketing strategies

Having pursued the various steps of the planning cycle described in this chapter, and having applied the various analytical tools

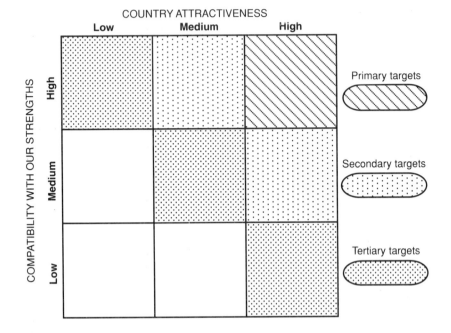

Figure 10.11 Matrix for screening the most attractive international markets

Criteria of attractiveness

Examples:

• The country is large.
• It is stable.
• It has high per capita income.
• It possesses an efficient
  distribution system.

Criteria of compatibility

Examples:

• The country is known to us
  through previous marketing
  contacts.
• Our flag fits.
• We already have distribution
  channels.
• Our brands are known there.

involved, the marketer is probably ready to finalize his or her
strategies in respect of each of the objectives set. This means that the
time has come to 'blend' the marketing mix for each of the segments
selected. A range of options are open for development:

Product

● Expand the range (e.g. additional sizes).
● Deepen the range (e.g. more colours in a particular size).

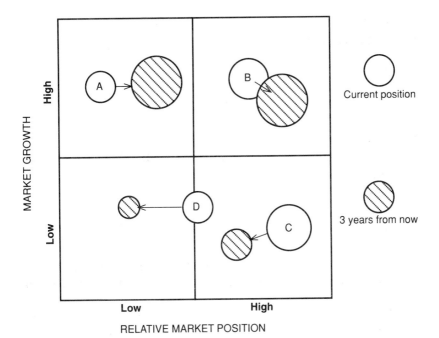

Figure 10.12 The Boston matrix as a predictive device

- Change the quality, features and benefits.
- Redesign or modernize the product.
- Consolidate the range (by cutting out less popular lines).
- Introduce/remove/extend branding.

Price

- Set price for market penetration.
- Skimming policy.
- Alter discount structure.
- Change price, terms or conditions.

Promotion

- Change advertising.
- Change selling strategy.

- Change the mix of advertising and selling.
- Change sales promotions.
- Change point-of-sale displays.

Place

- Change channels.
- Change balance between use of intermediaries and own sales force.
- Change service levels.
- Change packaging/unitization.
- Change logistics and physical distribution.

Clearly, a combination of all these strategic options can provide an enormous array of individual 'mix recipes'. The scope for selecting creative mixes is vast.

Once the strategy underpinning the marketing objectives has been determined, the preparation of the operational plan encompassing individual activities such as advertising, selling and distribution is a fairly simple, albeit detailed, process.

MARKETING PLANNING AUDIT

Score
0 1 2

1. **Does a systematic marketing planning process exist in the firm?**

   (a) No. We simply prepare annual
   budgets.   (*Score 0*)
   (b) Yes. Once a year all departments produce a 3-year plan incorporating estimated revenue and
   expenditure.   (*Score 1*)
   (c) Yes. Our planning cycle is well established. It is an iterative process during which a thorough SWOT analysis takes place. A top-down and bottom-up dialogue takes place throughout before strategies are
   evolved.   (*Score 2*)

   ▶

2. **How are marketing objectives arrived at in the company?**

(a) We extrapolate from recent years'
performance.   (*Score 0*)
(b) We use gap analysis to establish the size of the
marketing task we face.   (*Score 1*)
(c) We use gap analysis and respond to it by allocating
enough marketing resources to close the
gap.   (*Score 2*)

3. **Does the planning cycle allow for contingencies?**

(a) No. Our budgets are firm and any shortfalls must
be made up during the unexpired period of the
plan.   (*Score 0*)
(b) We allow deviations from the plans but not in
excess of 10 per cent. In the event of significant
deviations we review the plans at the end of the
year.   (*Score 1*)
(c) Our plans are designed to cope with contingencies
in a systematic way. All significant deviations are
monitored and the implications analyzed and
incorporated in modified and updated
plans.   (*Score 2*)

4. **Who is responsible for preparing the marketing plans?**

(a) We are simply told from above what we have to
achieve.   (*Score 0*)
(b) We have a corporate planning officer at the centre
who invites all departments, including marketing, to
submit their plans. The officer then aggregates them
all into a company plan.   (*Score 1*)
(c) The CEO considers that he/she is responsible for
the preparation of company plans. Our corporate
planner is seen as his/her administrative extension. At
the same time the widest participation in the process
is sought.   (*Score 2*)

5. **Are the plans expressed in quantitative or narrative format?**

(a) Our budgets are presented in figures
only.   (*Score 0*)

▶

(b) Our plans are mostly quantitative in nature, but some narrative about our perceived SWOT is incorporated therein.   *(Score 1)*

(c) The plans contain a judicious mix of narrative and figures. The former seeks to summarize the input upon which the plans are based. We ascribe considerable value to an intelligent narrative describing the build-up to the objectives and strategy.   *(Score 2)*

6. **Are the plans widely communicated?**

(a) No. Only heads of department possess full details of the budgets. We consider that our plans are top secret.   *(Score 0)*

(b) Yes. Plans are distributed fairly widely. Individuals only get those portions for which they are responsible.   *(Score 1)*

(c) Plans are widely communicated. Heads of department are requested to share the challenges and opportunities on a continuing basis with members of their organizations.   *(Score 2)*

7. **How clear are the firm's marketing objectives and strategies?**

(a) They are expressed in rather vague terms.   *(Score 0)*

(b) The objectives are clearly stated, but the strategies for achieving them are somewhat inconclusive.   *(Score 1)*

(c) They are clear and compatible with corporate mission and objectives. The strategies selected are crisp and unequivocal.   *(Score 2)*

8. **Does the company use the following analytical tools during its marketing planning cycle: gap analysis, segmentation, critical success factor analysis, product life-cycle analysis, market share analysis, the directional policy matrix, and the Ansoff matrix?**

(a) We never use any of these.   *(Score 0)*

(b) We use only some of these (up to four).   *(Score 1)*

(c) We use most of these tools (over four)

systematically and have adapted them to our
needs.   *(Score 2)*

9. **How much attention is given during the marketing
    planning cycle to competitive analysis?**

    (a) None. We believe that we know enough about our
    competitors.   *(Score 0)*
    (b) We check details about our competitors and their
    activities once a year.   *(Score 1)*
    (c) We monitor competitive practices throughout the
    year. In fact we have a small competitive intelligence
    unit charged with the task of maintaining a full and
    up-to-date dossier about our competitors. This dossier
    forms an integral part of the marketing audit
    process.   *(Score 2)*

10. **Does the company monitor and evaluate the
    attainment of results spelt out in the marketing plans?**

    (a) We only measure results in terms of profit and
    loss.   *(Score 0)*
    (b) We have control procedures which help to
    highlight deviations from plan.   *(Score 1)*
    (c) Our monitoring system flags up deviations from
    plans, and contingency steps spring into
    action.   *(Score 2)*

The maximum score possible is 20. Very few companies could achieve
such a score. Lower scores can be interpreted as follows:

15–20 **Excellent**
10–14 **Good to very good.**
 5–9   **Fair**
 0–4   **Poor**

11

Marketing control

An American proverb says: 'When you are up to your neck in alligators, it is not easy to remember that the original objective was to drain the swamp.' Control systems are not only designed to measure results and effectiveness. They are also meant to act as reminders, at all times, of what the original aims of the whole programme were. They provide the tiller that can help to ensure that corrective measures are taken when the need arises. Many marketers consider control procedures as the least stimulating part of the whole process. They forget that in fact they represent an integral part of that process.

Different types of control

The overall control process is quite straightforward, as Figure 11.1 illustrates. Where effective control procedures exist, each action is measured. If a deviation from preset objectives is identified, corrective action is undertaken, leading to a renewed and/or better action. In a dynamic world, by a continual repetition of this process the original situation is capable of being improved several-fold.

Bearing in mind the integrating nature of marketing, the various levels of management involved and its time dimension, control of marketing activities can be more complex than the simple model shown in Figure 11.1. What is needed is a model which recognizes the various elements involved in the planning and operational loops, and the relationships among them (see Figure 11.2).

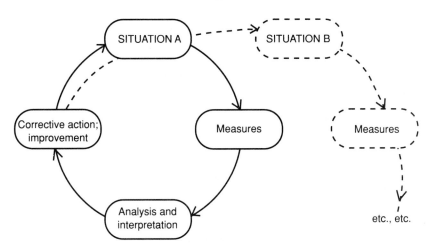

Figure 11.1 The basic control process

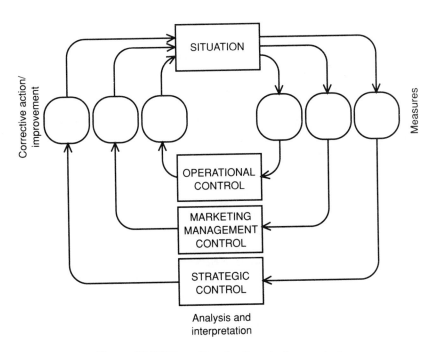

Figure 11.2 Different levels of marketing control

The control systems must encompass the following:

- Achievement of strategic plans.
- Managerial effectiveness.
- Measurement of operational programmes.

These control loops serve different parts of the organization and different levels of the hierarchy, but ideally they should blend together into a cohesive and well-integrated total structure. This way one can ensure that the input that underpins them is consistent and harmonious. All the intelligence-gathering undertaken by the firm can then be fully exploited by all.

In order to understand the types of measure which can be used to feed these control loops, we will look at each one in turn.

Strategic control

Control of the company at this level is particularly important in a world in which markets and environments are so volatile. A point to remember is that control procedures feed the input for the future planning cycle. To that extent control and input gathering are where the loop joins up and the new cycle begins. What needs to be kept under constant review is perhaps best summed up by Figure 11.3, which is based on the work of Michael Porter.

At the strategic level the company survives by outflanking its current rivals and anticipating the changing conditions which may occur as a result of new entrants, substitute products and the changing powers of buyers. All these areas must be monitored continuously. The firm's antennae must scan the horizon for signals as to the direction from which the biggest threats may emanate. The source of threats varies from one type of business to another. Experience has shown that new entrants and new technologies often work hand in hand. It is often quite difficult to spot the inherent threat when a new technology is first announced. Yet new technologies may suddenly be translated into marketing threats of major proportions.

At the corporate level it is critical that the overall strategy is kept under review. Just as products and services experience ever-shortening life-cycles, so do corporate strategies. In the not too distant past a company could enjoy the fruits of a well-conceived

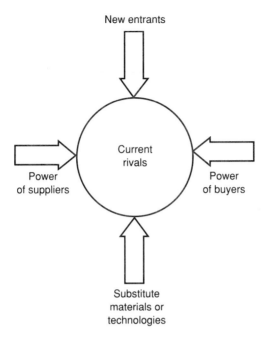

New entrants

Power
of suppliers

Current
rivals

Power
of buyers

Substitute
materials or
technologies

Figure 11.3 Monitoring the impact of competitive pressures on the firm's strategies

competitive advantage for quite a while. A unique strategy could set the company apart from its rivals for a number of years. Today, with all the impact of global communication and information technology, a firm's strategic lead may be cut from years to a very short period. The control system must maintain a vigilant eye on developments in this area. The model provided in Figure 11.3 represents a framework for such vigilance.

For the shorter term one way to develop and maintain a strategy which helps to separate the firm from its present-day rivals is the benchmarking method. It is a technique which provides management with valuable control insights into the firm's standing on a number of criteria:

- Critical success criteria are established for a given market or industry, such as returns on capital, productivity, capacity versus output, and sales volume per sales person.
- The performance of the most successful players in that industry are now analyzed against the criteria thus identified.

- The analyzing firm now compares its own performance against each one of the criteria thus identified for measurement. This kind of interfirm comparison helps to highlight strengths and weaknesses and pave the way for future corrective measures.

More specifically, the people belonging to the strategic level must control the following items:

- The effectiveness of the customer philosophy.
- The attainment of the firm's marketing strategy, in whatever terms it was expressed in the first place.
- The attainment of the marketing objectives.
- The appropriateness of the marketing organization.
- The quality of the marketing intelligence.
- General operational efficiency.

Through a series of audit questionnaires similar to those incorporated in this book, top management can monitor and measure the position of the firm in these areas and identify marketing problems. Some companies have actually developed a marketing controller position charged with the task of monitoring the level of performance of macro-marketing activities and plans.

Managerial effectiveness and efficiency control

Effectiveness is concerned with doing the right things. Efficiency is concerned with doing them well. While top management in its control procedures is particularly interested in monitoring that the right things are being done, the management level is also concerned with the level of efficiency achieved.

Those responsible for managing the marketing function must develop control procedures for measuring both the effectiveness and the efficiency of the various elements of the mix, and in particular those areas which impact upon the achievement of results. In this connection the most significant areas are sales, distribution and promotion.

These will be discussed in some detail. Other areas of expenditure and cost allocation can be controlled and measured, but it is outside the scope of this book to look at all of them.

Sales

Methods of controlling the sales effort will, of course, vary from company to company. In Chapter 9 a large list of possible standards of performance was reviewed. Whichever measures one decides to choose depends on the nature of the business and the marketplace. The sales pyramid described in Figure 11.4 provides a valuable system for monitoring levels of performance, especially in the industrial sector. It is based on the concept that an erosion rate exists between actual sales and the various stages of the selling effort.

Whatever sales are attained must be related to the number of proposals submitted to customers. This in turn is a function of the number of visits, which, in turn arises from the number of initial contacts. The pyramid results from the fact that not all initial contacts lead to visits, and not all visits lead to a proposal being requested and submitted. Finally, only a portion of the proposals results in orders being taken.

If a company's sales pyramid approximates to the one shown in Figure 11.4 then clearly the key sales efficiency controls will be as follows:

- Number of new contacts per week.
- Contacts to visits conversion ratio.
- Visits to proposals ratio.
- Proposal to orders radio.

Figure 11.4 The sales pyramid (for industrial goods)

Each one of these pieces of information will be essential for management control. If kept over time they could help to pinpoint where problems arise. Furthermore, these measures can provide clear guidance regarding the nature of the corrective actions which are required.

New contacts down

This problem can be solved through an increase in telephone selling activities; improved telephone skills; revised communication mix (e.g. mail shots, direct response advertising) and so on.

Contacts to visits down

This situation may be improved through communication skills training; improved 'Identikit' of the perfect customers for targeting purposes; better sales aids; and improved description of cost/benefit to customers.

Visits to proposals down

This problem may be tackled through improved selling skills; better motivational stimuli; and permission to lengthen the duration of sales calls, especially where the prospect profile looks right.

Proposals to orders down

This may call for an improvement in proposal quality and presentation skills; and better interfirm analysis with a view to highlighting the company's own strengths and competences.

These are just a few examples designed to illustrate how control procedures are more than simply an instrument for beating sales staff over the head. They can provide a powerful system for honing the whole selling task and making it into a more efficient and well-managed function.

It must also be remembered that it might be necessary to monitor sales costs in terms of average cost per call, entertainment expenses versus results, and cost of field sales as a proportion of total sales effort. Having this type of information available can provide a significant opportunity to keep the selling operation under control.

Advertising

We have already seen in Chapter 7 how difficult it is to measure advertising results. The point was made that measurement and control are much easier when the objectives are crystal clear from the start. Otherwise the task is so complex that many marketers do not bother to make the attempt. In such circumstances it is true to say that the advertising effort is not properly controlled and the results may be suboptimal.

It is important to keep a rigorous check on what advertising is costing and what it is achieving. Measures which can be used to control advertising efficiency include the following:

- Cost per 1,000 customers reached.
- Media effectiveness comparisons.
- Impact on customers.
- Retention rate of message.
- Attitude change to product/service.
- Enquiries resulting from advertising.

Most of this information cannot be obtained from internal sources and requires market research to provide the necessary feedback. Since this can be costly, it is essential that the company is clear in its own mind regarding what it wants to measure and why. Good control of just one or two 'levers' will be far more valuable than fuzzy control of a wide range of factors.

Distribution

For many years, distribution and the costs associated with it did not receive adequate attention from managerial control procedures. In the last few years there has been much fuller recognition of the importance of monitoring the costs and efficiency of distribution and logistics systems.

A significant improvement has taken place in the level of awareness of the impact that an efficient distribution system can have on customer satisfaction. Computer technology has also made considerable inroads into this area of marketing management. Control information can be made available virtually on line and at the press of a button.

The most important efficiency controls are as follows:

- Inventory levels/stock turnover.
- Stock-out situations.
- Customer complaints.
- Warehouse efficiency ratings.

- Physical distribution costs.

Operational controls

At this level the main concern is the measurement of profitability and returns in relation to the various operational tasks undertaken.

Profitability

Talk about profits often tends to refer to the total profit of the enterprise. It is useful to remember that, if every component of the process attains its contribution objective, the ultimate aggregate result will be what the firm has chosen as its overall profit objective. Moreover, it is always useful to know what are the bits that make up the total. Understanding the relationship between profits at the micro-level and profits at the macro-level helps to control the whole process.

In order to achieve such an aim it is important to understand some of the key ratios associated with the management of a business. In the context of this book we can explore only a few of these.

From a corporate vantage point, one should attempt to measure each product line of the business in terms of return on capital employed. Profits *per se* do not tell us how efficiently the profits have been reached. Return on capital employed can be expressed in the following equation:

$$\frac{R}{CE}$$

where R is the return or net revenue before tax and CE is the capital employed.

This ratio can be expanded into two secondary ratios:

$$\frac{R}{CE} = \frac{R}{S} \times \frac{S}{CE}$$

i.e. return on sales times sales per capital employed.

$\frac{R}{S}$ can in turn be written as: $\quad \dfrac{\text{Sales} - \text{Cost of goods sold}}{\text{Sales (i.e. Volume} \times \text{Price)}}$

Cost of goods sold = Production costs + Marketing costs
+ Administration costs

Similarly:

$$\frac{S}{CE} = \frac{\text{Sales}}{\text{Working capital (i.e. stock} + \text{Fixed assets (i.e. land,}}$$
$$+ \text{debtors} + \text{cash, etc.)} \quad \text{buildings plant, etc.)}$$

These simple ratios can form the basis of analysis, which in turn can raise questions relating to possible corrective measures.

Suppose, for example, that profitability has been found to drift downwards. What steps might be taken to regain the earlier and more satisfactory position? One's thinking process may run as follows:

1. Is the falling $\frac{R}{CE}$ due to falling $\frac{R}{S}$ or falling $\frac{S}{CE}$?

2. If it is $\frac{R}{S}$ then to what extent will the situation be restored by:

    (a) increasing sales volume
    (b) increasing price
    (c) reducing costs of goods sold
    (d) a combination of the above?

3. If it is $\frac{S}{CE}$ then is that due to:

    $$\frac{S}{\text{Working capital } (WC)} \quad \text{or} \quad \frac{S}{\text{Fixed assets } (FA)} ?$$

4. If it is $\frac{S}{WC}$ then is it because there has been a change in:

    $$\frac{\text{Sales}}{\text{Stocks}} \quad \text{or} \quad \frac{\text{Sales}}{\text{Debtors}} \quad \text{or} \quad \frac{\text{Sales}}{\text{Work in progress}} ?$$

5. If it is $\frac{S}{FA}$ then does this represent an underuse of the fixed asset capacity or a change in asset balance whereby the proportion $\frac{FA}{\text{Total assets}}$ is increasing non-productively?

By using such an analytical framework, it is relatively easy to home in on the problem area(s) and take corrective action. However, the main implication is that marketing personnel must learn to understand some of the basic accountancy concepts which underpin these management control ratios. Moreover, it also means that strong communication and mutual understanding must exist between members of the marketing team and their accountancy colleagues.

Another necessary ingredient is to ensure that the ratio information is made available within the company in a user-friendly and easily decodable format. In particular, it is vitally important that the allocation of indirect costs to the various product groups or channels is made in a fair and logical fashion. Too many companies allocate such costs in an arbitrary way, and this makes control procedures far less meaningful.

The last point can be illustrated by considering the simple case of a company which manufactures three product lines: 'Plax', 'Tablex' and 'Healex'. A simple profit and loss statement, as shown in Table 11.1, provides an overview of the firm's results but gives very little control information.

What would be much more useful from the point of view of controlling the operation is to have some concept of how the expenses were used up by the three product lines. Table 11.2 shows how the cost of sales might be allocated against functional activities. Each cost element must be apportioned to reflect the way resources are being used. It might be on the basis of floor space used by each product or by some other criterion of allocation, such as the amount of services consumed.

It is now necessary to relate these functional expenses to the product lines, as shown in Table 11.3.

Having established the average cost for each chosen functional unit, it now becomes possible to present the original product and loss statement that appeared in Table 11.1 in a way which provides a vastly improved prospect of monitoring profitability (see Table 11.4).

Once the time costs are allocated to the various product lines, it can be seen that Tablex makes something in excess of three-quarters of total profits. Plax accounts for the rest. Healex accounts for a loss of

Table 11.1 Simple profit and loss statement (£)

Sales		240,000
Cost of goods		156,000
Gross profit		84,000
Expenses (cost of sales)		
Salaries	37,200	
Rent	12,000	
Materials	14,000	
Total	63,200	63,200
Net profit		20,800

Table 11.2 Allocating expenses to functional areas (£)

	Total	Selling	Advertising	Delivery	Administration
Salaries	37,200	20,400	4,800	5,600	6,400
Rent	12,000	400	1,600	7,600	2,400
Materials	14,000	1,600	6,000	5,600	800
Total	63,200	22,400	12,400	18,800	9,600

Table 11.3 Allocating functional costs to products

	Selling (no. of calls in period)	Advertising (no of adverts)	Distribution (no. of deliveries)	Administration (no. of orders 'sets')
Products:				
Plax	250	40	70	50
Tablex	120	30	25	20
Healex	80	20	15	10
Total	450	90	110	80
Functional expenses	£22,400	£12,400	£18,800	£9,600
Average cost/ unit (approximate)	£50/call	£138/advert	£171/delivery	£120/order

Table 11.4 Profit and loss statement showing costs allocated per product (£)

	Plax	Tablex	Healex	Total
Sales	120,000	80,000	40,000	240,000
Cost of goods	78,000	46,000	32,000	156,000
Gross profit (A)	42,000	34,000	8,000	84,000
Expenses				
Selling (£50/call)	12,445	5,975	3,980	22,400
Advertising (£138/advert)	5,510	4,130	2,760	12,400
Distribution (£171/delivery)	11,963	4,273	2,564	18,800
Admin. (£120/order)	6,000	2,400	1,200	9,600
Total expenses (B)	35,918	16,778	10,504	63,200
Net profit/loss (A–B)	6,082	17,222	(2,504)	20,800

£2,504 for the period under consideration and is therefore a strong candidate for some corrective measure.

The exact nature of the action to be taken will depend upon the make-up of the organization. With regard to Healex it might be deemed reasonable either to increase sales or to reduce costs, or perhaps adopt a policy which would embrace both. It must be borne in mind that all products make a contribution towards covering the overheads of the business. Therefore an oversimplistic solution like 'dropping' Healex should not be contemplated without a much greater level of analysis.

The aim of this brief description of ratio analysis was to highlight the importance of understanding where the marketing costs are being incurred and how they should be monitored and controlled. Marketers who only spend money without controlling the payoffs cannot be described as effective. The cycle must always be completed through a rigorous and meaningful evaluation of results.

MARKETING CONTROL AUDIT

Score
0 1 2

1. **Does the company control its marketing activities?**

   (a) No. We believe that sales speak for themselves.   (*Score 0*)
   (b) We control marketing results spasmodically.   (*Score 1*)
   (c) Yes. We have developed control procedures which can be used systematically and regularly.   (*Score 2*)

2. **Which part of the marketing process does the company control (if any)?**

   (a) If we ever control anything it is sales.   (*Score 0*)
   (b) All those activities which are easily measurable.   (*Score 1*)
   (c) Every activity which involves us in costs or the allocation of resources.   (*Score 2*)

3. **To what extent does the company use its control procedures in improving the management of the marketing function?**

   (a) To the extent that it is being used at all it is used to reward or criticize members of the sales force.   (*Score 0*)

▶

(b) To help to assemble future plans. *(Score 1)*
(c) To take corrective measures, if necessary, during
the year, also provide an input for future
plans. *(Score 2)*

4. **Are marketing strategies measured and evaluated?**

(a) No. *(Score 0)*
(b) Yes, but in vague terms. *(Score 1)*
(c) Strategies are constantly under review. The aim, at
all times, is to measure the attainment of critical
success factors defined in the plans. *(Score 2)*

5. **Does the company attempt to monitor the
effectiveness of the marketing mix?**

(a) No. We believe that the marketing mix is all right
in theory only *(Score 0)*
(b) Yes, but not in a systematic way. *(Score 1)*
(c) Yes. We monitor the behaviour of the mix over the
life-cycle of the product in a systematic way. Product
managers understand the concept and use
it. *(Score 2)*

6. **Does the company control the effectiveness of its
product portfolio?**

(a) No. We know when a product is in
trouble. *(Score 0)*
(b) We attempt to use the various matrices stemming
from the Boston matrix from time to time, but find
them only partially useful. *(Score 1)*
(c) We invest a lot of effort in understanding our
product mix with a view to identifying priorities for
attention and product development, prior to problems
arising. *(Score 2)*

7. **Does the company attempt to measure its
competitiveness *vis-à-vis* other rivals?**

(a) We know all about our competitors' pricing
policy. *(Score 0)*
(b) We maintain a dossier about each one of our
competitors. *(Score 1)*
(c) We monitor the competitive scene on a regular
basis. This includes all the forces which constitute

competitive pressures, including new entrants, the
power of suppliers, the power of buyers and
substitutes.   (*Score 2*)

8.   **Does the company control the level of efficiency of its
marketing tools, other than selling?**

(a) No. Controlling the sales effort is complicated
enough.   (*Score 0*)
(b) Yes. We attempt from time to time to gauge the
efficiency of our distribution and
advertising.   (*Score 1*)
(c) Wherever money is spent we design control
procedures from the very outset. The rule in our
company is that no resources can be spent without
knowing how to measure ultimate
results.   (*Score 2*)

9.   **Does the accounts department get involved in
marketing control?**

(a) Certainly not. It is none of their
business.   (*Score 0*)
(b) Sometimes. Only if the marketing department
invites them to do so.   (*Score 1*)
(c) The accounts department and marketing work as a
team. They are both interested in controlling the
efficiency of costs associated with marketing
activities.   (*Score 2*)

10.   **Who participates in the process of developing control
procedures?**

(a) To the extent that we have such procedures they
are instigated by the sales manager.   (*Score 0*)
(b) By the marketing director and the top
team.   (*Score 1*)
(c) We believe in the value of control and therefore
design such systems with the broadest participation.
In fact the control of expenditure in our company is
considered as part of our 'shared
values'.   (*Score 2*)

The maximum score possible is 20. Very few companies could achieve such a score. Lower scores can be interpreted as follows:

15–20	**Excellent**
10–14	**Good to very good.**
5–9	**Fair**
0–4	**Poor**

12

Organizing for marketing

Most established companies would admit that if they could start life afresh they would not organize themselves in the way they are currently structured. It is rather like the rambler who, having lost his way, stopped a passer-by for direction and got the succinct reply: 'If I wanted to walk to Swiftwick, sir, I wouldn't be starting from here!'

Organizations evolve over time. The idea of being able to start from scratch and design the 'perfect' new structure may be appealing, but it is hardly practical. An organizational infrastructure is in place and its total replacement may cause considerable disruption to the flow of goods from the marketing company to its customers. Moreover, one must remember that in a dynamic world what looks like a perfect organization today may prove unsustainable within a short time. Marketing organizations must be capable of responding to environmental changes. In fact it is true to say that a company which is able to adapt its structure in response to market expediencies may enjoy a significant advantage.

The development of organizations

A brief review of where it all starts may provide a useful framework.

The pioneering phase

Most organizations start life when an entrepreneur has an idea which he or she wants to exploit and to make money. The entrepreneur's commitment and enthusiasm are such that somehow the necessary capital is raised to get started. At this stage little or no thought is given to organizational matters. The owner-manager is the centre of all company activities and decisions. To the extent that an organization exists, it looks like a wheel or a spider's web – the 'boss' is at the centre and the various operational functions are located at the ends of the spokes of the wheel. Little happens without the consent of the boss. In reality, the organization is an extension of its founder's mind and power.

Typically, such organizations are informal, extremely flexible and dynamic. Clearly, they do not all succeed. However, those that do benefit from access to considerable marketing knowledge, and provided the initial concept was sound they can be very profitable. The boss can come close to the customers (for in many such situations he or she is in fact the only salesperson) and knows their needs intimately. Probably the same person doubles up as the head of production and can move from function to function with the greatest of ease. Moreover, customer contact is highly personalized and the company often behaves in a customer-focused way. What customers want, within reason, they get.

Such organizations can function well and grow steadily. Nonetheless growth is the inevitable seed of potential crisis. The owner-manager becomes overextended. By spreading one's personal time and attention too thinly over many functions and activities, what was an organizational strength can easily become a major weakness. This is the point at which pioneering enterprises are liable not to survive the first major crisis. This is the occasion when the owner-manager has to learn to manage change and develop the skills of delegation. The successful promulgation of such a change is an essential stepping-stone towards company renewal.

The scientific management phase

A proper management structure is now needed. Tasks must be defined and responsibilities allocated. The rules of what is commonly called *scientific management* must be applied. This in turn means that the owner-manager must abdicate from many of the operational tasks which he or she had enjoyed running, and which had helped to create and maintain a special relationship with customers. This often leads to some frustration among loyal customers, who had been accustomed to dealing direct with the boss at all times. Departments grow and sometimes 'empires' are built. Communication among departments gradually deteriorates and this can have a serious effect on customer satisfaction. Another crisis is in the making.

Integrated organization

Two possible routes can be taken to overcome the crisis:

- Breaking the company into smaller, more manageable units, thereby recapturing the benefits of the earlier pioneering phase.
- Striving to find a structure which can combine the flexibility, creativity and dynamism of the pioneering phase with the intelligent use of the professionalism which characterized the productive phase of scientific management.

The latter option envisages a better understanding of human motivation and behaviour. Management development plans must be conceived, plans must cease to be meaningless sets of numbers, but must include well-considered narratives explaining the rationale for missions and strategies. The business exists to satisfy the customers, and therefore all departments and all functions must operate in an integrated fashion towards that end. The boss can now be compared to the cox of a rowing boat, the captain of a football team or the conductor of an orchestra. Integrated teamwork is the foundation upon which effective teams are now built.

Figure 12.1 summarizes the phases of organizational development described above, including the points of crisis that so many companies have to face. Obviously, marketing has a pivotal role to play in such an evolution.

Throughout the organizational evolution firms have to recognize that effectiveness depends on two major factors: (a) responsiveness to customers and (b) concern for organization and control. A firm that succeeds in being excellent in both areas is clearly a winner. However, in reality the introduction of scientific management often tends to dilute the firm's ability to respond to customers and their needs. A bureaucratic phase is often the result of such an evolution. It is important that management takes steps to shorten this period and also attempts to neutralize its dangers.

Figure 12.2 describes the four quadrants in which companies may find themselves during the organizational evolution period. The ideal quadrant to be in is no. 2. As stated earlier, few companies can move directly from quadrant 1 to quadrant 2. One thing is crystal clear: firms falling in quadrant 3 – namely, those that are neither

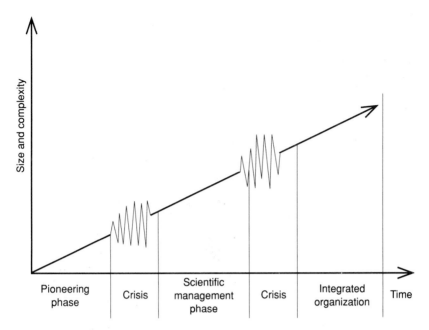

Figure 12.1 Phases of organizational development

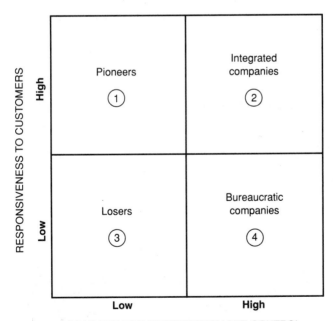

Figure 12.2 The evolution of organizations

responsive to customers nor concerned with the proper functioning of the organization, supported by control procedures – have very little future. They are potential losers. The shift from quadrant 4 to quadrant 2 is often characterized by the introduction of 'customer care' programmes and 'citizen/customer charters'. The aim is to reinstate the firm's responsiveness to customers and their needs.

The subactivities of an effective marketing organization

Marketing encompasses a myriad of subactivities. Not every company has to pursue all these activities. Moreover, the importance of the various activities to the success of the overall marketing effort varies from firm to firm. The structure must reflect these nuances. In some companies, 'design' is a vital component of the mix and therefore design management should be given a place at or near the 'top table'.

In a truly marketing-orientated company one must go back to basics and place the customer under a microscope with a view to finding out what it is he or she really wants and expects (see Figure 12.3).

Figure 12.3 Evaluating the attributes that customers are looking for

As we have seen earlier, rational buyers do not part with their money until they are satisfied that a number of elements pertaining to the company's offering are in place. The ability to identify the relative importance of these elements in the eyes of the customer is a most valuable preamble to the organizational process. A few of these elements represent functions with which the customer will come into contact. Others are hidden from the customer's direct gaze, but their output affects the customer and therefore must be organized in the most effective way.

A simple prioritization list for analysis is provided in Figure 12.4. The list is probably not a comprehensive one: marketers in different industries may think of other tasks to be added to the list. Figure 12.4 simply attempts to illustrate how the importance of marketing tasks can be compared in a judgmental manner and priorities established. Items scoring high figures should receive greater attention during the organization design process than those gaining low scores. A few of the latter tasks can probably be ignored in the short term and amalgamated with a few others under the heading of 'marketing services' or similar.

Before attempting to structure a marketing organization it is worth recalling that the management process consists of four distinct, yet interrelated and continuous steps:

1. Input gathering.
2. Objectives setting supported by strategies.
3. Operations.
4. Control and measurement.

At the control/measurement stage one gains fresh 'input' for the next cycle. Input can be updated and adjusted, and the cycle recommences. The process is cybernetic and dynamic. Organization development and training must be at the heart of the cycle, since they are a vital part of all the activities falling under these four headings. It is helpful to understand the organic relationship and interconnectedness of the four tranches of the marketing cycle before one undertakes the task of placing personnel and resources into an organizational framework.

Figure 12.5 provides a conceptual description of such a framework. All one needs to do now is to operationalize it by placing flesh on this schematic skeleton. It is important always to bear in mind that the organization chart which finally emerges is no more than a symbolic analogue of the firm's structure. Like a map of the London

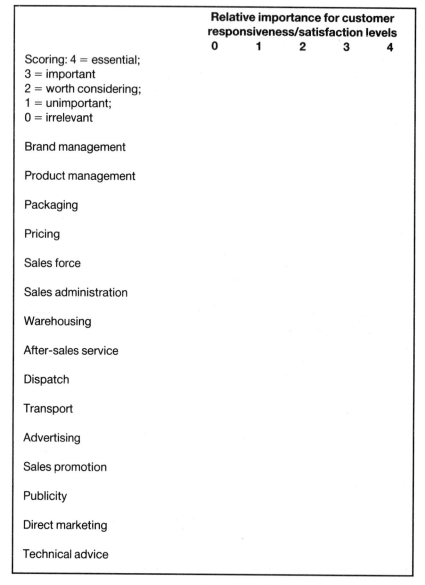

Figure 12.4 Priorities for organizational development

Underground a chart only attempts to portray reality. It does not show where the levers of power are vested, nor the true political centres of gravity. It is an aid to finding one's way among diverse responsibilities, accountabilities and personalities.

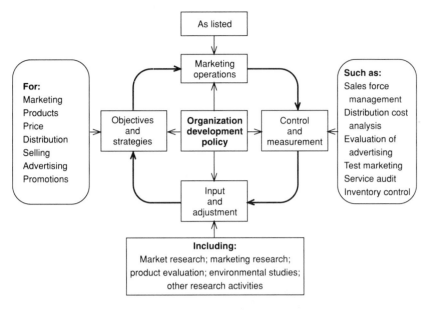

Figure 12.5 Total subactivities of the marketing organization

---

Types of marketing organization

During the pioneering phase companies are unlikely to have formal organizations. Nonetheless if the management is effective and reflects upon what needs to be achieved, it is likely to fulfil the necessary tasks envisaged by the marketing effort. One person may be undertaking all the subactivities, but in aggregate a cohesive job can be done.

During subsequent phases of the corporate life-cycle a number of alternative structures usually emerge. They fall into fairly distinct patterns.

Marketing organization based on functions

This kind of structure is often found in companies with a limited product range and where the market coverage needed is not geographically widespread. In its simplest form the structure looks like the one described in Figure 12.6.

The input-gathering task is provided by the market research department. Objective setting and strategy are masterminded by the

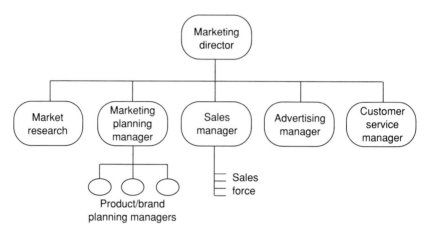

Figure 12.6 Marketing organization based on functions

marketing planning manager under the direct supervision of the marketing director and as an extension of his or her role. All the other functions shown are 'operational'. The marketing director will doubtless be concerned with control and measurement, either alone or with the help of one of the individuals below, probably the planning person.

Problems may arise if the product range expands or if the distribution becomes complex and the products need to be sold through different types of outlet. When this happens it puts tremendous pressure on the sales force. They find it difficult to cope with product knowledge on the one hand, and the intricacies of a diverse system of distribution on the other. Selling to cash-and-carry outlets is very different from the normal retail trade and certainly from industrial customers. Rare is the person who can cope with all three situations.

Marketing organization based on product groupings

The main aim of such an approach is to satisfy the special requirements of the products and their supporting technologies. Products are diverse and complex, and represent the key to the firm's competitive advantage. Product knowledge underlies the development of an effective relationship with customers.

The dedication of resources to product groupings can bring a number of benefits due to specialization and focus. The downside is that if left alone the various product groups may develop a separate and independent existence, and at that point it may become more difficult to exploit the synergy among the groups, either through the development of a common corporate identity and communication or through innovation. Moreover, activities like market research or advertising may tend to be duplicated with an inevitable extra cost. Figure 12.7 describes a typical structure for this kind of organization.

The structure for product group B in the diagram is replicated for the other product groups. Sometimes a senior manager, such as a corporate advertising manager, is appointed in order to supervise and coordinate the activities of the advertising managers in the various product groups. At this point the normal problems associated with the existence of 'line' and 'staff' roles at corporate and unit levels rear their head.

Unlike the earlier functional structure, whoever is responsible here for objectives setting and planning is likely to be the person responsible for controlling the process and monitoring the results.

Marketing organization based on market/ customer groupings

Here markets, such as user industries, or customer groups, such as schools, hotels and hospitals, provide the rationale for the marketing organization.

In Figure 12.8 the input gathering and operational functions are clustered around specific markets or customer groupings. The

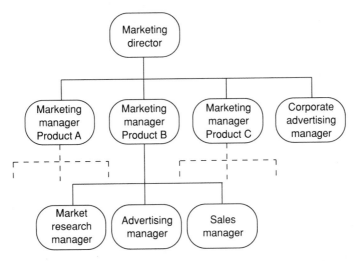

Figure 12.7 Marketing organization based on product groupings

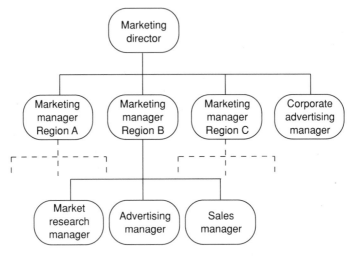

Figure 12.8 Marketing organization based on market/customer groupings

organization is designed to exploit specialization and knowledge of well-defined segments. The problem occurs when there are too many markets or customer groups to be serviced. One danger is that too many sales forces have to be formed. The other danger is that an organization that concentrates upon specific markets (e.g. cars, oil and marine) is often blinkered against detecting new opportunities in other markets (e.g. aerospace).

Marketing organization based on geographical regions

Companies that need to market their products in wide geographical areas would find the structure shown in Figure 12.9 useful. It is particularly apposite in cases where the product range is limited or homogeneous, and where many regions need to be covered with some speed. Such a structure is relevant to a company selling its products in many countries. Each country becomes self-contained and may develop its own functional infrastructure. On the other hand, the company runs the risk that when each region/country attempts to become self-sufficient, the synergy among the regions gets diluted and the opportunity of achieving economies of scale is missed.

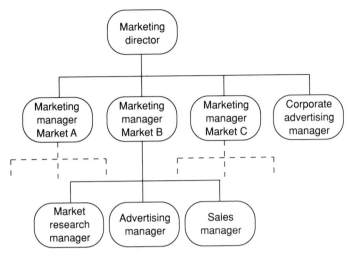

Figure 12.9 Marketing organization based on geography/regions

Marketing organizations based on channels of distribution

In certain circumstances the structure shown in Figure 12.10 can be a useful way of organizing the marketing function. It is particularly appropriate in the case of a company that has a range of products that can be sold both in the retail trade and to industrial users. Thus, for example, a manufacturer of building products may sell direct to large construction companies; to small builders through builder-merchants; and to the consumer through DIY outlets. Clearly, each one of these channels will need to be organized differently.

As with all the preceding organizational types, there might be corporate advertising and/or market research positions at the centre, with some functional counterparts at the divisions. The relationships between the people at the centre and those at the operating divisions must be clarified and the limits to their respective authority clearly understood. Otherwise communication problems may easily arise.

The type of organization described in Figure 12.10 can function well only when the channels are well defined and distinctly different. The major weakness is that it can limit the firm's horizons to existing channels and prevent the marketing organization from exploring innovative approaches to distribution.

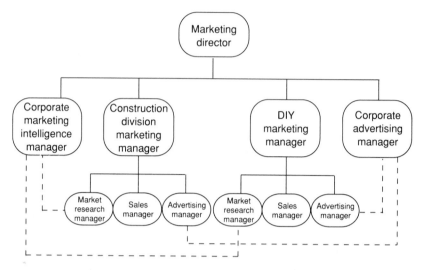

Figure 12.10 Marketing organization based on channels

Centralization versus decentralization

The perennial problem is how to strike a balance between marketing tasks which are performed at the centre and those that could best be undertaken at the operating divisions or branches. Companies operating with a number of separate production facilities, manufacturing a range of disparate products, must grapple with this kind of dilemma. A decision must be taken, at a fairly early date, as to which subactivities must be managed at head office and which should be pursued in the 'outposts'. Many variations can be conceived and there is no hard-and-fast rule as to which solution is the best for all situations. A number of approaches can be considered.

Figure 12.11 describes a number of permutations. In Figure 12.11(a) the head office takes responsibility for input gathering, setting objectives and strategies, and monitoring and controlling performance in the various units. The units are left to manage the operational functions of the mix within a set of objectives provided by head office.

Figure 12.11(b) illustrates a smaller head office role. Operating units are responsible for both input and operations. Head office looks after objectives setting and monitoring/control.

Figure 12.11(c) shows head office playing only a monitoring and controlling role. All other activities are managed by the units.

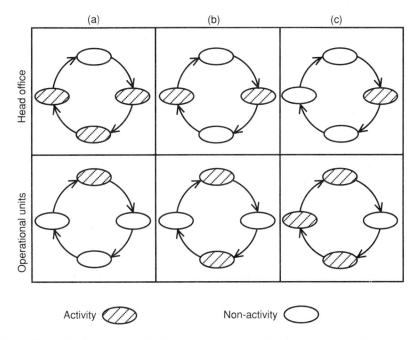

Note: All activities shown relate to Figure 12.5: the box at the bottom of each diagram
represents 'input', moving to 'objectives', 'operations' and 'control/measurement'.

Figure 12.11 Dividing functional tasks among head office and operating units

The point to remember is that, with decentralization, somewhere along the line duplication of effort takes place. Let us take advertising as an example. Two options exist: (a) central personnel at head office can service all the outlying units; or (b) each unit can develop its own advertising competence and pesonnel, with head office acting in a purely advisory capacity. In overall cost the latter solution may prove much more expensive. On the other hand, the quality of service and speed of reaction to events can be much superior. There is no simple answer to this conundrum. Each company must reflect upon the matter, consider the advantages and disadvantages, and conduct a cost–benefit analysis before choosing a structure.

Marketing organizations at the integrated phase of development

The various marketing organizations described above represent a classical range of structures that companies have adopted over the years with mixed success. No structure is ever perfect for all situations. A structure is only as effective as its ability to meet results and objectives. At the pioneering phase companies can achieve excellence without formal organizations.

Sooner or later one finds that hybrid structures emerge based on a mixture of one or more of the models described. It is worth remembering that creativity can also play an important role in organization design. Marketing people are supposed to be creative, yet not many examples of highly imaginative structures can be found in the case study literature.

One of the few creative ideas that have emerged in the field of organization development is the so-called *matrix organization*. It was received with excitement at first, but subsequently rejected by many companies for the simple reason that managers found the concept too complex and ridden with communication problems. However, it is probably worth considering when a firm has reached its integrated marketing phase.

The aim is to dovetail the needs of both products and markets in a way which is flexible and dynamic. This double-pronged approach, illustrated in Figure 12.12, produces a number of functional inter-relationships (in this example, as many as nine). Where these 'junctions' occur, the maximum knowledge and experience of both strands – products and markets – can be brought to bear. Between them they ought to be able to optimize the company's impact on every market situation and to identify opportunities.

In conventional chart form the matrix organization would look like the one shown in Figure 12.13.

While the approach has been seen by many company strategists as an answer to a number of organizational problems, experience has proved that it can work well only in mature and enlightened companies. It is of value to companies that are normally good at communication and where politics does not play a significant role in the firm's climate. Moreover, if one decides to experiment with the matrix notion, it must be crystal clear who is responsible for results. If product management is thus responsible, market management assumes a 'staff' role and vice versa. One cannot ascribe the responsibility for results to the two axes at the same time.

The matrix organization is a concept that offers exciting possibilities but should not be adopted by the faint-hearted, or by those who are not capable of dealing with flexible and somewhat vague structures.

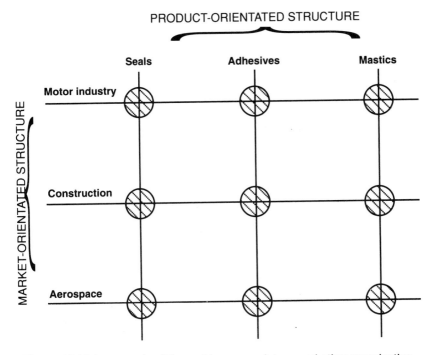

Figure 12.12 An example of the matrix approach to a marketing organization (a polymer company)

Main considerations

The quality of organizations resides not in the neatness of the charts but in the effectiveness of personal performance and the clarity of purpose. Before selecting a structure for development a number of basic principles ought to be borne in mind:

- Lines of authority and responsibility must be clear and unambiguous.
- The structure must be conducive to an efficient, speedy and accurate communication.
- Coordination of subactivities must be attainable without too much effort.
- The chosen approach must pay attention and cater for the company's priority areas, the marketing 'centres of gravity'.

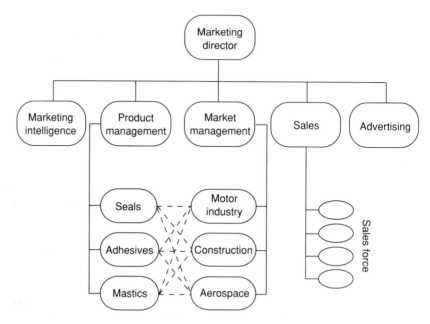

Figure 12.13 Matrix-style organization structure

- Those who have to make the marketing organization work must feel empathetic towards its purpose and aims. No organization can be effective if the people working in it dislike it.

Of all these points, perhaps the last is the most significant. It is the human side of an enterprise which is the company's ultimate strength and source of creativity. Without the whole-hearted commitment of its staff any marketing organization, regardless of its conceptual subtlety, is doomed to failure.

MARKETING ORGANIZATION AUDIT

Score
0 1 2

1. **How has the firm's marketing organization evolved?**

   (a) It has evolved over time with little
   thought. *(Score 0)*
   (b) It has developed in response to identified
   weaknesses. *(Score 1)*
   (c) It has been designed in an integrated fashion and
   always in response to the needs prescribed by the
   marketing plans. *(Score 2)*

2. **Is the marketing organization ever changed?**

   (a) No. We believe that changes are
   disruptive. *(Score 0)*
   (b) Yes. We feel that a change is as good as a
   rest. *(Score 1)*
   (c) We regard an organization as a dynamic tool for
   achieving objectives. As the objectives change we
   review the organization. *(Score 2)*

3. **When developing an organization are the needs of
   communication considered?**

   (a) We feel that an effective marketing organization
   will take care of communication. *(Score 0)*
   (b) We emphasize the importance of interfunctional
   communication. *(Score 1)*
   (c) We design an organizational system which can
   cope with and support the benefits of an effective
   communication downwards, upwards and
   sideways. *(Score 2)*

4. **Does the firm produce a formal chart for the
   marketing organization?**

   (a) No. People know what they have to do and who
   they are responsible to. *(Score 0)*
   (b) Yes. We have a very elegant and clearly produced
   chart. *(Score 1)*
   (c) Yes. Our organizational charts are clear and
   communicated widely. All jobs have clear descriptions
   and they are updated when circumstances
   demand. *(Score 2)*

5. **Are lines of authority clear?**

(a) No. We believe that vagueness can be a valuable element in an effective organization.   *(Score 0)*
(b) Yes. This is why we have an organizational chart. It says it all.   *(Score 1)*
(c) Yes. People in the marketing organization know full well (i) who they are responsible to, and (ii) for what. In addition to the chart each person has a clear job description that sets it all out.   *(Score 2)*

6. **Is the organization capable of exploiting marketing 'synergy' among the various strategic units?**

(a) No. Profit centres are totally distinct.   *(Score 0)*
(b) The benefits of synergy are fully understood, but little is done to exploit them.   *(Score 1)*
(c) A system exists for identifying areas in which the joint strength can be capitalized upon and ideas cross-fertilized.   *(Score 2)*

7. **Are members of the marketing team consulted about changes which will affect the organization?**

(a) No. Changes are announced when the need arises.   *(Score 0)*
(b) Consultation takes place after the event in order to remove problems and/or alleviate anxieties.   *(Score 1)*
(c) Full consultation takes place to ensure that commitment to the new structure is gained.   *(Score 2)*

8. **In selecting an organizational structure are the needs/ expectations of customers considered?**

(a) No. It is purely an internal matter.   *(Score 0)*
(b) We tell our customers about our new structure.   *(Score 1)*
(c) Our aim is always to ensure that the structure is capable of being empathetic with our customers and their expectations.   *(Score 2)*

▶

9. **Does the marketing organization encompass a recognition of marketing 'centres of gravity'?**

    (a) No. We cannot see the need for such a
    step.   *(Score 0)*
    (b) Yes. This is the main task of the marketing
    director/manager.   *(Score 1)*
    (c) Yes. The plan seeks to identify the 'stars' of the
    future and the organization reflects it
    fully.   *(Score 2)*

10. **Are the various subactivities of the marketing effort integrated?**

    (a) No. We cannot see the need for such a
    step.   *(Score 0)*
    (b) Yes. This is the main task of the marketing
    director/manager.   *(Score 1)*
    (c) Yes. We consider all the subactivities of the
    marketing function as members of one team. We feel
    that an integrated team is stronger than its component
    parts.   *(Score 2)*

The maximum score possible is 20. Very few companies could achieve such a score. Lower scores can be interpreted as follows:

15–20	**Excellent**
10–14	**Good to very good.**
5–9	**Fair**
0–4	**Poor**

13

Marketing integration

The word 'integration' has been mentioned many times in previous chapters and in the various audit questionnaires. It is one of the areas which are often neglected by marketers and which can cause untold problems for the organization and its marketing effort. Marketers must never forget that they are members of a diverse team which possesses a variety of skills and resources as well as organizational constraints. Marketing does not live alone and everything that the function undertakes must be dovetailed with these resources and limitations to fit into a cohesive blueprint for action.

The Shorter Oxford Dictionary defines the word 'integration' as 'the making up of a whole by adding together or combining the separate parts or elements'. On the face of it, this sounds like a very simple concept which does not justify a whole chapter. Yet in the business world it represents one of the major challenges that can make the difference between effectiveness and suboptimal performance. The ability to achieve an integrative process among the many forces that make an organization function can provide the firm with the cutting edge that should enable it to steer its plans and operations from policy determination to successful implementation.

Oddly enough, it appears that modern managers are less effective at the integration game than managers from 50 years ago. A brief moment of reflection should explain the reasons for such a phenomenon, and perhaps highlight a few useful lessons that can be learnt.

Modern technology and managerial methods have developed at such a rate that many managers find themselves operating in highly specialized functions. This increasing specialization has meant that in many areas barriers have sprung up among functions to the detriment of overall corporate effectiveness. It is virtually impossible for one manager, however brilliant and well informed, to master the complex and multidisciplinary knowledge that is available in the modern organization. Communication barriers develop not through malice or the desire for self-aggrandizement, but simply through a gap in knowledge or fear of the mysterious and the complex. Thus, production people often tend to isolate themselves from the machinations of the marketing department simply to avoid exposing themselves to ridicule. By the same token the finance manager looks askance at the costly and often inexplicable goings-on in the R & D department. Specialization has created a confidence gap among the various organs of the enterprise, and this in turn has become the cause of hidden conflicts and poor integration.

Our industrial ancestors had fewer problems in this area. Managing a business was a less complex process: the demarcation between functions was blurred. Present-day techniques and sophistication did not exist, with the result that the manager of that era was capable of acquiring full knowledge of every nook and cranny of the firm and its environment and facilities. With a comprehensive understanding of the enterprise such a manager was in full charge of all the variables and was able to integrate them into a cohesive and well-structured whole.

It is hoped that many non-marketing personnel will read this book. It is important to explain that this chapter is not seeking to prove that marketing is an elitist function which initiates and overrides the firm's overall policy and direction. Nonetheless readers, irrespective of their functional affiliation, should be reminded that the firm's main role is to undertake the supply of goods and services which are needed or desired by the customer, and in the process of so doing to meet the firm's objectives. This is the essence of the 'marketing concept'.

Any manager who is prepared to accept this fundamental truth must recognize that marketing is the locomotive that pulls all the carriages of the organization towards a destination. Viewed in this light, marketing has a coordinating and integrating role which ensures that all other functions perform their respective tasks in a homogeneous way. This part of the marketing task is often neglected or not fully appreciated, especially by non-marketing personnel. If integration is to be attained, everybody must participate in the process.

The meaning and scope of integration

What is meant by 'integration'? Integration with what? The whole subject will be viewed here from the vantage point of the marketing director, although it can be viewed from the perspective of each functional head in turn.

To the marketing director the word 'integration' should convey three distinct, albeit interrelated, tasks:

- The integration of marketing planning with the overall strategic planning of the firm. This we can call the *macro-integration* process.
- The integration of all the subactivities of the marketing department.
- The various ingredients of the marketing mix.

Macro-integration

In Chapter 10 we explored the importance of adhering to a planning hierarchy which commences with a mission and ends with programmes and budgets. The value of the planning cycle is to strike a logical and cohesive relationship among all the 'bricks' that make up a corporate plan. During the planning process contradictions must be ventilated and eliminated. This is probably one of the most difficult tasks, due to the fact that most organizations do not have a high-level 'focal point' charged with the task of promulgating an effective integration of the subplans. Integration seldom happens by itself – it calls for considerable pressure and persuasion from key people at the top. Without such an initiative from the strategic level of the firm, the chances of having the various elements of the corporate plan integrated into a cohesive whole are fairly slender.

When talking about the need to integrate the various 'bricks' of the planning edifice, one must remember that this entails two interrelated tasks:

- The integration of the 'top-down' and/or 'bottom-up' plans.
- The integration of the horizontal functional plans.

Figure 13.1 describes these two aspects in a diagrammatic form. Integration is achieved when both the vertical and horizontal planning modules hang together in one logical and well-structured

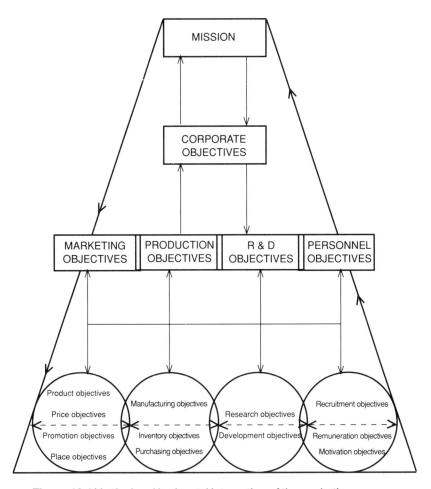

Figure 13.1 Vertical and horizontal integration of the marketing process

whole. When one is unable to pick up contradictions, either vertically or horizontally, the plans have proved their true worth.

Integrating the vertical plans

Integration can be said to have been achieved when all the activities
of the firm, from mission to consumer satisfaction, can be traced step
by step without ever hitting a logical cul-de-sac. Thus, if one looks at
'place' objectives one should be able to trace them to marketing
objectives, trace these to corporate objectives and these, in turn, to
the firm's mission.

Whether one starts from the top and works downwards or vice versa, it should not be possible to locate a flaw in this iterative logic. If the corporate plan prescribes a market share objective (for reasons which are compatible with the marketing audit which has been undertaken, and, it is hoped, after verifying the feasibility of attaining such an objective), the marketing plan must reflect such an objective. It would be absurd for the marketing department to feel that what is stated in the corporate plan does not bind it in its own plans. Furthermore, if the route to increased market share is the cost advantage route, this must be reflected in the pricing policy plan.

Integrating the horizontal plans

Equally important is the need to integrate the various plans horizontally. Marketing plans must be fully congruent with those of other functions.

As an example, let us imagine that one of the aims of the marketing effort is to increase market share for a specific product, through a complete revamp of the sales force. Obviously, the personnel function must reflect this in its personnel objectives as well as in its recruitment and training subplans. It is quite remarkable how often such an obvious concept is lacking in a firm's process of integrating the plans.

Similarly, if the marketing plans talk about newer and better products, the rules of horizontal integration would be met if the R & D department picked up the message and incorporated the appropriate objective in its own plans. Otherwise one of the major benefits of preparing plans would be completely nullified.

Plans are well integrated when the person who studies them can follow the way functional plans and subplans hang together both vertically and horizontally. This is one of the most significant tasks for whoever is in charge of preparing the corporate plans.

Integration of the subactivities of the marketing department

An analogy can be drawn between the way a company is run and an orchestra. The plans represent the music score. The chief executive officer is the conductor. The head of marketing, by virtue of his or her coordinative role, is the first violin, namely the leader of the orchestra. The competence of the first violin is of paramount importance for a successful orchestra. This does not mean that one can tolerate mediocrity among the other instruments, but if the leadership is poor the orchestra is unlikely to excel. An effective orchestra adheres to the score and responds to the conductor's cues regarding tempo and dynamics. Each instrument or group of instruments comes in at the appropriate moment and the orchestra produces the sound which was envisaged by the composer and is interpreted by the conductor. Mistakes do occur, but as long as the instruments play together and with the right spirit and motivation the results should be pleasing.

As we saw in Chapters 10 and 12, marketing consists of a number of subactivities that fall into four interrelated categories: input gathering, objective setting, operations and control.

Figure 13.2 summarizes once more the interrelationship among these areas of activity. They have been described fairly fully in previous chapters. The important point to highlight in the context of marketing integration is their interdependence. If any one of these activities is out of step with the others, the whole ceases to be a cohesive and integrated assemblage. Thus if the input gathered is unrelated to the planning process, the objectives set may be based on wrong premises and assumptions. In turn the operational activities are likely to be conducted without clear objectives and direction. Inevitably, there will be little point in measuring results.

Integration is achieved in this area when the marketing subactivities are so dovetailed as to perform their respective tasks in ways which support each other – and also the marketing effort as a whole. All this has to happen with the underlying aim of attaining the firm's overall objectives. On paper this is easy enough; in practice it calls for leadership and a determined and well-considered allocation of tasks, supported by clear task descriptions. A well-integrated team, representing the four subgroupings described, can impart to the marketing organization a most powerful competitive edge.

A simple case history should help to highlight the kinds of problem that can arise when poor integration takes place.

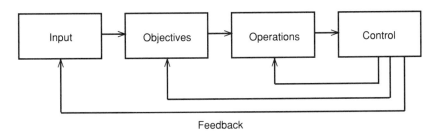

Feedback

Figure 13.2 The interrelationship among the various subfunctions of marketing

---

CASE STUDY
Aurora Pharmaceuticals

The company markets a combination of 'ethical drugs' and over-the-counter products. It has a simple functional structure.

A very active market research department is responsible for collecting market information and undertaking marketing studies. This department initiates its own surveys and seldom solicits guidance from the departments it seeks to serve. Many of these research projects are interesting and cover areas which hitherto nobody seems to have researched. However, in many instances these projects are of limited use to the various 'brand' departments. This represents the first integration weakness.

Planning is carried out by a series of 'brand managers'. They seldom prescribe specific research needs to the market research department. The detailed plans are submitted to the marketing director, but they are seldom discussed among the brand managers themselves or with the sales manager.

The sales manager receives little guidance in the selling priorities to be given to each product. The result is that he directs his sales force to apply equal effort to all products. This is unfortunate insofar as his strategy fails to take notice of the realities of the portfolio. The 'stars' receive the same amount of selling effort as the 'dogs'.

The promotion people are given budgets for each brand, but they have no idea what communication objectives are required for each brand. The campaigns are creative, but because of the absence of clear advertising objectives, their effectiveness is not being measured.

Potentially the team is capable of performing well. They know their instruments; they even know the score. However, the lack of integration from the top makes them perform at a suboptimal level.

The cure is simple. All that is needed is clear 'conducting' and direction from above with a well-defined allocation of tasks supported by job descriptions. Internal communication has to be improved through briefing sessions and dialogue. The message must be loud and clear: the team must work as a team and not as a bunch of single operators.

Integration among the various ingredients of the marketing mix

Enough has been said throughout this book to stress the importance of having a well-integrated marketing mix. Once again it is a very simple notion to understand. It is more difficult to implement. It is all very well choosing the right ingredients, but if they are not properly integrated the whole effort is futile. Figure 13.3 illustrates the point.

As was emphasized before, the mix represents a number of important ingredients which require money and effort aimed at satisfying customers' needs. These ingredients must be designed to be in state of total harmony with the marketplace as well as among themselves. Any single ingredient of the mix which is out of empathy with the rest can upset the whole assemblage. The product, price and place may all be perfect in relation to the target audience. Yet the whole effort may prove to be ineffective owing to a poor promotional strategy. The latter may simply fail to communicate the right messages to the right audiences. This is obviously a failure in the integration of the mix.

Mix integration problems may result from a myriad of causes. For example:

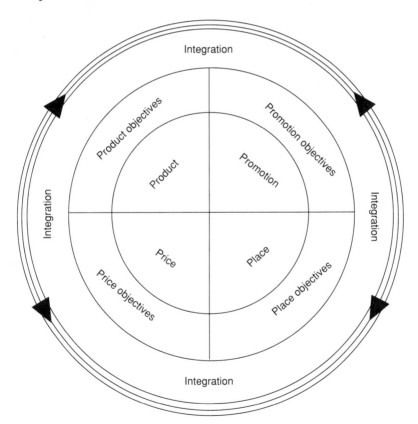

Figure 13.3 Integration of marketing mix ingredients

- **Price does not reflect the image ascribed to the product itself:**
  Thus, if the product is meant to convey luxury and quality
  features and the price is too low, an integration problem is sure to
  follow. For many years Jaguar sold its cars at prices which were
  totally inconsistent with the image that they purported to convey.

- **Promotional mix is inconsistent with the product and its price:** If
  British Airways were daft enough to advertise its Concorde
  service in newspapers read by C1, C2, D and E socioeconomic
  groupings, they should not be surprised if the results proved
  disastrous.

- **Distribution strategy is incompatible with the product:** This is
  almost a blinding glimpse of the obvious. Nevertheless quite
  often integration problems arise from a mismatch between
  product image and its concomitant price and the channel of
  distribution selected.

- **Promotion and place are poorly integrated:** An advertising campaign which conveys a 'downmarket' feel may make it very
  difficult to push a product through the top-end luxury stores for
  the simple reason that confusion in the eyes of the customers, as
  well as the store management, is the result of poor integration.

Many other examples of lack of integration and the resultant problems from the mix could be listed.

The overall message is fairly simple: the essence of successful
marketing demands that the various relationships that exist
upwards/downwards and internally in the marketing organization
are carefully thought out, and that a full attempt at integration is
planned and executed. The rewards can be very significant both for
the company and for its customers.

MARKETING INTEGRATION AUDIT

Score
0 1 2

1. **Is the company aware of the need to pay attention to the subject of marketing integration?**

   (a) No.   *(Score 0)*
   (b) Yes. We understand it in theory, but do not devote much time to its practical
   implications.   *(Score 1)*
   (c) Yes. It is an important part of the firm's philosophy and shared values.   *(Score 2)*

2. **When is the subject of integration discussed and reflected upon?**

   (a) Never.   *(Score 0)*
   (b) Once a year during the planning
   cycle.   *(Score 1)*
   (c) This is an issue which is being looked at and discussed throughout the year. Everybody is constantly reminded of the need to attain maximum integration in all directions and at all
   times.   *(Score 2)*

3. **Are the marketing plans integrated with the firm's corporate and strategic plans?**

   (a) The point is never raised.   *(Score 0)*
   (b) An attempt is made from time to time to ensure that marketing plans and corporate plans hang
   together.   *(Score 1)*
   (c) The whole process of preparing corporate plans and marketing plans is carried out in an integrated fashion. The concept is well understood and adhered
   to.   *(Score 2)*

4. **Does the company endeavour to integrate plans for marketing with other functions?**

   (a) No. The question does not arise.   *(Score 0)*
   (b) Functional heads are there when plans are
   presented.   *(Score 1)*
   (c) The question of interfunctional integration is of paramount importance. One person is charged with

▶

the task of ensuring that integration problems are fully
ventilated.   *(Score 2)*

5. **Are steps taken to ensure that the subactivities of
    marketing are fully integrated?**

    (a) No.   *(Score 0)*
    (b) Sometimes, but not in a systematic
    manner.   *(Score 1)*
    (c) Yes. The marketing director/manager considers
    this issue as an important part of his/her job. The
    subject receives constant attention.   *(Score 2)*

6. **Are marketing mix ingredients looked at with a view
    to attaining their full integration?**

    (a) The need does not arise.   *(Score 0)*
    (b) The subject of integration is considered when
    problems are brought to our notice.   *(Score 1)*
    (c) Full recognition of the value of such an integration
    pervades the company at all times.   *(Score 2)*

7. **When briefing outside advisers, such as advertising
    agencies or market research firms, are the needs of
    integration highlighted?**

    (a) No.   *(Score 0)*
    (b) Yes. We expect them to alert us to the need to
    integrate what they are doing with our
    objectives.   *(Score 1)*
    (c) All our briefing documents provide sufficient
    details about our plans and aims to ensure that
    outsiders understand where their services slot in. The
    need for such integration is always
    emphasized.   *(Score 2)*

8. **Does top management refer to the need to think in
    terms of integration?**

    (a) No.   *(Score 0)*
    (b) The marketing director/manager
    does.   *(Score 1)*
    (c) The whole message stems from the very top. It is
    part of the firm's climate and culture. *(Score 2)*

▶

Score
0 1 2

9. **To what extent does the firm incorporate the integration philosophy into its training and development programmes?**

(a) We do not train. *(Score 0)*
(b) The subject is never mentioned. If those who run programmes for us raise the issue, so much the better. *(Score 1)*
(c) We always insist that the subject forms an integral part of any programme we conduct, or which is conducted on our behalf. *(Score 2)*

10. **Does the company control and monitor the level of integration that is taking place?**

(a) No. *(Score 0)*
(b) Only when problems arise as a result of lack of integration and it is clearly perceived that corrective measures are needed in this area. *(Score 1)*
(c) Our system of appraisal and evaluation includes clear statements about the level of integration that managers have planned for and attained. *(Score 2)*

The maximum score possible is 20. Very few companies could achieve such a score. Lower scores can be interpreted as follows:

15–20 **Excellent**
10–14 **Good to very good.**
5–9 **Fair**
0–4 **Poor**

References and further reading

Adams, J.D. (ed.) (1986) *Transforming Leadership: From vision to results*, Alexandria, Va: Miles River Press.

Ansoff, Igor (1965) *Corporate Strategy*, New York: McGraw-Hill.

Bowersox, Donald J., and Bixby Cooper, M. (1992) *Strategic Marketing Channel Management*, New York: McGraw-Hill.

Bowman, Cliff (1990) *The Essence of Strategic Management*, Hemel Hempstead: Prentice Hall.

Chisnall, Peter (1992) *Marketing Research*, 4th edn, New York: McGraw-Hill.

Christopher, C., Majaro, S., and McDonald, M. (1987) *Strategy Search*, Aldershot: Gower.

Christopher, Martin (1991) *The Customer Service Planner*, Oxford: Butterworth-Heinemann.

de Chernatony, Leslie, and McDonald, Malcolm H.B. (1992) *Creating Powerful Brands*, Oxford: Butterworth-Heinemann.

Drucker, Peter F. (1973) *Management: Tasks, responsibilities, practices*, New York: Harper & Row.

Fraser-Robinson, John (1989) *The Secrets of Effective Direct Mail*, New York: McGraw-Hill.

Kotler, Philip (1991) *Marketing Management: Analysis, planning and control*, 7th edn, Hemel Hempstead: Prentice Hall.

Lavidge, Robert J., and Steiner, Gary A. (1961) 'A Model for Predictive measurement of Advertising Effectiveness', *Journal of Marketing*, Oct XXV.

McDonald, Malcolm H.B. (1991) *The Marketing Planner*, Oxford: Butterworth-Heinemann.

Majaro, Simon (1991a) *Managing Ideas for Profit: The creative gap*, London: McGraw-Hill.

Majaro, Simon (1991b) *The Creative Marketer*, Oxford: Butterworth-Heinemann.

Nellis, Joseph G., and Parker, David (1990) *The Essence of Economy*, Hemel Hempstead: Prentice Hall.

Parker, Marjorie (1990) *Creating Shared Vision*, Clarendon Hills, Illinois: Dialog Int. Ltd.

Peters, T.J., and Waterman, R.H. (1982) *In Search of Excellence*, New York: Harper & Row.

Pinchot, G. (1985) *Intrapreneuring*, New York: Harper & Row.

Porter, M.E. (1985) *Competitive Advantage: Creating and sustaining superior performance*, New York: The Free Press.

Rossiter, John R. (1993) *Advertising and Promotion Management*, 3rd edn, New York: McGraw-Hill.

Stanton, William J., and Etzel, Michael J. (1991) *Fundamentals of Marketing*, 9th edn, New York: McGraw-Hill.

White, Roderick (1993) *Advertising: What it is and how to do it*, 3rd edn, New York: McGraw Hill.

Index

account executive (salesperson's
    role), 165
achievement (sales force
    performance criteria, 160–2
action (AIDA framework), 123
action communication, 122–3
activities, sales force, 162–3
ad hoc research projects, 50
advertising
    action communication, 122–3
    DAGMAR communication, 122–3,
    129
    efficiency control, 214–15
    promotional mix, 121–4, 127–31
'affordability', 100
ageing products
    buying time for, 79–80
    see also decline stage
AIDA framework, 123
Ansoff matrix, 192–3
anticipating customer requirement,
    20–1
antitrust legislation, 99
assumptions (planning process), 184
atmosphere (media selection),
    130–1
attention (AIDA framework), 123
audit questionaires, 2–3, 212
    distribution/logistics, 155–7
    input-gathering, 60–3
    marketing-orientated, 12–15
    marketing control, 220–3

marketing integration, 253–5
marketing mix, 37–9
marketing planning, 204–7
pricing policy, 115–17
product management, 89–92
promotional mix, 136–9
sales management, 174–7

bar coding, 154
barriers to marketing planning
    process, 179–80
behavioural models (promotional
    mix), 123
'below-the-line' activities, 121
benchmarking, 151–2, 211
Boston Consulting Group, 76, 77
Boston matrix, 76–9, 83, 200, 203
brainstorming sessions, 190
brand-switching models, 59, 60
branding, 87–9
'breadwinning' products, 75, 76
break-even point, 101–2
British Rates and Data (BRAD), 130
bureaucratic companies, 226–7
'business-to-business' environment
    (decision-making unit),
    167–8
business definition, 182
business growth rate, 76, 77
business portfolio analysis, 76,
    200–1, 202, 203
buyers, 7, 17–18, 167

buying behaviour, 194, 229
buying time (ageing products), 79

case studies
    marketing integration, 250
    pricing policy, 107–8
cash cows (Boston matrix), 77–8, 80,
        104, 201
centralization, 236–7
channels
    distribution, 140–1, 144–7, 235
    marketing, 141–3
charities (marketing task), 22
Chartered Institute of Marketing, 10,
        16, 65
climate (of firm), 179
'cognitive dissonance', 122
commodity marketing, 81
communication
    DAGMAR, 122–3, 129
    direct marketing, 121, 133–5
    marketing mix, 29–30
    models, 123–4
    plan (preparing), 135–6
    process, 21, 118–20
communications (distribution), 150
comparative cost (advertising
        media), 130
competences, distinctive, 182
competition, perfect, 97
competitions (direct marketing), 134
competitive advantage, 3, 7, 20, 103,
        104, 190, 193, 211
competitive position
    developing, 80–2, 83
    relative, 76, 77
competitive practices, 46
competitive pressures (impact
        monitored), 210, 211
computers, 154, 215
conjoint analysis, 108–11
consultants (salespeople as), 163, 164
consumer goods, 17–18, 19, 88
context (for market planning), 181–4
control systems, *see* marketing
        control
core product, 82, 103
corporate attitude, 11–15
corporate objectives, 181, 183–4
corporate plan, *see* marketing
        planning

corporate strategies, 183–4
corporate values, 153
cost-benefit analysis, 43–5, 237
cost/impact matrix, 43, 44
cost-plus pricing, 100–1
costs, 130, 150
    distribution, 140–1, 215–16
    expenditure elasticities, 28–9
    functional expenses, 218–19
    indirect, 101, 149
    inventory, 148–9
    leadership, 80–1
    pricing and, 100–2
    of salesperson, 171, 172–4
counselling (by salespeople), 163,
        164
country attractiveness, 200, 202
creativity (and innovation), 7–8
crisis points, 226–7
critical success factor analysis, 197–8,
        211
culture, customer service, 152–4
customer
    buying behaviour, 194, 229
    databanks, 133, 134–5
    decision-making unit, 6–7, 17–19,
        167–8, 169
    direct marketing, 133–5
    dossiers, 167–8
    environment, 46–8
    groupings, 233–4
    market segmentation, 193–5
    motivation, 194
    penetration, 161
    'perfect', 165–7, 214
    perspective (price), 99–100, 107–11
    profit and loss accounts (study)
        (comparative study), 172–3
    requirements, 17–22, 81–2, 228–9,
        230
    satisfaction, 6–9, 149, 215, 230
    typology, 194–5
customer service, 150–1
    culture, 152–4
    level, inventory and, 149
    matrix, 152

DAGMAR communication, 122–3, 129
data, 49
    collection, 50–1, 53
    interpretation, 50–1, 54

databanks, 133, 134–5
de-marketing skills, 104–5
decentralization, 236–7
deciders, 7, 17–18, 167
decision-making unit, 6–7, 17–19,
    167–8, 169
decline stage (product), 69, 70, 73,
    75–6, 79–80, 104–5
    deleting old products, 86–7
Delphi method (demand forecast),
    56–7
demand forecasting, 54–60
demand and supply, 94–7, 98
desire (AIDA framework), 123
detailed programmes (planning
    process), 185–6
deterministic models, 60
development
    integrated phase, 237–9
    new products, 82–6
    of organizations, 224–8
developments in distribution, 154
differentiation (competitive
    position), 80, 81
digital marketing, 133–4
direct mail, 133, 134–5
direct marketing, 121, 133–5
direct selling, 133
directional policy matrix, 76, 200
discounts, 103, 112–13
distinctive competences, 182
distribution
    depots, 148
    efficiency control, 215–16
distribution channel, 140–1
    marketing organizations based on,
        235–6
    motivation, 146–7
    power in, 144–5
distribution and logistics
    channel motivation, 146–7
    cost, 140–1
    customer service, 150–4
    developments, 154
    intermediaries, 143–4
    logistics, 147–50
    marketing channels, 141–3
    policy audit, 155–7
    power, 144–5
diversification, 192, 193
dogs (Boston matrix), 77–8, 86

downward forces (prices), 113–14
Drucker, Peter, 4, 64
dynamic models (prediction), 59

economies of scale, 99, 154, 234
efficiency control, 212–16
elasticities (analysis), 28–9
elasticity of demand, 95–6
electronic media (digital marketing),
    133–4
electronic point of sale, 154
elementary stage (pricing), 105–6
enlightened stage (pricing), 105–6
entrepreneur (pioneering phase),
    224–5
environment (marketing profile),
    46–8
EPOS systems, 154
evolution
    of organizations, 224–8
    pricing orientation and, 105–6
    see also development
expenditure elasticities, 28–9
expenses (sales force), 162
expertise (demand forecasting), 55,
    57
exponential smoothing, 58
external factors (marketing profile),
    47–8
extrapolation (demand forecasts), 54,
    55, 58

facilities (distribution), 148
fairness (objectives), 160
feedback, 119, 186
'feel good' factor, 81
forecast revenue, 191
forecasting demand, 54–60
forecasting techniques, 188, 200–1
'four Ps model', 22–3, 25, 31–3, 47–8,
    140, 202–4
    see also place; price; product;
        promotion
free samples, 132
functional approach, 16–23, 231–2
functional expenses, 218–19
functional tasks, 236–7
future, indications for, 182

gap analysis, 188, 190–2
gatekeepers, 7, 18, 167

generic products, 70, 87–8
geographical regions, 234–5
goods, 17–18, 19, 88, 213–14
goods incentives, 146–7
graphical model, 59
group discussions, 57
growth stage (product), 69–70, 103

handling costs, 150
hierarchy of planning, 181–4
holistic approach, 1, 3–9
horizontal integration, 246–7, 248

'iceberg' model, 153
identifying customer requirements,
        17–20
image, 87, 89
    pricing and, 111–12
impact/cost matrix, 43, 44
incentives, 103, 132–3, 146–7
indirect costs, 101, 149
industrial goods, 18–19, 213–14
industry type, 33–4
influencers, 7, 17–18, 167
influencing process, 124, 127–9
information, 7, 49, 150
    internal, 168–70
information technology, 211
innovation, 7–8, 80–2, 83
'innovators', 103, 194
input-gathering, 40, 184
    areas/quantity, 41–5
    audit, 60–3
    intelligence, 48–52
    marketing profile analysis, 46–8
    marketing research, 52–4
    methods of demand forecasting,
        54–60
institutions (marketing profile), 46
intangible requirements, customer,
        19–20, 21, 81–2, 103
integrated communication
        programme, 168, 169
integrated organization, 226–8
integrated phase of development,
        237–9
integration, 244–5
    audit, 253–5
    meaning and scope, 246–52
intelligence, value of, 48–52
interest (AIDA framework), 123

interference (in communication
        process), 120
intermediaries, 143–4, 148
internal factors (marketing profile),
        47–8
internal information, 168–70
international marketing, 73
introduction of product, 69, 103
intuition (demand forecasting), 54,
        55–7
inventory, 148–9
inventory control, 154
investment, 149, 183
    recovery process, 71–3

job titles, 29–30
'joining', 164–5
'junk mail', 133, 134
jury of executive opinion, 56
jury of informed/expert opinion, 57

knowledge, 7
    see also information; input-
        gathering
Kotler, Philip, 58

'laggards', 194
Lavidge, Robert J., 123–4
law of diminishing returns, 28, 29,
        59, 171
least squares method, 58
legal system, 46
'likelihood to buy' matrix, 88
line managers, 188
linear models (prediction), 59
local stockholding, 148
logistics of distribution, 140, 147–50

macro-integration, 246–8
mail order companies, 133
Majaro, Simon, 84
management process, 16–17
managerial effectiveness, 212–16
manufacturer–intermediary
        relationship, 143–4
manufacturer distribution, *see*
        distribution and logistics
manufacturer power, 144–5
manufacturer's price perception,
        99–100
mapping (and positioning), 195–7

margins (sales force objectives),
  161–2
market
  considerations (channels), 143
  extension, 192, 193
  groupings, 233–4
  growth rate, 76, 77
  leadership, 145
  -orientated structure, 238–9
  penetration, 161, 191–2, 193
  research, 52–4, 215
  segmentation, 193–5, 200–1
market share, 76–8, 82–3, 103, 104,
  145
  analysis, 199–200
marketing
  audit, 184, 188
  channels, 141–3
  direct, 133–5
  effective (input), *see* input-
    gathering
  holistic approach, 1, 3–9
  integration, *see* integration
  objectives, 184–6, 193
  -orientation, 11–15
  role (holistic approach), 3–9
marketing concept
  definitions, 10
  marketing-orientated audit, 12–15
  marketing as corporate attitude,
    11–12
  marketing as function, 16–23
marketing control
  audit, 220–3
  different types, 208–10
  managerial effectiveness, 212–16
  operational controls, 216–20
  strategic control, 210–12
marketing information system, 51–2
marketing mix, 21, 24–9, 46
  analysis, 30–6
  audit, 37–9
  'four Ps model', 22–3, 25, 31–3,
    47–8, 202–4
  integration of ingredients, 250–2
marketing organizations
  audit, 241–3
  centralization, 236–7
  development of, 224–8
  integrated phase, 237–9
  main considerations, 239–40

subactivities, 228–31
  types of, 231–6
marketing plan (communication
  plan), 135–6
marketing planning, 178
  aids to, 188–201
  audit, 204–7
  benefits, 179–80
  process, 180–8
  strategy-formulation, 201–4
marketing profile analysis, 46–8
marketing programmes
  existing, 34–6
  new, 31–4
marketing research process, 52–4
marketing strategies, 185
  formulating, 201–4
Marks and Spencer, 16
matrix organization, 238–9, 240
mature stage (pricing), 69–70, 104,
  105–6
'me-too' product, 88, 111
measurability (objectives), 159
media selection (advertising), 130–1
message channels, 118–20
military campaign analogy, 31, 48
'mismanagement curve', 70–1
mission statement, 182
money incentives, 146–7
monitoring procedures, 186–7,
  210–12
monopoly pricing, 97, 99
motivation, channel, 146–7
motivation, customer, 194
'motivational' discounts, 112
multiple regression model, 59

network analysis technique, 59
new products, 82–6, 192, 193
niche market, 81, 82
nonlinear models (prediction), 59

objectives
  corporate, 181, 183, 184
  marketing, 185
  promotion, 121–4, 125–6
  of sales force, 158–65
  of sales promotions, 132, 136
old products (deleting), 86–7
oligopoly pricing, 99
operational controls, 216–20

opportunities (SWOT analysis), 184, 186, 193, 197–8
organization (role), 182
organizational 'iceberg', 153
organizational model (levels), 1–2
organizations, *see* marketing organizations
original equipment manufacturers, 26–7
overheads, 101, 149
owner-manager, 225

'packages', 131, 167
packaging system, 150
Pareto curve/analysis, 75–6
perfect competition, 97
'perfect' customer, 165–7, 214
perfect market, 96, 97
performance criteria (sales), 160, 161–2
performance levels (sales), 170–1
personal selling, *see* selling
Peters, T.J., 4–5, 6, 8
physical distribution, 148
Pinchot, Gifford, 3
pioneering phase, 105, 224–5, 226–7, 231, 238
place, 140, 142, 204
    see also distribution and logistics; 'four Ps model'
planning, *see* marketing planning
pooled individual estimates method (demand forecasting), 57
Porter, Michael, 3, 210
portfolio of products
    management of, 79–87
    need for balance, 73–9
    price and, 105–7
positioning (and mapping), 195–7
power (distribution channel), 144–5
pre-testing (sales), 132
predictive models, 54, 55, 58–60
price
    -demand relationship, 94
    differentiation, 89
    effect of supply/demand, 96–7
    equivalence, 108
    in marketing strategies, 203
price and pricing policy, 93
    audit, 115–17
    costs, 100–2

customer perspective, 107–11
discounts, 112–13
image and, 111–12
monopoly pricing, 97, 99
oligopoly pricing, 99
product life-cycle, 103–5, 106
product portfolio, 105–7
summary, 113–14
supply/demand, 94–7, 98
viewpoints, 99–100
'priceometer', 113–14
'primary demand', 122
primitive stage (pricing), 105–6
priorities, 229, 230
privatized public utilities, 99
proactive marketing plans, 190
product
    costs, 140–1
    development, 82–6, 192, 193
    differentiation, 111–12
    groupings, 232–3
    image, 87, 89, 111–12
    marketing strategies, 202–3
    -orientated structure, 238–9
    positioning benefit, 108–9
    profit and loss accounts, 173–4
    screening procedure, 83, 84, 86
product life-cycle, 66–7
    analysis, 198
    communication models, 123
    extending, 79–80
    price and, 103–5, 106
    review of, 68–79
product management audit, 89–92
product portfolio
    management of, 79–87
    need for balance, 73–9
    price and, 105–7
product policy and planning, 64–7
    branding, 87–9
    product life-cycle, 68–79
    product management audit, 89–92
    product portfolio, 79–87
'product surround', 82
productivity, 191
    developing competitive position, 80–2, 83
    sales force, 158, 165–71
profile analysis, 46–8
profit and loss account (of salesperson), 172–4

profitability, 22–3, 73–4, 183
operational controls, 216–20
project definition, 52
promotion
marketing strategies, 203–4
objectives, 121–4, 125–7
see also 'four Ps model'
promotional channels, 120–1
promotional mix
advertising, 124, 127–31
audit, 136–9
communication plan, 135–6
communication process, 118–20
direct marketing, 133–5
promotion objectives, 121–7
promotional channels, 120–1
promotions, 131–3
promotional offers, 103, 132–3
publicity, 121
pull strategy (channel motivation),
146
push strategy (channel motivation),
146

question marks (Boston matrix), 77–8

RAND Corporation, 56
ratio analysis, 216–20
reactive marketing plans, 190
receiver (communication), 118–20
regions, 234–5
regression and correlation, 58
rejuvenation process (ageing
products), 79–80
relevance (objectives), 159–60
report stage (market research), 54
research plan, 53
research projects, 43–5, 50
resource allocation, 27
responsibility allocation, 27–8
restrictive practices, 145
retailer power, 144–5
return on capital employed, 216–17
return on investment, 183
risk-reduction, 83–4

sales (efficiency control, 213–14
sales force
audit, 174–7
productivity, 165–71
profit and loss account, 172–4

role/objectives, 158–65
size, 171–2
'star' performers, 170–1
sales promotions, 121, 131–3
sales pyramid (industrial goods), 213–14
sales revenue elasticities, 28–9
sales volume, 161
samples (promotions), 132
'satellite' model, 8–9
satellite television, 133–4
'satisfiers', 22–3, 25, 202–4
satisfying customer requirements,
21–2
saturation stage, 69, 73, 104–5
scenarios, 188–90
scientific management phase, 225–7
screening process (new products),
83, 84, 86
seasonal products, 74
segment attractiveness, 200–1
'selective demand', 122
selling, 121
changing role, 160, 162–5
sales force (role), 158–65
sales force productivity, 165–71
sales force size, 171–2
sales management audit, 174–7
salesperson's profit and loss
account', 172–4
sender (communication), 118–20
service department, 27–8
service incentives, 147
seven Ss framework, 4–6, 8
shared values, 5, 9, 153, 179
snakes and ladders game, 124, 127–9
special offers, 103, 132–3
Standard Industrial Classification
(SIC), 166
standardization, international, 73
'star' performers (sales), 170–1
stars (Boston matrix), 77–8, 80–2, 201
static models (prediction), 59
statistical methods, 188
Steiner, Gary A., 123–4
stochastic models (prediction), 60
stock levels, 148–9, 154
storage costs, 148–9, 150
strategic control, 210–12
strategies
corporate, 183–4
marketing, 185, 201–4

strengths (SWOT analysis), 184, 186,
      193, 197–8
subactivities, 228–31
   integration of, 248–50
supermarket checkouts, 154
suppliers, 143
   price perception, 99–100
supply and demand, 94–7, 98
SWOT analysis, 184, 186, 193, 197–8
synergy, 223, 234
system attributes, 109–11

tangible requirements, customer,
      19–20, 21, 81–2
target area, 152
target audience, 54, 124, 127–30
target customers, 142–3, 165–7
target revenue, 191
technology, 210–11
telemarketing, 133, 134
'tellmanship', 164
threats (SWOT analysis), 184, 186,
      193, 197–8

time, utility of, 140, 142
time series, 58
'total package' distribution, 154
transport, 148

unique product, 87–8
unitization, 150
upward forces (prices), 113, 114
users, 7, 17–18, 167
utility of place/time, 140, 142

values, 5, 9, 153, 179
vertical integration, 246–8
visioning process, 188–90
volume of sales, 161

warehousing, 148
warranty period, 27
Waterman, R.H., 4–5, 6, 8
weaknesses (SWOT analysis), 184,
      186, 193, 197–8
wholesaler power, 144–5